A **dic·tio·na·ry**
of **MADE-UP**
LANGUAGES

From Adûnaic to Elvish,
Zaum to Klingon—
The Anwa (Real) Origins of Invented Lexicons

STEPHEN D. ROGERS

adamsmedia
Avon, Massachusetts

Acknowledgments

I'd like to thank Peter Archer and the team at Adams Media. Thanks also go out to Andrew Montalbano and Jessica Polny for their help and to Christine Johnson and Analise Rogers for their forbearance. Is now not a good time to mention Volume 2?

Published by
Adams Media, a division of F+W Media, Inc.
57 Littlefield Street, Avon, MA 02322. U.S.A.
www.adamsmedia.com

ISBN 10: 1-4405-2817-9
ISBN 13: 978-1-4405-2817-0
eISBN 10: 1-4405-3039-4
eISBN 13: 978-1-4405-3039-5

Printed in the United States of America.

10   9   8   7   6   5   4   3   2   1

Library of Congress Cataloging-in-Publication Data
is available from the publisher.

Many of the designations used by manufacturers and sellers to distinguish their product are claimed as trademarks. Where those designations appear in this book and Adams Media was aware of a trademark claim, the designations have been printed with initial capital letters.

This book is available at quantity discounts for bulk purchases.
For information, please call 1-800-289-0963.

Contents

Introduction

Perhaps you've wondered what's involved in inventing a new language.

You've come to the right place.

This dictionary is divided into three sections. In the first, and longest, I'll take you on a tour of more than a hundred languages that have been invented for political, artistic, or logical reasons. I'll then walk you through the steps you might follow to construct your own language. Then we'll examine more than a dozen language games that people have developed.

THE PURPOSE OF LANGUAGE

What exactly is a made-up language? It is one that someone invents rather than one that arises naturally in the real world.

People invent languages for many reasons:

+ **To give themselves and others a challenge**
+ **To give depth to a fictional civilization**
+ **To explore ideas, such as how a society might be if the native tongue contained no words having to do with time**
+ **To offer people an auxiliary language that is nationally neutral**
+ **To allow communication between speakers of other languages**
+ **To fix faults in the languages that already exist**

Without a shared language, we lose the ability to connect with others. We are isolated.

As social creatures, we humans have developed many means of communication. We gather and talk. We write messages that can bridge space and time. We invent the telegraph, the telephone, the texting device.

Being social creatures, we are in many ways defined by our use of language. Try to separate language from any activity we perform. Even those that may be done in silence are described in language, both internally when we consider the activity and externally when we share what we've experienced.

Over time, we bond with others who share our language—to the point where we will consider those who speak a different shared language as outsiders. We identify ourselves by our language.

What's your primary language? To what group does this make you belong? How does this language reinforce your connection to the people who speak the same language? How does this language separate you from others who don't speak the same language?

I speak English. I assume you speak English, if only as a second language. That we both speak English does not necessarily mean that we can always understand each other. English has dialects, accents, and regionalisms. (Do you drink soda, pop, or tonic? Do you eat a sub, a hero, or a hoagie?)

We adjust our language depending on with whom we're communicating. We talk differently to family members than to strangers, and to people older or younger than we are. We pick up nomenclature and jargon from the subcultures with which we interact. A professor uses different words from those of a plumber—not necessarily better ones, just different. Our words, and the experiences that those words represent, create a way of viewing the world.

According to the sixteenth edition of *Ethnologue: Languages of the World* (2009), there are over 6,900 living languages. There are countless dead or extinct languages that were once spoken on a daily basis. (Dead languages, such as Latin, are now used only for scientific, legal, or religious purposes. Extinct languages, such as Anglo-Saxon, have disappeared because of the evolution of the language or the extinction of its speakers.)

A CONSTRUCTED LANGUAGE

A language is an ordered process of naming things—physical things, emotional things, and mental things—and describing their actions with and their relationships to one another. Although we generally don't have names for things that don't exist, we're able to make up such names, should the need arise.

For instance, if you were asked the name of the big cat with the two horns, you'd probably say there's no such thing. But now that the image of a big cat with two horns is in your head, a part of your brain proposes, judges, and rejects possible names for this imaginary beast. Saber-horned cat? Bullcat? Hornfang?

What would you call a bunch of them? (It's important to know whether you're facing one or a pride. A pack? A gang?) What would you call their offspring?

Whatever you call this two-horned cat, if you communicate the name to others, and if the term catches on and becomes the "official" name, you've coined a word. The cat doesn't have to exist, but you can cause the verbal image of it to gain currency. (Remember words like *vampire* and *dragon*?)

To begin naming things, whether real or imaginary, is to begin to create a unique language. You're not alone. The Language Creation Society (*www.conlang .org*) won't even hazard a guess as to how many languages have been made up or how many of those constructed languages are currently in use.

CREATING A GRAMMAR

Making up new names or words for actions or descriptions isn't the only part of creating a language. The different elements of the language must have an ordered relationship to one another. We call this "grammar." Grammar allows us to combine groups of words to create meanings. Constructed languages must do the same thing: They create a morphology (a structure of meaning for various words within the language), syntax (how to combine those words into sentences), and phonology (how those words and phrases and sentences sound). In a natural language such as English, morphology, syntax, and phonology grow up gradually over time, influenced by other languages and the spread of English. In a constructed language, the creator or creators must invent these things, basing them upon an existing or a newly created foundation.

I make up words as I point at things. *Staz* is *pen* and *hin* is *cup*. Have I created a language? Not yet, because I don't have a grammar—just a vocabulary.

I decide that adding an *-a* means the pen is mine, adding an *-e* means the pen is yours, adding an *-i* means the pen belongs to someone else, adding an *-o* means the pen belongs to everybody, and adding a *-u* means the pen belongs to nobody. Now I'm beginning to develop a syntax, one of the elements of grammar. I can continue with this, adding a morphology and a phonology, and at the end of it I'll have a constructed language (or *conlang*).

The made-up languages that appear in this dictionary were created by people who went through just such a process. In some cases it took someone a lifetime. In other cases, the creator built a language that was perhaps added to by others. The resultant languages in either case are often models of beauty and complexity.

MADE-UP LANGUAGES

Because this dictionary is a printed work, we'll focus on languages designed to be written and/or spoken. Most are, for simplicity's sake. That said, there's no reason a language needs to meet this criteria. (Obvious exceptions are sign language and computer languages.)

Human biology dictates how we communicate verbally. The range of available sounds is determined by the shape of one's jaw, teeth, tongue, and lips, not to mention the nature of the human respiratory system. We also don't bother making sounds that others can't hear. There's no reason to suppose that alien life forms would speak in a language that humans would be capable of reproducing.

As you read this book, you'll meet some writers who made only the barest outlines of their constructed languages. Other writers (notably J. R. R. Tolkien) developed a full-blown language that can be written, spoken, and signed—if not presented in mime—complete with phonological charts, dictionaries, and etymologies.

THE SAPIR-WHORF HYPOTHESIS

One concept that runs through the thinking of many who create languages is the Sapir-Whorf Hypothesis. This theory of linguistic relativity states that language determines, or at least influences, thought. If a language has no words for *I* or personal ownership, can the speakers of that language be selfish? If a language has no future tenses, can the speakers of that language understand the concept of the future? How would a society differ if the language spoken did not differentiate between the sexes?

Which comes first: the worldview or the language? Once both are in place (as much as they ever can be said to reach such a static state), will changing the language alter the worldview of those who speak it?

Many writers test linguistic relativity theories in a controlled setting. That control, unfortunately, guarantees that the results are not accurate. In George Orwell's *Nineteen Eighty-Four*, we don't learn whether the state's attempt to control thought by controlling language would really work—an extreme statement of Sapir-Whorf—as much as we learn Orwell's thoughts on the subject.

STRUCTURE OF *THE DICTIONARY OF MADE-UP LANGUAGES*

In the following entries, material will be presented as in this order:

+ Language
+ Spoken By
+ Documented By
+ Behind the Words
+ Derivation of the Language

- Characteristics of the Language
- A Taste of the Language
- Some Useful Phrases
- Numbering System
- Philological Fact(s)
- In Their Own Words
- If You're Interested in Learning the Language
- For More Information

When available, translations are provided of two texts: the Lord's Prayer and the Babel Text. The latter, taken from the Bible, is used extensively by creators of constructed languages to showcase their masterpieces. In English it reads as follows:

Now the whole world had one language and a common speech. As men moved eastward, they found a plain in Shinar and settled there. They said to each other, "Come, let's make bricks and bake them thoroughly." They used brick instead of stone, and tar for mortar.

Then they said, "Come, let us build ourselves a city, with a tower that reaches to the heavens, so that we may make a name for ourselves and not be scattered over the face of the whole earth."

But the Lord came down to see the city and the tower that the men were building. And the Lord said, "If as one people speaking the same language they have begun to do this, then nothing they plan to do will be impossible for them. Come, let us go down and confuse their language so they will not understand each other."

So the Lord scattered them from there over all the Earth, and they stopped building the city. That is why it was Babel—because the Lord confused the language of the whole world. From there the Lord scattered them over the face of the whole Earth.

Note: The inclusion of these translations in this dictionary should not be misconstrued as an advocacy of any particular religion or the marginalization of any other belief system.

PART I
MADE-UP
LANGUAGES

Adûnaic

SPOKEN BY

Adûnaic was the language of the Men of Númenor during the Second Age.

DOCUMENTED BY

J. R. R. Tolkien (1892–1973) explored many languages and cultures as he told the stories of Middle-earth: *The Hobbit* (1937), *The Fellowship of the Ring* (1954), *The Two Towers* (1954), and *The Return of the King* (1955). (The last three are collectively called *The Lord of the Rings*.) After his death, his son Christopher Tolkien (1924–) edited *The Silmarillion* (1977) with the help of Guy Gavriel Kay (1954–). Christopher Tolkien then deeply analyzed his father's notebooks, letters, and drafts to produce an extended study of Middle-earth and its creation: *The Book of Lost Tales, Part One* (1983), *The Book of Lost Tales, Part Two* (1984), *The Lays of Beleriand* (1985), *The Shaping of Middle-earth* (1986), *The Lost Road and Other Writings* (1987), *The Return of the Shadow (The History of The Lord of the Rings, Part One)* (1988), *The Treason of Isengard (The History of The Lord of the Rings, Part Two)* (1989), *The War of the Ring (The History of The Lord of the Rings, Part Three)* (1990), *Sauron Defeated (The History of The Lord of the Rings, Part Four)* (1992), *Morgoth's Ring (The Later Silmarillion, Part One)* (1993), *The War of the Jewels (The Later Silmarillion, Part Two)* (1994), and *The Peoples of Middle-earth* (1996).

BEHIND THE WORDS

Númenor was the great island kingdom in the West of the world, described by Tolkien in *The Silmarillion* and other writings. It was given to the Edain, the fathers of men, by the Valar in return for their assistance in the War of the Jewel against the evil Morgoth.

Although the Edain, the men of Númenor, were at first wise and kingly, in time they were corrupted by the evil Sauron, a former servant of Morgoth, who poisoned the ear of the king of Númenor. The Númenoreans attempted to make war against the Valar in order to become immortal, like the Elves. However, the result of the war was the destruction of Númenor itself. Only a small fragment of the Númenoreans, those who had opposed the war and the temptations of Sauron, survived and traveled to Middle-earth, where they founded the great realms of Arnor and Gondor.

The story of Númenor was part of the broader story of Middle-earth and the rise and fall of the race of kings of the West. Some of this story is contained in *The Silmarillion*. *Unfinished Tales*, containing pieces written by Tolkien and collected after his death by his son Christopher, includes a detailed description of Númenor. The last fragment of Númenoreans left in Middle-earth at the time of the War of the Ring (the events described in *The Lord of the Rings*) was the Dúnedain, whose chief, Aragorn son of Arathorn, at the end of the war became the king of Gondor. He married Arwen, daughter of Elrond, son of Eärendil, the first king of Númenor.

Adûnaic was considered somewhat less prestigious than the Elvish tongues Quenya and Sindarin, both of which were in widespread use in Númenor. Later, when the Númenoreans became increasingly estranged from the Elves, some Númenorean monarchs forbade the use of Quenya and Sindarin and insisted upon the universal use of Adûnaic.

DERIVATION OF THE LANGUAGE
Adûnaic derived from the Bëorian and Hadorian dialects of Taliska.

CHARACTERISTICS OF THE LANGUAGE

+ Adûnaic favors the subject-verb-object construction.
+ Nouns can be singular, dual, or plural.
+ Nouns can have a normal form, a subjective form, and an objective form.
+ Verbs can be biconsonantal, triconsonantal, or derivatives.
+ Adûnaic recognizes four grammatical genders: masculine, feminine, common (masculine and/or feminine), and neuter.

A TASTE OF THE LANGUAGE
agan (noun)—death
anî (noun)—woman
anû (noun)—man
azgarâ (verb)—to wage war
balak (noun)—ship
bêl (verb)—to love
hîn (noun)—child
pûh (noun)—breath
ûrê (noun)—sun
zadan (noun)—house

SOME USEFUL PHRASES
Ki-bitha Adûnâyê? (Do you speak Adûnaic?)
Zadân anNi zadân anKi. (My home is your home.)
Zagrahê ya! (Kill them!)
Nûphan! (Idiot!)
Bâ kitabdahê! (Don't touch me!)

PHILOLOGICAL FACTS

➤ Adûnaic was the everyday language spoken by Númenoreans. As a result, when they began to establish trading ports on the shores of Middle-earth, the language spread throughout Middle-earth, where it gradually fused with other tongues, particularly Dwarvish, to form Westron, the Common Speech. Hence the comment of Faramir (one that didn't make it into the finished manuscript of *The Lord of the Rings*) that "all speech of men in this world is Elvish in descent."

➤ Tolkien created Adûnaic shortly after World War II, while he was further developing the story of Númenor. He wrote a partial account of it, "Lowdham's Report on the Adûnaic Language," which was later published by Christopher Tolkien in *Sauron Defeated*. However, he seems to have been ambiguous about it and at one point played with the idea that the Númenoreans never had their own language but instead were exclusively speakers of Elvish. Eventually, after changing his mind two or three times, he settled on the explanation of Adûnaic provided above.

FOR MORE INFORMATION

Review the works listed above, the resources listed in the bibliography, and the web pages: "Adûnaic—the vernacular of Númenor" (*www.folk.uib.no/hnohf/adunaic.htm*), "Ardalambion" (*www.folk.uib.no/hnohf/*), "Cirth" (*www.omniglot.com/writing/cirth.htm*), "How many languages did J.R.R. Tolkien make?" (*www.folk.uib.no/hnohf/howmany.htm*), "J. R. R. Tolkien: A Biographical Sketch" (*www.tolkiensociety.org/tolkien/biography.html*), "Lalaith's Guide to Adûnaic Grammar" (*www.lalaith.vpsurf.de/Tolkien/Grammar.html*), "Sarati alphabet" (*www.omniglot.com/writing/sarati.htm*), "The Silmarillion" (*www.en.wikipedia.org/wiki/The_Silmarillion*), and "Tengwar" (*www.omniglot.com/writing/tengwar.htm*).

UNIVERSAL TRANSLATOR

In the video game *Tales of Eternia* (2000), the characters travel to Merle and receive an Orz Earring, which works as universal translator.

Aklo

Aklo was first used by the Serpent Men, some 1.5 million years ago.

DOCUMENTED BY
Arthur Machen (1863–1947) introduced Aklo in his short story "The White People" (1899). H. P. Lovecraft (1890–1937) then referenced the language in his short stories "The Dunwich Horror" (1928) and "The Haunter of the Dark" (1935). Forty years later, Robert Shea (1933–1994) and Robert Anton Wilson (1932–2007) brought Aklo back in *The Illuminatus! Trilogy*, which consists of *The Eye in the Pyramid*, *The Golden Apple*, and *Leviathan* (all originally published separately in 1975). Still later, Alan Moore (1953–) used Aklo in his story "The Courtyard" (2003). Moore's story was an extension of the Cthulhu Mythos, the extensive body of work created by Lovecraft and his disciples.

BEHIND THE WORDS
The Aklo language was one of a series of strange languages and rituals that Machen mentioned in his short story, "The White People." Much of the story, which is in the form of the diary of a young girl, refers to hidden knowledge, the pursuit of which drives humans insane.

Aklo is the forbidden language of occult texts and incantations. No examples of the language actually appear in print; the authors who employed it maintained the fiction that because Aklo is forbidden, and some careless reader might incant a spell capable of calling forth evil, the language must forever remain hidden.

Arthur Machen was a Welsh writer of mythic supernatural tales of horror. Machen influenced not only contemporaries Oscar Wilde and Arthur Conan Doyle but also future writers such as H. P. Lovecraft, who wrote weird fantasy and horror often concerned with forbidden knowledge.

The supernatural power of Machen's Aklo meshed with the mythos Lovecraft set out to create. Robert Shea and Robert Anton Wilson then used Aklo to underpin their satirical take on mystical philosophies and conspiracy theories in their trilogy. Alan Moore brought the language back to its beginning:

> *Indeed to cast a spell is simply to spell, to manipulate words, to change people's consciousness, and this is why I believe that an artist or writer is the closest thing in the contemporary world to a shaman.*

PHILOLOGICAL FACT

➤ Aklo is one of the few languages to be used by many authors in their own works. First developed in 1899 by Arthur Machen, Aklo was used by others, culminating in its use more than a hundred years later by the graphic novelist Alan Moore. Colin Wilson (1931–), the English philosopher and novelist, used Machen and Lovecraft as elements in his short novel, *The Return of the Lloigor* (1969/1974) and mentions Machen's preoccupation with the strange and the supernatural.

FOR MORE INFORMATION

Review the works listed above, the resources listed in the bibliography, and the websites: "Arthur Machen" (*www.litgothic.com/Authors/machen.html*), "The *Financial Times* namechecks H. P. Lovecraft and talks about the fictional language Aklo" (*www.thelovecraftsman.com/2011/04 /financial-times-namechecks-hp-lovecraft.html*), and "The H. P. Lovecraft Archive" (*www.hplovecraft .com*)

SPEAKING OF LANGUAGES

Linguistics is our best tool for bringing about social change and [science fiction] is our best tool for testing such changes before they are implemented in the real world. Therefore the conjunction of the two is desirable and should be useful.

—Suzette Haden Elgin

Amtorian

SPOKEN BY

Amtorian is the language of the Amtorians, who live on the planet Amtor (Venus). Although some Amtorians gather in the most basic societies and others are technically advanced, all speak the same language.

DOCUMENTED BY

Edgar Rice Burroughs (1875–1950) wrote about Carson Napier traveling to Venus and experiencing adventures with the Amtorians in *Pirates of Venus* (1934), *Lost on Venus* (1935), *Carson of Venus* (1946), *Escape on Venus* (1946), and *The Wizard of Venus* (1964).

BEHIND THE WORDS

Amtorian is the only language spoken on the planet Amtor (Venus). Amtorian seems to resist any development of local dialects or regionalisms and doesn't change over time as a result of generational tinkerings. One might call Amtorian "a living dead language."

CHARACTERISTICS OF THE LANGUAGE

In Amtorian, complex words are constructed by compounding nouns.

A TASTE OF THE LANGUAGE

an (noun)—bird
fal (verb)—to kill
faltar (noun)—pirate ship
gan (noun)—man
notar (noun)—ship

PHILOLOGICAL FACTS

➤ Carson Napier (Burroughs's character in *Pirates of Venus*) describes Amtorian: "I found the language easy to master, but I shall not at this time attempt to describe it fully. The alphabet consists of twenty-four characters, five of which represent vowel sounds, and these are the only vowel sounds that the Venusians' vocal cords seem able to articulate. The characters of the alphabet all have the same value, there being no capital letters. Their system of punctuation differs from ours and is more practical; for example, before you start to read a sentence you know whether it is exclamatory, interrogative, a reply to an interrogation, or a simple statement. Characters having values similar to the comma and semicolon are used much as we use these two; they have no colon; their character that functions as does our period follows each sentence, their question mark and exclamation point preceding the sentences the nature of which they determine."

➤ Edgar Rice Burroughs also wrote extensively about Barsoom (Mars), the jungle (the Tarzan series), and the hollow center of the Earth (the Pellucidar series). His adventures were not confined to imaginary worlds, however, as he also wrote contemporary novels, westerns, and historicals.

➤ Amtor, or Venus, was a setting Burroughs came to somewhat later than Barsoom. His first Venusian novel, featuring the hero Carson Napier, was published in 1931. Burroughs created a world that was scientifically advanced in some respects and deeply backward in others. Atomic-powered ships plied the planet's seas, which were filled with strange, hostile creatures. The planet had magnificent cities, though one, Kormor, was populated by reanimated corpses.

FOR MORE INFORMATION
Review the works listed above, the resources listed in the bibliography, and the websites: "Anthropology on Amtor" (*www.erbzine.com/mag14/1495.html*) and "Pirates of Venus" (*www.en.wikipedia.org/wiki/Pirates_of_Venus*).

SPEAKING OF LANGUAGES

Language shapes the way we think and determines what we can think about.

—Benjamin Lee Whorf

Ancient

SPOKEN BY

The language Ancient is spoken by The Ancients, the Ori, and the Athosians in the Pegasus Galaxy.

DOCUMENTED BY

The film *Stargate* (1994) introduced the story, which was continued in the television shows *Stargate SG-1* (1997–2007), *Stargate: Atlantis* (2004–2009), and *SGU Stargate Universe* (2009–2011). There have also been Stargate games, Stargate comics, Stargate books, and two direct-to-DVD films as well as an animated series, *Stargate: Infinity* (2002–2003).

BEHIND THE WORDS

Millions of years ago, in an unnamed galaxy, the Alterans divided along philosophical lines. The Ancients' worldview, based on a scientific outlook, stressed free will, while the Ori maintained a rigid religious outlook. As the tension between the two sides became unbearable, the Ancients left that galaxy rather than go to war.

The Ancients eventually settled in Avalon (the Milky Way galaxy), where they built an empire that they seeded with Stargates. These allowed the Ancients to quickly move around the galaxy. One of the planets they colonized was called Terra (Earth), and so the human race is believed by some to be descendants of the Ancients.

CHARACTERISTICS OF THE LANGUAGE

+ Ancient is similar to Latin and thus is probably a forerunner of that language.
+ Characters in the Ancient alphabet are blocky and contained within a vertical, rectangular shape.
+ Ancient does not divide words or sentences with spaces or punctuation marks.
+ The letters *f* and *u* use the same symbol.

A TASTE OF THE LANGUAGE

Amacuse (noun)—friends
Ameria (noun)—ark
Anquietas (noun)—Ancients
Astria Porta (noun)—Stargate
Avernakis (noun)—universe
Cozars (noun)—legs
Cruvis (adjective)—wrong
Derentis (adjective)—crazy, insane
Euge (adjective)—good
Glaciuse (noun)—ice

Illack (noun)—path, way
Incursis (noun)—attack, invasion
Lacun (adjective)—lost, hidden
Navo (adjective)—new
Pare (noun)—fathers
Puto (verb)—to believe, to think
Sanctus (adjective)—hallowed, sacred
Sua (noun)—sun
Thessara (noun)—treasure
Ventio (noun)—wind

SOME USEFUL PHRASES

Aveo, Amacuse (Goodbye, my friends.)
Comdo asordo. (Please help.)
Ego deserdi asordo. (I desire help.)

Mia clementia, denar esto. (Have mercy. I was blind, but now I see.)
On na matta netario. (This is really unnecessary.)

NUMBERING SYSTEM

The Ancients use a base-eight numbering system.

PHILOLOGICAL FACTS

➤ Some examples of Ancient text that appeared in the *Stargate* television shows were translated by fans and discovered to be jokes. Once this information reached the Internet and the producers realized the show was being made to look camp, the policies for creating Ancient text were changed.

➤ The Ancients traveled to the Pegasus galaxy, some 3 million light years from the Milky Way, after abandoning our Milky Way galaxy. They scattered human life throughout Pegasus, though most of it remains on a relatively low technological level. The Athosians live on the planet Athos and pray regularly to their ancestors, the Ancients.

FOR MORE INFORMATION

Review the works listed above, the resources listed in the bibliography, and the web pages: "Ancient (Stargate)" (*www.en.wikipedia.org/wiki/Ancient_(Stargate)*) and "Ancient Language" (*http://stargate.wikia.com/wiki/Ancient_language*).

UNIVERSAL TRANSLATOR

In the Star Wars universe (*Star Wars: Episode IV: A New Hope* [1977], *Episode V: The Empire Strikes Back* [1980], *Episode VI: Return of the Jedi* [1983], *Episode I: The Phantom Menace* [1999], *Episode II: Attack of the Clones* [2002], and *Episode III: Revenge of the Sith* [2005]), most creatures speak the universal language Galactic Base, also known as English. Several races (such as the Wookies, Hutt, and Ewoks) do speak their own languages, but nobody ever really seems to mind. Given the ease with which everybody understands everybody else, it comes as even more of a surprise when C-3PO boasts in *Episode IV: A New Hope* that he's "fluent in over 6 million forms of communication."

Ancient Language

SPOKEN BY
Originally, all beings in Alagaësia spoke the Ancient Language, but eventually, only elves, dwarfs, Grey Folk, and some humans continued to do so.

DOCUMENTED BY
Christopher Paolini (1983–) introduced the teenage Eragon and his dragon, Saphira, in *Eragon* (2003), continuing The Inheritance Cycle with *Eldest* (2005), *Brisingr* (2008), and *Inheritance* (2011).

BEHIND THE WORDS
Christopher Paolini wrote the following regarding the creation of the language:

Since my parents owned a dictionary of word origins, I pulled it off the shelf and flipped through it. Eventually I found an obscure Old Norse word, brisingr, that meant fire, and I loved it so much, I decided to base the rest of my language on Old Norse. To find more words, I went online and dug up various Old Norse dictionaries, although I have been known to invent a word now and then when the story requires it! As far as the grammar and pronunciation of my "ancient language" go, they bear absolutely no resemblance to Old Norse as I wanted to give it my own twist.

CHARACTERISTICS OF THE LANGUAGE
+ Adjectives in the Ancient Language are placed after the nouns they describe.
+ Verbs are past simple, present simple, or future simple.
+ When two nouns are joined together, the descriptive noun comes first.
+ The prefix *äf-* when added to verbs changes the connotation from neutral to negative.
+ The Ancient Language follows a subject-verb-object structure.

A TASTE OF THE LANGUAGE

adurna (noun)—water
agaetí (noun)—celebration
älfa (noun)—elf
älfr (pronoun)—he
älfrinn (pronoun)—she
deloi (noun)—earth
fyrn (noun)—war
hjarta (noun)—heart
illian (adjective)—happiness
ilumëo (noun)—truth

maela (adjective)—quiet
orúm (noun)—serpent
raudhr (adjective)—red
solus (noun)—sun
thringa (noun)—rain
treavam (noun)—tree
vinr (noun)—friend
vollar (noun)—plains, fields, ground
wyrda (noun)—fate
zar'rac (noun)—pain

SOME USEFUL PHRASES

Atra du evarínya ono varda. (May the stars watch over you.)
Du grind huildr! (Hold the gate!)
Eka aí fricai un Shur'tugal! (I am a Rider and a friend!)
Eyddr eyreya onr! (Empty your ears!)
Sé onr sverdar sitja hvass! (May your swords stay sharp!)

PHILOLOGICAL FACTS

➤ Homeschooled Christopher Paolini graduated from high school at fifteen and began work on *Eragon*. The book was eventually self-published, and a copy was discovered by Carl Hiaasen's stepson. Hiaasen brought the book to the attention of his publisher, who offered to publish and distribute the book.

➤ The first word of the ancient language that Eragon learns in *Eragon* is *brisingr*, which became the title of the third book in the series. (*Brisingr* means *fire*.)

➤ One characteristic of the Ancient Language is that it was directly linked to magic. Each act of magic required a specific word. The more words one knew, the greater his magical abilities. Further, the Ancient Language did not permit a lie to be spoken in it; thus everything spoken in the Ancient Language was necessarily true (though the truth could, occasionally, be twisted or misinterpreted). Thus it became a favorite language for oaths or other compacts that required absolute honesty on both sides.

A name spoken in the Ancient Language was a *true name*, and speaking it allowed the speaker to control the person or creature being named.

However, as revealed in the novel *Brisingr*, a person's true name could be changed. If this change was made, the person was freed from all compulsions imposed under his previous true name.

FOR MORE INFORMATION

Review the works listed above, the resources listed in the bibliography, and the web pages: "Ancient Language" (*http://inheritance.wikia.com/wiki/Ancient_Language*), "The Author" (*www.alagaesia.com/christopherpaolini.htm*), and "Audio News: Christopher Paolini and Brisingr News!" (*www.randomhouse.com/audio/news/audio_news/christopher_paolini_and_brisin.html*).

UNIVERSAL TRANSLATOR

In the film *The Last Starfighter* (1984), teenager Alex Rogan is given a chip on his shoulder that allows him to understand the languages spoken by the nonhuman races.

Angley

SPOKEN BY

Angley is spoken by the people living in the Domain of Skyholm, which is located in the area formerly known as France.

DOCUMENTED BY

Poul Anderson (1926–2001) made up three languages in *Orion Shall Rise* (1983): Angley, Ingliss, and Unglish. While each of the languages is rooted in English, each is nearly indecipherable to speakers of the other two languages, owing to ways the languages developed over centuries of separation.

BEHIND THE WORDS

Several hundred years after a nuclear war, people—and nations—still have to find ways to deal with each other.

DERIVATION OF THE LANGUAGE

Angley is derived from English and French.

PHILOLOGICAL FACTS

➤ The novel *Orion Shall Rise* is set in an Earth previously ravaged by a nuclear war and divided into a series of societies. These include the Northwest Union, located in the Pacific Northwest of North America; the Five Nations of the Mong, located in middle America; the Maurai Federation, existing in the Pacific and encompassing the former nation of New Zealand; and the Domain of Skyholm, which includes much of what had previously been Western Europe.

➤ *Orion Shall Rise* revisits a world Poul Anderson used in three earlier short stories—"The Sky People" (1959), "Progress" (1961), and "Windmill" (1973)—and the time-travel novel *There Will Be Time* (1972).

FOR MORE INFORMATION

Review the works listed above, the resources listed in the bibliography, and the web pages: "Maurai" (*http://en.wikipedia.org/wiki/Maurai*) and "Thoughts on Poul Anderson" (*www.scifibookspot.com/markley/?p=48*).

Anglic [Galactic empire]

SPOKEN BY

Anglic was spoken by the Galactics in Poul Anderson's Technic History series, nearly 3,000 years of history packed into sixteen books published from 1958 to 1989: *War of the Wing-Men (The Man Who Counts)* (1958), *Let the Spacemen Beware (The Night Face)* (1963), *Trader to the Stars* (1964), *Agent of the Terran Empire* (1965), *Flandry of Terra* (1965), *The Trouble Twisters* (1966), *Satan's World* (1969), *The Day of Their Return* (1973), *The People of the Wind* (1973), *A Knight of Ghosts and Shadows* (1974), *Mirkheim* (1977), *The Earth Book of Stormgate* (1978), *A Stone in Heaven* (1979), *The Long Night* (1983), *The Game of Empire* (1985), and *The Saturn Game* (1989).

DOCUMENTED BY

Poul Anderson (1926–2001) was a Science Fiction Writers of America Grandmaster and seven-time winner of the Hugo (awarded by the attendees of Worldcon). He wrote many of the constructed languages covered by this dictionary. The Technic History stories trace the rise and fall of a civilization from the exuberant adventures of Nicolas van Rijn to Dominic Flandry's efforts to defeat the fated doom.

BEHIND THE WORDS

Stories of the Polesotechnic League period featured Nicholas van Rijn; those of the Terran Empire period featured Dominic Flandry. Still other stories and novels of the series featured David Falkayn and a cast of stand-alones. The novels cover nearly 5,000 years of history.

PHILOLOGICAL FACTS

➤ Poul Anderson's daughter is married to science fiction writer Greg Bear, one of only two authors to win best Novel, best Novella, best Novelette, and best Short Story—all four Nebula categories recognized by the Science Fiction Writers of America.

➤ Chronologically, the first major figure Anderson wrote about in the series was Nicolas van Rijn, a merchant prince of the Polesotechnic League. The character was somewhat of a combination of Falstaff and Machiavelli.

Concerning him, Anderson wrote, "While some readers couldn't stand this burly, beery, uninhibited merchant prince, on the whole he was probably the most popular character I ever hit upon, and the stories about him enjoyed a long and lusty run." Anderson's saga also included the adventures of the spy captain Sir Dominic Flandry, who was active in the period when the Galactic Empire was beginning its long, slow decline into darkness.

FOR MORE INFORMATION

Review the works listed above, the resources listed in the bibliography, and the web pages: "Thoughts on Poul Anderson" (*www.scifibookspot.com/markley/?p=48*) and "Van Rijnisms Contest" (*www.baen.com/contests-april2.asp*).

SPEAKING OF LANGUAGES

Words—so innocent and powerless as they are, as standing in a dictionary, how potent for good and evil they become in the hands of one who knows how to combine them.

—Nathaniel Hawthorne

Anglic [Civilization of the Five Galaxies]

SPOKEN BY
Anglic is spoken by humans, who are only one of 112 races included in The Uplift universe.

DOCUMENTED BY
David Brin (1950–) chronicles the story of an Earth regarded as primitive by alien races who consider chimpanzees, dolphins, and dogs the most worthwhile species on the planet.

BEHIND THE WORDS
In the Uplift universe, a patron species will help prepare a nonuplifted species to achieve intergalactic travel. These patron species speak one of twelve Standard Galactic Languages and think little of the Anglic spoken on Earth. The story unfolds over six books: *Sundiver* (1980), *Startide Rising* (1983), *The Uplift War* (1987), *Brightness Reef* (1995), *Infinity's Shore* (1996), and *Heaven's Reach* (1998).

DERIVATION OF THE LANGUAGE
Anglic is derived from English, Chinese, and Japanese.

CHARACTERISTICS OF THE LANGUAGE

+ Anglic is a typical ambiguous and clumsy Earth language.

PHILOLOGICAL FACTS

➤ David Brin has a Bachelor of Science degree in astronomy, a Master of Science degree in applied physics, and a Doctor of Philosophy degree in space science. He has written more than twenty novels and collections of short stories as well as presented papers on a variety of philosophical, political, and technical subjects.

➤ The process of "Uplift," by which a species is genetically modified by another species, "binds" the client species to its patron for up to 100,000 years. Uplift was thought to have been begun by an ancient race known only as the Progenitors. Humans deny that they are a client species and are convinced that they arrived at their present level of sentience through evolution—a belief that most of the rest of the galactic civilizations sneer at. Through this convention, Brin has been able to discuss such issues in the series as evolution, political power, and "species-ism."

FOR MORE INFORMATION

Review the works listed above, the resources listed in the bibliography and the web pages: "List of Uplift Universe species" (*http://en.wikipedia.org/wiki/List_of_Uplift_Universe_species*) and "Tomorrow Happens" (*www.davidbrin.com*).

SPEAKING OF LANGUAGES

I feel impelled to speak today in a language that in a sense is new, one which I, who have spent so much of my life in the military profession, would have preferred never to use. That new language is the language of atomic warfare.

—Dwight D. Eisenhower

Anglo-French [Lord Darcy stories]

SPOKEN BY
Anglo-French is spoken by the people of the country formed by the union of England and France.

DOCUMENTED BY
Randall Garrett (1927–1987) allows Lord Darcy to juggle dual-investigative duties as chief forensic investigator for the Duke of Normandy and special investigator for the High Court of Chivalry in stories that take place in an alternate version of the contemporary world: *Too Many Magicians* (1966), *Murder and Magic* (1979), and *Lord Darcy Investigates* (1981).

BEHIND THE WORDS
In the Lord Darcy alternate-history stories, France and the British Isles have merged into the Anglo-French (Angevin) Empire. While magic is a given in this world, society is less technologically advanced than its nonalternative counterpart. There is considerable political tension between the Angevin empire and the slowly expanding Polish empire, which often leads to Darcy becoming involved in espionage activities.

DERIVATION OF THE LANGUAGE
Anglo-French is derived from English and French.

PHILOLOGICAL FACTS

➤ For the last seven years of his life, Randall Garrett suffered from a debilitating disease that made it increasingly difficult for him to work. After his death, the Lord Darcy stories were continued by his friend Michael Kurland (1938–).

➤ Garrett's stories were part of the genre called Steampunk, in which magic and advanced science coexist with such late-nineteenth-century elements as revolvers and steam trains. In Garrett's stories, the character of Lord Darcy was akin to Sherlock Holmes, and he was assisted in his investigations by a Dr. Watson–like character, Master Sean O'Lochlainn, a licensed sorcerer. Michael Kurland, in his continuation of the series, also paid tribute to Sir

Arthur Conan Doyle's fictional detective in the title of his first Lord Darcy novel, *A Study in Sorcery* (Conan Doyle's first Sherlock Holmes novel was, of course, *A Study in Scarlet*).

FOR MORE INFORMATION

Review the works listed above, the resources listed in the bibliography and the web page: "Lord Darcy by Randall Garrett" (*www.webscription.net/chapters/0743435486/0743435486.htm*).

SPEAKING OF LANGUAGES

Language is a process of free creation; its laws and principles are fixed, but the manner in which the principles of generation are used is free and infinitely varied. Even the interpretation and use of words involves a process of free creation.

—Noam Chomsky

Anglo-French [*The Shield of Time*]

SPOKEN BY

The inhabitants of an alternate future speak Anglo-French in *The Shield of Time* (1991), the tenth book in the Time Patrol series.

DOCUMENTED BY

Poul Anderson (1926–2001) wrote about the Time Patrol, a group commissioned to fix paradoxes caused by time travel.

BEHIND THE WORDS

In reality, the Hundred Years' War is the name given by historians to a long series of conflicts between England and France, from 1337 to 1453. Victories swayed back and forth between the two sides, although the French kings of the House of Valois eventually succeeded in reducing England's holdings in France, and by 1453's Battle of Castillon, France may be said to have won the war. In Anderson's alternate history, England won the Hundred Years' War.

PHILOLOGICAL FACT

➤ Although English and French derived from two different linguistic streams (French is a Romance language, descended from Latin, whereas English's early roots are Germanic), they have much in common. This is partly due to the proximity of England and France and the extensive traffic between the two; it is more specifically due to the fact that in 1066 William, Duke of Normandy, conquered England after defeating Harold Godwinson at the Battle of Hastings. The outcome was an influx of French words, which in many cases crowded out the earlier Anglo-Saxon terms. The end result was a language that was a hybrid between Germanic Anglo-Saxon and Latinate French.

FOR MORE INFORMATION

Review the work listed above, the resources listed in the bibliography, and the web pages: "The Shield of Time" (*www.amazon.com/Shield-Time-Poul-Anderson/dp/0812510003*) and "Thoughts on Poul Anderson" (*www.scifibookspot.com/markley/?p=48*).

asa'pili

SPOKEN BY

The asa'pili language is spoken by the peoples of bolo'bolo.

DOCUMENTED BY

The anonymous Swiss author p.m. used asa'pili in *bolo'bolo* (1983).

BEHIND THE WORDS

The language represents the author's interpretation of a utopian agricultural world.

CHARACTERISTICS OF THE LANGUAGE

+ Repeating a noun changes the noun from specific to general. For example, while *suvu* refers to a particular body of water, *suvu'suvu* refers to water in general.

A TASTE OF THE LANGUAGE

asa (noun)—earth, world

bete (noun)—medicine, health

bolo (noun)—community, village, tribe

buni (noun)—gift, present

dala (noun)—council, assembly

dudi (noun)—foreigner, observer

gano (noun)—house, building, dwelling

kana (noun)—household, hunting party, family, gang

kene (noun)—communal work

kodu (noun)—agriculture, nature, sustenance

munu (noun)—reputation

nugo (noun)—death, suicide pill

pali (noun)—energy, fuel

sadi (noun)—market, stock market, fair

sibi (noun)—craft, art, industry

sila (noun)—hospitality, tolerance, mutual aid

suvu (noun)—water, water supply, well, baths

taku (noun)—personal property, secret

yaka (noun)—disagreement, war, duel

yalu (noun)—food, cuisine

PHILOLOGICAL FACTS

➤ The anonymous author chose the initials *p.* and *m.* because they represented the biggest sections of the Zurich telephone book.

➤ While many constructed languages are developed in part to create a language free of ambiguity, many of the words in asa'pili have multiple meanings. This may be related to bolo'bolo being an anarchist society. A *bolo* is the creator's term for an autonomous social unit—something like a tribe, in this case composed of several hundred people.

➤ The terms *anarchy* and *anarchist* are often used to revile an action or person, but they have a very precise political meaning and philosophy. An anarchist seeks a society in which the state does not exist and in which people are organized in as decentralized a structure as is possible. The term has been around since the seventeenth century and has found modern supporters in many of the libertarians of today's political movements.

FOR MORE INFORMATION

Review the work listed above, the resources listed in the bibliography, and the web page: "P.M. (author)" (*http://en.wikipedia.org/wiki/P.M._(author)*).

SPEAKING OF LANGUAGES

At some point in the next century the number of invented languages will probably overtake the number of surviving natural languages.

—Cullen Murphy

Atlantean

SPOKEN BY
The citizens of Atlantis speak Atlantean.

DOCUMENTED BY
The Atlantean society is described in *Atlantis: The Lost Empire* (2001), Disney's animated tale of a young Milo Thatch (voiced by Michael J. Fox), who sets out to find the lost continent.

BEHIND THE WORDS
Atlantean is the original language from which all languages on Earth are developed.

DERIVATION OF THE LANGUAGE
Marc Okrand based Atlantean on Proto-Indo-European with a smattering of Chinese, Hebrew, Latin, and Greek.

CHARACTERISTICS OF THE LANGUAGE

+ The Atlantean alphabet does not have an uppercase and lowercase.
+ Atlantean sentences always follow a subject-object-verb format.
+ Six suffixes are used to indicate person and number: *-ik* (first person singular), *-en* (second person singular), *-ot* (third person singular), *-kem* (first person plural), *-eh* (second person plural, familiar and unfamiliar), and *-toh* (third person plural).
+ Adjectives follow nouns in Atlantean, but adverbs precede verbs.
+ Verbs can be inflected for ten tenses/aspects: simple present tense, present perfect tense, present obligatory tense, simple past tense, immediate past tense, past perfect tense, simple future tense, future possible tense, future perfect tense, and future obligatory tense.

A TASTE OF THE LANGUAGE
Atlantis (noun)—Atlantis
bernot (verb)—to bring

darim (noun)—time
gawid.in (adverb)—joyfully

gwis (pronoun)—we
kag (pronoun)—I
makit.tem (noun)—The King
moh (pronoun)—you
Negeb! (interjection)—Enter!
ser (adverb)—just

sob (pronoun)—they
ta.mil (adjective)—royal
tug.in (pronoun)—his
weydagosen (noun)—visitors
yob (noun)—crystal

NUMBERING SYSTEM

dihn—one
doot—two
say—three
kut—four
shah—five

luk—six
tohs—seven
yah—eight
niht—nine
Eh-khep—ten

PHILOLOGICAL FACTS

➤ Atlantean was written by Marc Okrand (the author of Klingon), who also assisted John Emerson with the design of the alphabet. While Leonard Nimoy was in the movie and had worked with Okrand on the Star Trek movies, Nimoy was not the person who originally suggested Okrand to Disney.

➤ Three writing systems were developed for Atlantean. First was the way Atlantean was written during the drafting of the script. Second was the way written Atlantean was portrayed in the film. Finally, a phonetic version was created that allowed the actors to more easily learn their lines.

➤ First mentioned by Plato around 360 B.C., Atlantis was originally supposed to have been located in the Mediterranean near the Pillars of Hercules. Others have suggested different sites for the legendary city, including the South Pacific and the Atlantic. The one point on which all legends agree is that the beautiful city was home to a highly advanced civilization that sank beneath the sea and was never seen again. The stories of Atlantis attracted the Nazis, looking for a lost race of Aryans, as well as some of the odder mystics of the twentieth century. (Edgar Cayce, for instance, predicted that Atlantis would rise from the ocean in 1968 or 1969.)

FOR MORE INFORMATION

Review the work listed above, the resources listed in the bibliography, and the web pages: "Atlantean language" (*www.bookrags.com/wiki/Atlantean_language*), "Atlantean language" (*http://en.wikipedia.org/wiki/Atlantean_language*), "Official Corpus" (*www.langmaker.com/atlanteancorpus.htm*), and "Talk:Atlantean language" (*http://en.wikipedia.org/wiki/Talk%3AAtlantean_language*).

SPEAKING OF LANGUAGES

We shall never understand one another until we reduce the language to seven words.

—Kahlil Gibran

Avarin

Avarin is spoken by the Avari, Elves who refused the call of Oromë to come to Valinor.

DOCUMENTED BY

J. R. R. Tolkien (1892–1973) explored many languages and cultures as he told the stories of Middle-earth: *The Hobbit* (1937), *The Fellowship of the Ring* (1954), *The Two Towers* (1954), and *The Return of the King* (1955). (The last three are collectively called *The Lord of the Rings.*) After his death, his son Christopher Tolkien (1924–) edited *The Silmarillion* (1977) with the help of Guy Gavriel Kay (1954–). Christopher Tolkien then deeply analyzed his father's notebooks, letters, and drafts to produce an extended study of Middle-earth and its creation: *The Book of Lost Tales, Part One* (1983), *The Book of Lost Tales, Part Two* (1984), *The Lays of Beleriand* (1985), *The Shaping of Middle-earth* (1986), *The Lost Road and Other Writings* (1987), *The Return of the Shadow (The History of The Lord of the Rings, Part One)* (1988), *The Treason of Isengard (The History of The Lord of the Rings, Part Two)* (1989), *The War of the Ring (The History of The Lord of the Rings, Part Three)* (1990), *Sauron Defeated (The History of The Lord of the Rings, Part Four)* (1992), *Morgoth's Ring (The Later Silmarillion, Part One)* (1993), *The War of the Jewels (The Later Silmarillion, Part Two)* (1994), and *The Peoples of Middle-earth* (1996).

BEHIND THE WORDS

Tolkien conceived of Valinor (also known as the Undying Lands) as a place where the immortal beings of Middle-earth could live free from the fear of Morgoth or any other enemy that might arise. When the Elves first awakened, the Valar summoned them to Valinor, and most of them followed Oromë. Those who resisted the call, out of fear or overcautiousness, remained in the area where they had first awakened, where they lived in the woods or caves. They became *wild* Elves and taught skills to the first men, though the Eldar (as those who had gone to Valinor were known) were far more skilled and taught men much when they returned to Middle-earth from exile.

DERIVATION OF THE LANGUAGE

Avarin is derived from Primitive Quendian.

A TASTE OF THE LANGUAGE

The following six words are the only ones Tolkien left his readers; he did not provide translations.

cuind	*kinn-lai*
hwenti	*penni*
kindi	*windan*

PHILOLOGICAL FACT

➤ According to Christopher Tolkien's *The War of the Jewels* (1994), J. R. R. Tolkien wrote about Avarin but only wrote those six words of Avarin. As each word has a different form, the language might have any many as six dialects.

FOR MORE INFORMATION

Review the works listed above, the resources listed in the bibliography, and the web pages: "Ardalambion" (*www.folk.uib.no/hnohf/*), "AVARIN—All Six Words" (*www.folk.uib.no/hnohf/avarin .htm*), "Cirth" (*www.omniglot.com/writing/cirth.htm*), "How many languages did J.R.R. Tolkien make?" (*www.folk.uib.no/hnohf/howmany.htm*), "J. R. R. Tolkien: A Biographical Sketch" (*www.tolkiensociety .org/tolkien/biography.html*), "Sarati alphabet" (*www.omniglot.com/writing/sarati.htm*), and "Tengwar" (*www.omniglot.com/writing/tengwar.htm*).

SPEAKING OF LANGUAGES

Change your language and you change your thoughts.

—Karl Albrecht

Babel-17

SPOKEN BY

The language Babel-17 was spoken by an agent of the Invaders.

DOCUMENTED BY

Samuel R. Delany (1942–) explored the Sapir-Whorf Hypothesis in *Babel-17* (1996) by creating a language that had the potential to manipulate people by manipulating the language they spoke.

BEHIND THE WORDS

During a war between the Alliance and the Invaders, Rydra Wong determines that sabotage is being committed by someone not even aware of the acts. She ultimately determines that the person was programmed to commit the crimes and then forget about them, owing to inherent qualities of the language Babel-17.

CHARACTERISTICS OF THE LANGUAGE

+ The language does not contain the pronouns *I* and *you*.
+ Babel-17 is capable of maintaining logical paradoxes.
+ Learning Babel-17 leads to a shift in your perceptions.

PHILOLOGICAL FACTS

➤ By the end of the story, Rydra Wong develops a version of the language that she calls Babel-18. She hopes this new language will be enough to convince speakers of the language to end the war.

➤ The Sapir-Whorf Hypothesis was first formulated in the mid-twentieth-century, primarily by Benjamin Lee Whorf. His thesis was that language actually determines the way in which its speakers perceive the world. He attempted to prove this by studying various Native American tribes and their worldviews, as reflected by their language. More recently, the Sapir-Whorf Hypothesis has been criticized by linguists such as Noam Chomsky and Steven Pinker as faulty and overly simplistic.

FOR MORE INFORMATION

Review the work listed above, the resources listed in the bibliography, and the web page: "Babel-17" (*http://en.wikipedia.org/wiki/Babel-17*).

SPEAKING OF LANGUAGES

Use what language you will, you can never say anything but what you are.

—Ralph Waldo Emerson

Baronh

SPOKEN BY

The language Baronh is spoken by the Abh, a race at war with the Four Nations Alliance of humankind.

DOCUMENTED BY

Morioka Hiroyuki (1962–) unfolds the story in *The Crest of the Stars* (a trilogy of novels that have been adapted into an anime series) and *Banner of the Stars* (currently four novels that have also been adapted into an anime series).

BEHIND THE WORDS

Japanese revolutionaries, who wanted to purify the language by omitting any foreign influences, started a colony where they synthesized the Abh, intending to use them as space slaves. However, the Abh revolted and created their own civilization. After the Abh won their freedom, they quickly developed their own language, Baronh.

DERIVATION OF THE LANGUAGE

Baronh is derived from ancient Japanese before the language was corrupted by outside influences.

CHARACTERISTICS OF THE LANGUAGE

+ Baronh uses the Ath alphabet, which contains twenty-eight symbols.
+ Nouns and pronouns have seven cases: nominative, accusative, genitive, dative, directive, ablative, and instrumental.
+ Baronh is an inflected language.
+ Some consonants become silent at the end of words.
+ Adjectives in Baronh follow the nouns they modify.

A TASTE OF THE LANGUAGE

achec (noun)—foot
baich (noun)—fuel

caisre (verb)—to run
dauth (noun)—summer

foc (noun)—fish
gamh (noun)—mountain
hora (adjective)—arrogant
idoch (noun)—life
laibebonh (noun)—food
muïc (noun)—winter
nae (verb)—to wash

oll (noun)—song
podainh (noun)—danger
ragre (verb)—to investigate
saibh (noun)—fang
tusaic (noun)—messenger
ulloute (verb)—to defeat
zoech (noun)—time

NUMBERING SYSTEM

ceutes (keut)—one
mats (mat)—two
bis—three
gos—four
lys—five

bus—six
das—seven
ga—eight
socnn (sokn)—nine
los—ten

PHILOLOGICAL FACTS

➤ Despite its origins in slavery to a highly authoritarian and racist society, Abh culture evolved to be loving and family centric. Although Abh generally reproduce through a gestation machine, it's not uncommon for them to gestate naturally as well. They are organized in three social roles: soldiers, businesspersons, and parents.

➤ An English translation of *Crest of the Stars* was published in anime form, in three volumes, by Tokyopop in 2006 and 2007.

FOR MORE INFORMATION

Review the works listed above, the resources listed in the bibliography, and the web pages: "The Abh Nation" (*www.abhnation.com/index.php?option=com_content&task=view&id=235&Itemid=*), "Banner of the Stars" (*http://en.wikipedia.org/wiki/Banner_of_the_Stars*), and "Hiroyuki Morioka" (*http://en.wikipedia.org/wiki/Hiroyuki_Morioka*).

SPEAKING OF LANGUAGES

Language is the armory of the human mind, and at once contains the trophies of its past and the weapons of its future conquests.

—Samuel Taylor Coleridge

Black Speech

SPOKEN BY
Black Speech is spoken by those who live in Mordor and serve under Dark Lord Sauron.

DOCUMENTED BY
J. R. R. Tolkien (1892–1973) explored many languages and cultures as he told the stories of Middle-earth: *The Hobbit* (1937), *The Fellowship of the Ring* (1954), *The Two Towers* (1954), and *The Return of the King* (1955). (The last three are collectively called *The Lord of the Rings.*) After his death, his son Christopher Tolkien (1924–) edited *The Silmarillion* (1977) with the help of Guy Gavriel Kay (1954–). Christopher Tolkien then deeply analyzed his father's notebooks, letters, and drafts to produce an extended study of Middle-earth and its creation: *The Book of Lost Tales, Part One* (1983), *The Book of Lost Tales, Part Two* (1984), *The Lays of Beleriand* (1985), *The Shaping of Middle-earth* (1986), *The Lost Road and Other Writings* (1987), *The Return of the Shadow (The History of The Lord of the Rings, Part One)* (1988), *The Treason of Isengard (The History of The Lord of the Rings, Part Two)* (1989), *The War of the Ring (The History of The Lord of the Rings, Part Three)* (1990), *Sauron Defeated (The History of The Lord of the Rings, Part Four)* (1992), *Morgoth's Ring (The Later Silmarillion, Part One)* (1993), *The War of the Jewels (The Later Silmarillion, Part Two)* (1994), and *The Peoples of Middle-earth* (1996).

BEHIND THE WORDS
Spoken by Dark Lord Sauron and his evil minions, Black Speech is perceived as so vile that Sauron's enemies will not dare speak the language.

DERIVATION OF THE LANGUAGE
Black Speech was created by Dark Lord Sauron for use by his forces.

CHARACTERISTICS OF THE LANGUAGE

+ Black Speech uses a subject-verb-object syntax.
+ There are no articles in Black Speech.
+ It does not use the letter *e*.

A TASTE OF THE LANGUAGE

agh (conjunction)—and

búrz (adjective)—dark

durbat (verb)—to rule

ghâsh (noun)—fire

gimbat (verb)—to find

hai (noun)—folk

krimpat (verb)—to bind

nazg (noun)—ring

snaga (noun)—slave

thrakat (verb)—to bring

PHILOLOGICAL FACTS

➤ The Dark Lord Sauron inscribed the One Ring with the following text:

Ash nazg durbatulûk, ash nazg gimbatul,

Ash nazg thrakatulûk agh burzum-ishi krimpatul.

(One ring to rule them all, one ring to find them,

One ring to bring them all and in the darkness bind them.)

➤ Tolkien said that Sauron himself used a pure form of the Black Speech, while his minions employed a debased form of it. In fact, the orcs seem to have spoken several languages or dialects, depending on where they came from. Thus, when Frodo and Sam overheard a conversation between two orcs in Mordor, the orcs were speaking the Common Language in order to more easily communicate with one another. The inscription on the One Ring quoted above was, presumably, in the pure form of the Black Speech.

IF YOU'RE INTERESTED IN LEARNING THE LANGUAGE

You don't want to learn Black Speech. You just don't.

FOR MORE INFORMATION

Review the works listed above, the resources listed in the bibliography, and the web pages: "Ardalambion" (*www.folk.uib.no/hnohf/*), "Cirth" (*www.omniglot.com/writing/cirth.htm*), "How many languages did J.R.R. Tolkien make?" (*www.folk.uib.no/hnohf/howmany.htm*), "J. R. R. Tolkien" (*http://en.wikipedia.org/wiki/J._R._R._Tolkien*), "J. R. R. Tolkien: A Biographical Sketch" (*www.tolkiensociety.org/tolkien/biography.html*), "Orkish and the Black Speech—base language for base purposes" (*www.uib.no/People/hnohf/orkish.htm*), "Sarati alphabet" (*www.omniglot.com/writing/sarati.htm*), "A Second Opinion on the Black Speech" (*www.uib.no/People/hnohf/blackspeech.htm*), and "Tengwar" (*www.omniglot.com/writing/tengwar.htm*).

Bokonon

Bokonon is spoken by those who practice the religion of Bokononism.

DOCUMENTED BY
Kurt Vonnegut (1922–2007) wrote about Bokononism in *Cat's Cradle* (1963).

BEHIND THE WORDS
The protagonist of *Cat's Cradle*, John, is working on a book describing what people were doing on the day the United States dropped an atomic bomb on Hiroshima, Japan. While researching the project, John ends up on San Lorenzo, a Caribbean island ruled by a mad dictator. Bokononism is a powerful religious movement on the island, one that John learns was created in order to control the island's people, though it is now illegal.

A TASTE OF THE LANGUAGE

boko-maru (noun)—the supreme act of worship

duprass (noun)—a karass of two people

foma (noun)—harmless lies

granfalloon (noun)—a false karass

karass (noun)—a group working to do God's will

pool-pah (noun)—wrath of God

saroon (verb)—to acquiesce to a vin-dit

sin-wat (noun)—someone who is selfish when it comes to love

stuppa (noun)—a fool

vin-dit (noun)—a sudden introduction to Bokononism

wampeter (noun)—one of two themes every karass has

Zah-mah-ki-bo (noun)—fate

PHILOLOGICAL FACT

➤ Kurt Vonnegut published a collection of essays under the title *Wampeters, Foma and Granfalloons* (1974). In the introduction he says, "Dear Reader: The title of this book is composed of three words from my novel *Cat's Cradle*. A *wampeter* is an object around which the lives of many otherwise unrelated people may revolve. The Holy Grail would be a case in point. *Foma* are harmless untruths, intended to comfort simple souls. An example: 'Prosperity is just around the corner.' A *granfalloon* is a proud and meaningless association of human beings. Taken together, the words form as good an umbrella as any for this collection of some of the reviews and essays I have written, a few of the speeches I have made."

FOR MORE INFORMATION
Review the works listed above, the resources listed in the bibliography, and the web pages: "Bokononism" (*http://en.wikipedia.org/wiki/Bokonon*), "Kurt Vonnegut" (*http://en.wikipedia.org/wiki/Kurt_Vonnegut*), and "Wampeters, Foma and Granfalloons" (*http://en.wikipedia.org/wiki/Wampeters,_Foma_and_Granfalloons*).

SPEAKING OF LANGUAGES

The limits of my language mean the limits of my world.

—Ludwig Wittgenstein

Live by the foma that makes you brave and kind and healthy and happy.

—From *The Books of Bokonon*

Bordurian

SPOKEN BY
Bordurian is spoken by the inhabitants of Borduria.

DOCUMENTED BY
Hergé (Georges Prosper Remi) (1907–1983) wrote and illustrated Tintin's adventures, using the fictional country Borduria in works like *The Adventures of Tintin: The Calculus Affair*.

BEHIND THE WORDS
Hergé wrote the adventures of Tintin starting in the late 1920s and thus placed the intrepid young reporter amidst events shaking the continent of Europe: the Russian Revolution, the rise of fascism in Germany, and the growing interwar tensions. To date, more than 350 million Tintin books have been sold.

In this story, Tintin and Haddock are trying to stop Bordurian agents from obtaining a sonic device that could be turned into a weapon.

DERIVATION OF THE LANGUAGE
The language used by the inhabitants of Borduria appears to have been largely modeled on Hungarian and Romanian, with some Polish and Albanian thrown in for good measure.

A TASTE OF THE LANGUAGE
amaïh! (interjection)—hail!
hôitgang (noun)—exit
mänhir (adjective)—mister
ointhfan (noun)—reception desk
opernska (noun)—opera
platz (noun)—plaza

Pristzy! (interjection)—Darn!
szonett (noun)—bell
sztôpp (interjection)—Stop!
tzhôl (noun)—customs
zsnôrr (noun)—moustache

PHILOLOGICAL FACT

➤ Borduria is located in the Balkans and referred to in several Tintin adventures. As depicted in *The Calculus Affair*, it seems a cross between a fascist state (leaders give the Nazi salute) and a Stalinist dictatorship.

FOR MORE INFORMATION

Review the works listed above, the resources listed in the bibliography, and the web pages: "Bordurian" (*http://en.wikipedia.org/wiki/Bordurian*) and "Tintin" (*http://en.wikipedia.org/wiki/Tintin_(character)*).

SPEAKING OF LANGUAGES

Any man who does not make himself proficient in at least two languages other than his own is a fool.

—Martin H. Fischer

Brithenig

SPOKEN BY
Brithenig is spoken by those who wish to learn the constructed language.

DOCUMENTED BY
Andrew Smith started inventing the Brithenig language in 1996.

BEHIND THE WORDS
Andrew Smith created Brithenig as an experiment to see how English might have developed differently if Latin had proved much more influential than Celtic. He then created a history for Kemr, the Kingdom of Cambria, as the place in the British Isles where Brithenig took root and flourished under the name Comroig.

DERIVATION OF THE LANGUAGE
Brithenig is derived from Latin.

CHARACTERISTICS OF THE LANGUAGE

+ In Brithenig words, the last syllable is stressed.
+ Adding *-th* to a verb makes the statement a command.

A TASTE OF THE LANGUAGE

ag (noun)—water
breich (noun)—arm
cafall (noun)—horse
can (noun)—dog
cel (noun)—sky
ciwdad (noun)—city
dent (noun)—tooth
efig (noun)—friend
eo (pronoun)—I
ew (noun)—egg
gwegl (adjective)—old

gwent (noun)—gwent
gwg (noun)—voice
gwid (noun)—life
gwirdd (adjective)—green
llaeth (noun)—milk
morth (noun)—death
nîr (adjective)—black
noeth (noun)—night
nôn (noun)—name
ogl (noun)—eye
origl (noun)—ear

padr (noun)—father
pedd (noun)—foot
pisc (noun)—fish

yscol (noun)—school
ysl (noun)—island
ystuil (noun)—star

SOME USEFUL PHRASES

Parola'gw Frithenig? (Do you speak Brithenig?)
Ke gos es gwstr nôn? (What is your name?)
Se ddeg a'w (Please.)
Greid (Thank you.)
Sa es nyll. (You're welcome; it's nothing.)

NUMBERING SYSTEM

yn—one
dew—two
trui—three
cathr—four
cinc—five

sei—six
seth—seven
oeth—eight
noe—nine
deg—ten

THE LORD'S PRAYER

Nustr Padr, ke sia i llo gel,
sia senghid tew nôn.
gwein tew rheon
sia ffaeth tew wolont,
syrs lla der sig i llo gel.
Dun nustr pan diwrnal a nu h-eidd;
e pharddun llo nustr phechad a nu,
si nu pharddunan llo nustr phechadur.
E ngheidd rhen di nu in ill temp di drial,
mai llifr nu di'll mal.
Per ill rheon, ill cofaeth e lla leir es ill tew,
per segl e segl. Amen.

PHILOLOGICAL FACT

➤ Andrew Smith decided to construct not only an alternate language but also an alternate timeline to accompany it. The result, constructed in collaboration with others, was Ill Bethisad. Its map of Europe bears a similarity to the real-world Europe, though with some striking differences. Norway and

Sweden, for example, have been conflated into a single country, called Scandinavian Realm. Spain is divided into Castille y Leon and Aragon. Italy is broken into Lombardy and San Marino in the north and Two Sicilys in the south, with the Holy See occupying the area around Rome.

FOR MORE INFORMATION

Review the resources listed in the bibliography and the web page: "The Page of Brithenig" (*http://steen.free.fr/brithenig/homepage.html*).

UNIVERSAL TRANSLATOR

In the podcast series *Fish Finders* (2008–09), Nick attempts to use a UTA (Universal Translator Assistant) to learn what dolphins are saying.

SPEAKING OF LANGUAGES

Viewed freely, the English language is the accretion and growth of every dialect, race, and range of time, and is both the free and compacted composition of all.

—Walt Whitman

Chapalli

SPOKEN BY

Chapalli is spoken by the Chapalli, a race whose empire has absorbed the Earth.

DOCUMENTED BY

Kate Elliott (1958–) writes about Tess Soerensen in the Jaran series: *Jaran* (1992), *An Earthly Crown* (1993), *His Conquering Sword* (1993), and *The Law of Becoming* (1994). (Kate Elliott is a pseudonym of Alis A. Rasmussen.)

CHARACTERISTICS OF THE LANGUAGE

+ Important elements of spoken Chapalli are the hand gestures used to give meaning to the words.

PHILOLOGICAL FACT

➤ On her official web page, Elliot promised that there would be more Jaran novels because "there's a lot more to write." However, as of this writing only the original four Jaran novels have been published.

FOR MORE INFORMATION

Review the works listed above, the resources listed in the bibliography, and the web pages: "Literature: Novels of The Jaran" (*http://tvtropes.org/pmwiki/pmwiki.php/Literature/NovelsOfTheJaran*) and "The World of Kate Elliott" (*www.kateelliott.com*).

■ UNIVERSAL TRANSLATOR ■

In countless stories, comics, films, shows, and games, the artistic medium acts as a universal translator, allowing the reader/viewer/player to understand foreign and alien communication in a conveniently understood language.

Common Eldarin

SPOKEN BY

Common Eldarin is spoken by the Eldar, the Elves who made the Great March to Valinor.

DOCUMENTED BY

J. R. R. Tolkien (1892–1973) explored many languages and cultures as he told the stories of Middle-earth: *The Hobbit* (1937), *The Fellowship of the Ring* (1954), *The Two Towers* (1954), and *The Return of the King* (1955). (The last three are collectively called *The Lord of the Rings.*) After his death, his son Christopher Tolkien (1924–) edited *The Silmarillion* (1977) with the help of Guy Gavriel Kay (1954–). Christopher Tolkien then deeply analyzed his father's notebooks, letters, and drafts to produce an extended study of Middle-earth and its creation: *The Book of Lost Tales, Part One* (1983), *The Book of Lost Tales, Part Two* (1984), *The Lays of Beleriand* (1985), *The Shaping of Middle-earth* (1986), *The Lost Road and Other Writings* (1987), *The Return of the Shadow (The History of The Lord of the Rings, Part One)* (1988), *The Treason of Isengard (The History of The Lord of the Rings, Part Two)* (1989), *The War of the Ring (The History of The Lord of the Rings, Part Three)* (1990), *Sauron Defeated (The History of The Lord of the Rings, Part Four)* (1992), *Morgoth's Ring (The Later Silmarillion, Part One)* (1993), *The War of the Jewels (The Later Silmarillion, Part Two)* (1994), and *The Peoples of Middle-earth* (1996).

BEHIND THE WORDS

The Elves were persuaded to leave the place of their creation and travel to Valinor, the Undying Lands, where they would be safe from harm. During the march to Valinor, many Elvish words were normalized, but the Elvish language still broke into dialects, eventually leading to Telerin.

DERIVATION OF THE LANGUAGE

Common Eldarin is derived from Primitive Quendian.

CHARACTERISTICS OF THE LANGUAGE

+ Common Eldarin had twelve monophthongs and ten diphthongs (two primary and eight secondary).

PHILOLOGICAL FACT

➤ Despite the affinity of many latter-day fantasy writers for Celtic culture, Tolkien drew for his inspiration from northern cultures. When he was still quite young, he decided to read the *Kalevala*, a Finnish epic poem, in its original language and so learned Finnish. "It was like discovering a complete wine-cellar filled with bottles of an amazing wine of a kind and flavour never tasted before. It quite intoxicated me," he wrote. Most of the names of characters in his books and the structures of many of his constructed languages were heavily influenced by cultures of northern Europe.

FOR MORE INFORMATION

Review the works listed above, the resources listed in the bibliography, and the web pages: "Ardalambion" (*www.folk.uib.no/hnohf/*), "Cirth" (*www.omniglot.com/writing/cirth.htm*), "Common Eldarin" (*www.tolkiengateway.net/wiki/Common_Eldarin*) "How many languages did J.R.R. Tolkien make?" (*www.folk.uib.no/hnohf/howmany.htm*), "J. R. R. Tolkien: A Biographical Sketch" (*www.tolkiensociety.org/tolkien/biography.html*), "Sarati alphabet" (*www.omniglot.com/writing/sarati.htm*), and "Tengwar" (*www.omniglot.com/writing/tengwar.htm*).

SPEAKING OF LANGUAGES

That woman speaks eight languages and can't say no in any of them.

—Dorothy Parker

D'ni

SPOKEN BY
D'ni is spoken by the subterranean characters in the games *Myst* and *Riven*, published by Cyan Inc.

DOCUMENTED BY
Richard A. Watson developed D'ni for the worlds of *Myst* and *Riven*, created by Rand and Robyn Miller, Chris Brandkamp, Chuck Carter, Richard Watson, Bonnie McDowall, and Ryan Miller.

DERIVATION OF THE LANGUAGE
D'ni is derived from the Ronay language, spoken by the Ronay of Garternay.

CHARACTERISTICS OF THE LANGUAGE

+ D'ni follows a subject-verb-object structure.
+ Nouns are formed by stem-(plural)-(possessor).
+ *Ril* negates any word that follows it.

A TASTE OF THE LANGUAGE

ano (noun)—water
barel (verb)—to make
çev (verb)—to thank
eder (verb)—to sleep
filað (noun)—top
gilo (noun)—plant
húr (verb)—to find
idsé (noun)—line
jima (noun)—prophecy
kera (adjective)—brave

lyima (adjective)—invisible
marent (verb)—to follow
na'grenis (adjective)—brittle
ošanin (adjective)—lost
pac (noun)—city
rís (verb)—to eat
šú (adjective)—dead
tam (noun)—fire
vog (noun)—nature
yar (noun)—day

SOME USEFUL PHRASES
bomahnshoo tomeht teh eest. (I will die here with them.)
rehm'lah sehkhehn poahnt bonooehts b'rigahsen. (The lizard has highly acidic saliva.)

pishoeet b'zoo gah bokehneet t'zoo tsahn. (They belong to me and they will be with me forever.)
votahr ah'shehm khehkamrov kehnehm. (I praise you for who you are.)
khahpo rehzuhnuh rildolgehlehnij gahth. (Perhaps the ending has not yet been written.)

NUMBERING SYSTEM

rún—zero
fa—one
brí—two
sen—three
tor—four
vat—five

vagafa—six
vagabrí—seven
vagasen—eight
vagator—nine
névú—ten

PHILOLOGICAL FACT

➤ *Myst* was one of the first video games to immerse the viewer in a virtual world. It quickly shot up in popularity, leading to a minor "*Myst* industry," with guides to the world, puzzle-solving aids, and even novels set in the world of Myst. In 2007 to 2008 it was available briefly as an online gaming world, but after the game was shut down, it became available as a free download.

FOR MORE INFORMATION

Review the works listed above, the resources listed in the bibliography, and the web pages: "D'ni" (*http://en.mystlore.com/wiki/D'ni*), "D'ni alphabet" (*www.omniglot.com/writing/dni.htm*), "D'ni Guild of Linguists - Word List" (*www.linguists.riedl.org/old/linguists-words.htm*), and "*Myst*" (*http://en.wikipedia.org/wiki/Myst*).

SPEAKING OF LANGUAGES

Slang is a language that rolls up its sleeves, spits on its hands and goes to work.

—Carl Sandburg

Dahmek

SPOKEN BY

Dahmek is spoken by the women on the planet Eho Dahma, in the Damiriak solar system.

DOCUMENTED BY

K Gerard Martin explored their world in the *Carreña* series: *Carreña 1: The Fall of Evanita*, *Carreña 2: Lamina*, and *Carreña 3: Imperative Birth*. The language is further described in *Cerafina's Damiriak Language Handbook*.

BEHIND THE WORDS

The Damiriak solar system is home to a race of women who live on three of the planets: Eho Miriam, Eho Dahma, and Nimsant. Eho Miriam was the home world, and people spoke Old Damariak until the men died off because of emissions from the sun, Seris. The women who colonized Eho Dahma developed the Dahmek language.

DERIVATION OF THE LANGUAGE

Dahmek descended from Old Damariak.

CHARACTERISTICS OF THE LANGUAGE

+ Words contain more consonants than vowels.
+ Dahmek uses a root-word construct.
+ Sentences follow a subject-verb-object structure.

A TASTE OF THE LANGUAGE

artelsk (verb)—to insist
beilbark (noun)—dagger
darlais (verb)—to enjoy
enrilushiarst (verb)—to interrogate
falirme (noun)—stream
giart (noun)—boss

haufu (adjective)—healthy
igalirf (noun)—incursion
kairsfp (noun)—jail
liaurk (verb)—to raid
miorpalirtu (adjective)—radioactive
naltripu (adjective)—faithful

olfesharlt (noun)—apartment
pelirp (noun)—mail
renf (noun)—sun
sharlade (adjective)—heroic

talurn (noun)—memory
ufert (noun)—identity
vaiforp (noun)—dinner
wiensf (noun)—home

PHILOLOGICAL FACTS

➤ Dahmek uses the Deibuth alphabet, which contains twenty-seven symbols, each with an upper- and lowercase form.

➤ A trailing *e* is added to words ending with the Deibuth letters corresponding to *w*, *b*, *v*, *m*, *d*, *dh*, *z*, *zh*, *g*, and *ng*. All three of the languages spoken in the Damiriak solar system use the same words for numbers.

IF YOU'RE INTERESTED IN LEARNING THE LANGUAGE

Pick up a copy of *Cerafina's Damiriak Language Handbook*, by K Gerard Martin, to learn more about Dahmek than you probably know about your native tongue.

FOR MORE INFORMATION

Review the works listed above and the resources listed in the bibliography.

SPEAKING OF LANGUAGES

I remain convinced that obstinate addiction to ordinary language in our private thoughts is one of the main obstacles to progress in philosophy.

—Bertrand Russell

The Divine Language

SPOKEN BY
The Divine Language is spoken by Leeloo, whose name means *stone* in that language.

DOCUMENTED BY
Luc Besson (1959–) and Milla Jovovich (1975–) developed The Divine Language for use in the movie *The Fifth Element* (1997).

BEHIND THE WORDS
The Mondoshawan are returning to Earth with the four stones capable of stopping the Great Evil when their ship is ambushed by the Mangalores. Earth scientists manage to reconstitute Leeloo, a supreme and perfect being, from the wreckage. Leeloo escapes and enlists the help of taxi-driver Korben Dallas to find the four stones, defeat the Great Evil, and save the Earth.

A TASTE OF THE LANGUAGE
algoulana (adjective)—brave
banalëto (verb)—to give
choncha (adjective)—beautiful
dilin'dilin (noun)—bell
escobar (noun)—priest
ferji (adjective)—rude
goummill (noun)—leg
handala (noun)—hand
itchewa (verb)—to turn
limoï (verb)—to listen

mina hinour (verb)—to kiss
mycket (adjective)—jealous
ogon (noun)—day
ou-man (noun)—person
ractamo (adjective)—huge
sassta'shima (noun)—spaceship
tokemata (verb)—to talk
tuna (noun)—home
vigo (verb)—to see
ydeo (verb)—to trust

SOME USEFUL PHRASES
Akta Gamat. (Never without my permission.)
Mu fryesh akta simoulai. (The action that you just took is offensive to me, and I consider it to be an evil act.)
Djala on hila djebet sän'ogonen? (What is today's date?)
Jeseï on mino kalatzen dolgamitba. (Autumn is my favorite time of year.)
Dot on do dolgaban. (There is no time.)

NUMBERING SYSTEM

amna—one

tba—two

kba—three

pat—four

sab—five

sat—six

chab—seven

rab—eight

fab—nine

ami—ten

PHILOLOGICAL FACTS

➤ During breaks in filming, Luc Besson and Milla Jovovich would hold conversations in The Divine Language and write letters to each other in the language.

➤ Luc Besson began work on the story that was to become *The Fifth Element* while still in high school. The outline for the story was reportedly 400 pages long, far too long for a screenplay, so Besson based his script on only the first part of the story. Despite the success of the film, there are no reported plans to make a movie of the latter part of Besson's outline.

FOR MORE INFORMATION

Review the work listed above, the resources listed in the bibliography, and the web pages: "The Divine Language" (*www.divinelanguage.webs.com/apps/photos/*) and "The Language of Leeloo" (*www.divinelanguage.com*).

SPEAKING OF LANGUAGES

The finest language is mostly made up of simple unimposing words.

—George Eliot

Doriathrin

SPOKEN BY

In Tolkien's Middle-earth, by the time of the events of The Lord of the Rings, Doriathrin was no longer spoken. The language was an ancient tongue that evolved alongside Old Noldorin, the two eventually becoming Sindarin (Grey-elven).

DOCUMENTED BY

J. R. R. Tolkien (1892–1973) explored many languages and cultures as he told the stories of Middle-earth: *The Hobbit* (1937), *The Fellowship of the Ring* (1954), *The Two Towers* (1954), and *The Return of the King* (1955). (The last three are collectively called *The Lord of the Rings*.) After his death, his son Christopher Tolkien (1924–) edited *The Silmarillion* (1977) with the help of Guy Gavriel Kay (1954–). Christopher Tolkien then deeply analyzed his father's notebooks, letters, and drafts to produce an extended study of Middle-earth and its creation: *The Book of Lost Tales, Part One* (1983), *The Book of Lost Tales, Part Two* (1984), *The Lays of Beleriand* (1985), *The Shaping of Middle-earth* (1986), *The Lost Road and Other Writings* (1987), *The Return of the Shadow (The History of The Lord of the Rings, Part One)* (1988), *The Treason of Isengard (The History of The Lord of the Rings, Part Two)* (1989), *The War of the Ring (The History of The Lord of the Rings, Part Three)* (1990), *Sauron Defeated (The History of The Lord of the Rings, Part Four)* (1992), *Morgoth's Ring (The Later Silmarillion, Part One)* (1993), *The War of the Jewels (The Later Silmarillion, Part Two)* (1994), and *The Peoples of Middle-earth* (1996).

BEHIND THE WORDS

Doriathrin was spoken at the court of King Thingol, father of Lúthien Tinúviel. Lúthien later married the human Beren; their story is told in Tolkien's *The Silmarillion*. From Lúthien was descended Arwen, daughter of Elrond, who, at the end of *Lord of the Rings*, married the human Aragorn, King Elessar of Gondor. Although Lúthien learned Beren's speech when she married him (and he asked her why, since her own tongue was more beautiful), her memory of her native language apparently remained. Doriathrin seems to have been closely related to Sindarin or even, perhaps, a form of it. This has led some scholars to suggest that Doriathrin was effectively a *dead* tongue, one that Tolkien had developed early in his work on Middle-earth and later abandoned.

CHARACTERISTICS OF THE LANGUAGE

+ Doriathrin uses -*in* to indicate plurality.
+ The alphabet does not have the umlauts found in Sindarin.

A TASTE OF THE LANGUAGE

dor (noun)—land

dorn (noun)—oak

drôg (noun)—wolf

durgul (noun)—sorcery

el (noun)—star

gad (noun)—fence

gald (noun)—tree

gell (noun)—sky

líw (noun)—fish

mab (noun)—hand

méd (adjective)—wet

ngorthin (adjective)—horrible

orth (noun)—mountain

radhon (adjective)—east

roth (noun)—cave

umboth (noun)—large pool

PHILOLOGICAL FACT

➤ In his introduction to *The Lost Road and Other Writings* Christopher Tolkien said of his father, "In his essay 'A Secret Vice' (*The Monsters and the Critics and Other Essays*, 1983, p. 198), my father wrote of his liking for Esperanto, a liking which, he said, arose 'not least because it is the creation ultimately of one man, not a philologist, and is therefore something like a "human language bereft of the inconveniences due to too many successive cooks"—which is as good a description of the ideal artificial language (in a particular sense) as I can give.'"

FOR MORE INFORMATION

Review the works listed above, the resources listed in the bibliography, and the web pages: "Ardalambion" (*www.folk.uib.no/hnohf/*), "Cirth" (*www.omniglot.com/writing/cirth.htm*), "Doriathrin—the mothertongue of Lúthien" (*www.folk.uib.no/hnohf/doriath.htm*), "How many languages did J.R.R. Tolkien make?" (*www.folk.uib.no/hnohf/howmany.htm*), "J. R. R. Tolkien: A Biographical Sketch" (*www.tolkiensociety.org/tolkien/biography.html*), "Sarati alphabet" (*www.omniglot.com/writing/sarati.htm*), and "Tengwar" (*www.omniglot.com/writing/tengwar.htm*).

Dothraki

SPOKEN BY

Dothraki is spoken by the nomadic horse warriors known as the Dothraki who live in the Dothraki Sea.

DOCUMENTED BY

HBO hired David J. Peterson to create the Dothraki language for the adaptation *Game of Thrones* (2011–), asking him to expand upon what George R. R. Martin (1948–) had built into his Ice and Fire series: *A Game of Thrones* (1996), *A Clash of Kings* (1998), *A Storm of Swords* (2000), *A Feast for Crows* (2005), and *A Dance with Dragons* (scheduled for 2011).

BEHIND THE WORDS

The action of the story takes place in the Seven Kingdoms of Westeros, where many fight to defend the realm . . . or take their place at its head.

DERIVATION OF THE LANGUAGE

David J. Peterson drew on Martin's work and added concepts from Russian, Turkish, Estonian, Inuktitut, and Swahili.

CHARACTERISTICS OF THE LANGUAGE

+ Dothraki has four vowels.
+ The language uses a subject-verb-object structure.

A TASTE OF THE LANGUAGE

ayena (noun)—bell
chakat (verb)—to be silent
dorv (noun)—goat
eveth (noun)—water
fire (noun)—ring
hadaen (noun)—food
indelat (verb)—to drink
jalan (noun)—moon

kaffat (verb)—to crush
lajat (verb)—to fight
mithri (noun)—rest
noreth (noun)—hair
ostat (verb)—to bite
qoy (noun)—blood
rhaggat (noun)—cart
shekh (noun)—sun

| *tokikes* (noun)—fool | *yatholat* (verb)—to rise |
| *vaes* (noun)—city | *zhikhak* (adjective)—sick |

NUMBERING SYSTEM

at—one	*zhinda*—six
akat—two	*fekh*—seven
sen—three	*ori*—eight
tor—four	*qazat*—nine
mek—five	*thi*—ten

PHILOLOGICAL FACTS

➤ David J. Peterson is president of the Language Creation Society, a group that exists to promote constructed languages. On its web page, *www.conlang .org*, you can purchase, among other things, T-shirts, beer-mug coasters, and iPhone cases. The society's mission is "to promote conlangs and conlanging through offering platforms for conlangers to publish high-quality work of interest to the community, raising awareness about conlanging amongst the general public, organizing work for professional conlangers and people in the entertainment industry interested in adding more depth to their alternative worlds, and providing a central place for reliable contacts and information to those seeking to learn more."

➤ George R. R. Martin began writing *A Song of Ice and Fire*, of which *Game of Thrones* is the first volume, in 1996. The series is planned to run to seven volumes, but as of 2011, Martin had published only five, with a gap of nearly six years between the appearance of volume 4 (*A Feast for Crows*) and volume 5 (*A Dance with Dragons*).

IF YOU'RE INTERESTED IN LEARNING THE LANGUAGE

A good place to start if you're interested in learning Dothraki is the unofficial web page of the language: *www.dothraki.org*.

FOR MORE INFORMATION

Review the works listed above, the resources listed in the bibliography, and the web pages: "David J. Peterson's Web Thing" (*www.dedalvs.com/index.html*), "Dothraki" (*www.dothraki.org*), "Dothraki Wiki" (*http://wiki.dothraki.org/dothraki/Main_Page*), and "A Song of Ice and Fire" (*http://en.wikipedia .org/wiki/A_Song_of_Ice_and_Fire*).

Eloi

Eloi is spoken by the Eloi people as portrayed in the film *The Time Machine* (2002).

DOCUMENTED BY
Screenwriter John Logan wrote the Eloi language for the 2002 movie.

BEHIND THE WORDS
The Time Machine (1895) by H. G. Wells (1866–1946) was turned into a film in 1960, but it wasn't until the 2002 version that the Eloi got to speak their own language. H. G. Wells coined the phrase "time machine" and introduced "the fourth dimension" as a way of viewing time.

PHILOLOGICAL FACT

➤ In his novel, Wells never quoted the Eloi and made clear that their language was, like them, soft and unobtrusive; he speaks of them "cooing" when the Time Traveller first meets them. Later it becomes clear that the Eloi are descendants of human beings but the human race has split apart: The subterranean Morlocks have taken with them the evil, animalistic tendencies, while the Eloi, though beautiful, are weak and helpless in the face of the Morlock threat. Wells is equally silent on the subject of the Morlock language, though they must presumably have had one, since they had also developed machinery.

FOR MORE INFORMATION
Review the work listed above, the resources listed in the bibliography, and the web pages: "Eloi" (*www.langmaker.com/eloi.htm*) and "The Time Machine" (*http://en.wikipedia.org/wiki/The_Time_Machine*).

SPEAKING OF LANGUAGES

"Why do you learn this language . . . if you don't use it?"

"It is a tradition we hand down. It must have meant something once."

—Mara, *The Time Machine* (film)

Our language has wisely sensed the two sides of being alone. It has created the word loneliness to express the pain of being alone. And it has created the word solitude to express the glory of being alone.

—Paul Tillich

Enchanta

SPOKEN BY
Enchanta is spoken by the inhabitants of Encantadia.

DOCUMENTED BY
Suzette Doctolero wrote the Filipino television series *Encantadia* (2005), which was followed by a prequel, *Etheria* (2005–2006).

A TASTE OF THE LANGUAGE

ado (noun)—father
ado (noun)—mother
a-junte (verb)—to sing
amaranteya (noun)—freedom

kantao (noun)—bracelet
neshda (verb)—to whisper
sanctre (noun)—death
ybarro (adjective)—brave

SOME USEFUL PHRASES

Avira voya uste. (Let me pass.)
Ekoshme. (Charge!)
Esva nastre sente. (Go and accept my blessings.)

PHILOLOGICAL FACT

➤ *Encantadia* was voted by Filipinos as their favorite television series in 2005 when it first aired. The story of the series is concerned with four princesses contending for a crown to the kingdom of Encantadia.

FOR MORE INFORMATION
Review the works listed above, the resources listed in the bibliography, and the web pages: "Enchanta" (*www.babylon.com/definition/enchanta/English*), "Enchanta" (*www.excathedra.multiply.com/journal/item/39*), and "Etheria" (*http://en.wikipedia.org/wiki/Etheria*).

Esperanto

SPOKEN BY

Esperanto is spoken by somewhere between 200 and 2,000,000 people, depending on whom you ask and whether they can understand the question.

DOCUMENTED BY

Doktoro Esperanto (pseudonym of L. L. Zamenhof) developed Esperanto to be an international language.

BEHIND THE WORDS

L. L. Zamenhof (1859–1917), a Byelorussian doctor, hoped to create a universal language that would bring people together in peace. He took ten years to develop the language; his first book written in Esperanto was published in 1887. He soon claimed adherents to his new language from around the world, and the first international congress of Esperanto speakers was held in France in 1905. World Wars I and II interrupted the spread of the language, especially because of the hostility of the Nazis, who viewed Esperanto as part of the international Jewish conspiracy denounced by Hitler.

Among its enthusiasts, there has been debate over the years as to whether Esperanto was intended to replace national languages or merely to be a useful supplement to them. Today, since Esperanto has never been adopted as the official language of a country, the latter point of view predominates. There are more than 100 periodicals published in Esperanto, along with thousands of books and millions of web pages.

DERIVATION OF THE LANGUAGE

Its lexicon derives primarily from Western European languages, while its syntax and morphology display strong Slavic influences.

—Universala Esperanto-Asocio

CHARACTERISTICS OF THE LANGUAGE

+ Esperanto has twenty-three consonants, five vowels, and two semivowels.
+ Words are developed by stringing together prefixes, roots, and suffixes.
+ Subjects, verbs, and objects can appear in any order.

A TASTE OF THE LANGUAGE

akvo (noun)—water
alkonduki (verb)—to bring
amiko (noun)—friend
birdo (noun)—bird
fajro (noun)—fire
hejmo (noun)—home
manĝi (verb)—to eat
morto (noun)—death
nutraĵo (noun)—food
piedo (noun)—foot

ponardo (noun)—dagger
ringo (noun)—ring
rivereto (noun)—stream
simplanimulo (noun)—fool
sonorilo (noun)—bell
suno (noun)—sun
somero (noun)—summer
travintri (noun)—winter
urbo (noun)—city
venki (verb)—to defeat

SOME USEFUL PHRASES

Kiel vi nomigas? (What is your name?)
Mi ŝatasrenkonti novajn homojn. (I like meeting new people.)
Mi amas vin. (I love you.)

Cu vi parolas Esperanton? (Do you speak Esperanto?)
Unu bieron, mi petas. (One beer, please.)

NUMBERING SYSTEM

unu—one
du—two
tri—three
kvar—four
kvin—five

ses—six
sep—seven
ok—eight
naŭ—nine
dek—ten

PHILOLOGICAL FACTS

➤ The film *Angoroj* (1964) was recorded entirely in Esperanto. Jacques-Louis Mahé, the director and producer, lost a large amount of money on the project and blamed Universala Esperanto-Asocio for the film's failure.

The film *Incubus* (1965) was the second film (after *Angoroj*) to be recorded entirely in Esperanto and stars William Shatner. Shatner, who learned some

Esperanto for the part, proved no better at the language than any of the other actors, causing a negative reaction from the Esperanto community.

➤ The *Concise Encyclopedia of the Original Literature of Esperanto 1887–2007* (by Geoffrey Sutton, Mondial, 2008) includes over 300 articles on the leading writers in Esperanto.

THE LORD'S PRAYER

Patro nia, kiu estas en la cielo,
sanktigata estu Via nomo.
Venu Via regno.
Farigu Via volo,
kiel en la cielo, tiel ankau sur la tero.
Nian panon ciutagan donu al ni hodiau.
Kaj pardonu al ni niajn suldojn,
kiel ankau ni pardonas al niaj suldantoj.
Kaj ne konduku nin en tenton,
sed liberigu nin de la malbono.
(Car Via estas la regno kaj la potenco
kaj la gloro eterne.)
Amen.

IF YOU'RE INTERESTED IN LEARNING THE LANGUAGE

The Esperanto-USA web page (*www.esperanto-usa.org*) is a good place to learn Esperanto and to order books, DVDs, and other training materials.

FOR MORE INFORMATION

Review the works listed above, the resources listed in the bibliography, and the web pages: "Angoroj" (*http://en.wikipedia.org/wiki/Angoroj*), "Doktoro Esperanto's Dream" (*www.english.illinois .edu/-people-/faculty/debaron/401/401%20files/esperanto.html*), "Esperanto USA" (*www.esperanto-usa.org*), and "Incubus (1966 film)" (*http://en.wikipedia.org/wiki/Incubus_(1966_film)*).

SPEAKING OF LANGUAGES

A special kind of beauty exists which is born in language, of language, and for language.

—Gaston Bachelard

Eunoia

SPOKEN BY

Eunoia is spoken by the Taelons, an alien race that comes to Earth seeking refuge.

DOCUMENTED BY

Linguist Christian Bök (1966–) used notes left by Gene Roddenberry (1921–1991) to design the language for the show *Earth: Final Conflict* (1997–2002).

BEHIND THE WORDS

In return for safe refuge, an advanced alien race, the Taelons, offer human beings access to advanced technologies. The Taelons, however, have a hidden agenda.

CHARACTERISTICS OF THE LANGUAGE

+ With a vowel-rich vocabulary, Eunoia has been described as sounding like both singing and sighing.
+ The language is always changing, mutating like a virus.
+ Eunoia uses *nounverbs* that combine idea and action.

PHILOLOGICAL FACTS

➤ Christian Bök wrote a book of poetry, *Eunoia* (2001), which is separated into five chapters, each titled with a single vowel. All the poems within a given chapter only use that chapter's vowel. *Eunoia* is also available online, flash or text (*http://archives.chbooks.com/online_books/eunoia*).

➤ *Eunoia* is one of the shortest words in the English language to contain all the vowels. The word means *beautiful thinking*.

FOR MORE INFORMATION

Review the works listed above, the resources listed in the bibliography, and the web pages: "Cultural Overview" (*http://classic-web.archive.org/web/20020211221231/taelons.com/lexicon/loverview.html*), "Linguistic Assumptions" (*http://classic-web.archive.org/web/20020211215830/taelons.com/lexicon/llinguist.html*), and "Preliminary Pronunciation" (*http://classic-web.archive.org/web/20020211221356/taelons.com/lexicon/lprelimin.html*).

Gargish

SPOKEN BY

Gargish is spoken by the Gargoyles in the massive multiplayer online game *Ultima Online: Stygian Abyss* (*www.uoherald.com/legacy/stygianabyss/*).

BEHIND THE WORDS

Gargoyles were the third playable race (after humans and elves) to appear in the Ultima Online universe, and *Stygian Abyss* is the eighth expansion pack for the game. It was released in 2009. Gargoyles are hairless creatures that are skilled at magic, combat, and crafts. They live in Ter Mur, a lush land beset by internal strife.

CHARACTERISTICS OF THE LANGUAGE

+ The Gargish alphabet consists of thirty symbols.

A TASTE OF THE LANGUAGE

alb (adjective)—white
an-lor-tim (noun)—night
flam (noun)—fire
flam-tim (noun)—summer
korp (noun)—death
lup (noun)—wolf
ov (noun)—egg
pisk (noun)—fish
por-char (noun)—leg
por-mír (noun)—river
ra (noun)—valor

reg (noun)—home
ru (adjective)—red
sarp (noun)—serpent
sil (noun)—star
summ (noun)—honor
sur (noun)—sun
turn (noun)—cave
vas-arb (noun)—tree
vid (verb)—to look
zú-tim (noun)—winter

SOME USEFUL PHRASES

Ánte esta terreg mánite múr anísh zen. (In that land live many strange creatures.)
A qua lemmúr wíste, an zen anku vol verde wís. (But as everyone knows, no creature without wings is truly intelligent.)
Tú rete ku klí axi: ún, or, esh us. (All begins with the three principles: Control, Passion, and Diligence.)

NUMBERING SYSTEM

pri—one
sek—two
qi—three
kuar—four

pen—five
ek—six
sem—seven
ok—eight

PHILOLOGICAL FACTS

➤ *Ultima Online* received eight entries in the *Guinness World Records: Gamer's Edition 2008.*

➤ The Ultimate Online encyclopedia comments that "the Gargoyles are often mistaken as demons but are in fact a proud mystical race with an ancient history." Their situation in Ter Mur is a particularly difficult one, since they are beset by challenges from both within and without. Inside Ter Mur, strange supernatural creatures from the Void are entering the land. Meanwhile, Ter Mur's natural resources are being drained, and the gargoyles must combat the threat from the Void while dealing with this problem.

IF YOU'RE INTERESTED IN LEARNING THE LANGUAGE

Do you feel like getting in touch with your inner gargoyle? Check out the *Ultima Online* site (*www.uo.com/archive/gargoyle*) to give voice to the urge.

FOR MORE INFORMATION

Review the works listed above, the resources listed in the bibliography, and the web pages: "Gargoyle Race" (*www.uoguide.com/Gargoyle_Race*), "The Language of the Gargoyles" (*www.uo.com/archive/gargoyle/*), and "Ter Mur" (*www.uoguide.com/Ter_Mur*).

SPEAKING OF LANGUAGES

Every legend, moreover, contains its residuum of truth, and the root function of language is to control the universe by describing it.

—James A. Baldwin

Glide

SPOKEN BY
Glide is spoken by the Glides.

DOCUMENTED BY
Diana Reed Slattery (*The Maze Game*, 2003) developed Glide to see how far language could deviate from the norm.

BEHIND THE WORDS
Hallucinogenic pollen from the blue water lily brings the language to the Glides some 4,000 years from now.

CHARACTERISTICS OF THE LANGUAGE

+ Glide is a representative language that cannot be spoken.
+ Glide consists of static and dynamic forms in two and three dimensions.

IF YOU'RE INTERESTED IN LEARNING THE LANGUAGE:
Whether you want to learn Glide or simply experience a visually dynamic language, trip on over to the Glide web page (*www.academy.rpi.edu/glide*).

PHILOLOGICAL FACT

➤ Slattery's novel *The Maze Game* tells the story of the origins of Glide like this: "The 27 glyphs of the Glide language emerged from the bottom muck of a vast lily pond. The pollen of the giant blue water lilies distilled into a powerful entheogen, the Wine of the Lilies. The pollen was harvested by small-bodied people who could scoop and glide from lily pad to lily pad smoothly and swiftly enough to avoid being tipped into the water, tangled in the roots, and consumed by the omnivorous lily. The Glides, breathing the raw pollen, cross-pollinated the lily as they harvested. The lily, in appreciation of their efforts, gave them a language, Glide, first as an extension of the gestures of harvesting and pollination, later in written form."

FOR MORE INFORMATION

Review the works listed above, the resources listed in the bibliography, and the web pages: "Conglanging: The Not-So-Secret Vice" (*www.realitysandwich.com/print/18617*), "The Glide Project" (*www.academy.rpi.edu/glide*), and "Xenolinguistics I: Aspects of Alien Art" (*http://mazerunner .wordpress.com/2008/02/22/xenolinguistics-i-aspects-of-alien-art*).

SPEAKING OF LANGUAGES

It is useful to the historian, among others, to be able to see the commonest forms of different phenomena, whether phonetic, morphological or other, and how language lives, carries on and changes over time.

—Ferdinand de Saussure

Glosa

SPOKEN BY

Glosa is spoken by those who wish to communicate through an auxiliary language.

DOCUMENTED BY

Interglossa was invented by a versatile scientist, Lancelot Hogben (1895–1975), who saw it as an auxiliary language (*auxlang*), one that would contribute to communication between speakers of different languages without requiring them to give up their native tongues. Ronald Clark and Wendy Ashby worked on Interglossa to make it easier to use. After Hogben died and could no longer approve their changes, Clark and Ashby broke off on their own with Glosa.

BEHIND THE WORDS

Glosa is an international auxiliary language. Ashby and Clark tested the language in the "laboratory" setting of their hometown until 1979, before going public.

DERIVATION OF THE LANGUAGE

Glosa is derived from Interglossa, another international language.

CHARACTERISTICS OF THE LANGUAGE

- Words always retain their original form, no matter what role they play in a sentence (that is, Glosa is a noninflected language).
- Grammatical function is determined by word order and by *operator words*, making it similar to Chinese and several other East Asian languages.
- Complex words are created by putting together basic words.
- Glosa uses a standard subject-verb-object structure.
- Pronunciation is similar to Italian, with some German influences.

A TASTE OF THE LANGUAGE

aqa (noun)—water
avi (noun)—bird
blada (noun)—dagger
civita (noun)—city

domi (noun)—home
fero (verb)—to bring
fluvi (noun)—river
frigi-tem (noun)—winter

heli (noun)—summer
koragi (adjective)—brave
morta (noun)—death
piro (noun)—fire
piski (noun)—fish
poda (noun)—leg

rubi (adjective)—red
serpenti (noun)—serpent
vespera-vora (noun)—dinner
vora (verb)—to eat
zona (noun)—ring

SOME USEFUL PHRASES
Qo-mode nomina/nima vi? (What is your name?)
Qe vi dice Glosa? (Do you speak Glosa?)

A vi eu-sani. (Here's to your health.)
Qo-mode iti vi? (How are you?)

NUMBERING SYSTEM
mo—one
bi—two
tri—three
tet—four
pen—five

six—six
set—seven
ok—eight
nona—nine
dek—ten

THE LORD'S PRAYER
Na parenta in Urani; na volu;
tu nima gene revero.
Tu krati veni; tu tende gene akti
epi Geo homo in Urani Place;
don a na nu-di na di-pane;
e Tu pardo na plu mali akti.
Metro na pardo mu; qui akti
mali de na.
E ne dirige na a plu moli ofere;
sed libe na ab mali.
Ka Tu tena u krati, u dina
e un eufamo pan tem.
Amen.

PHILOLOGICAL FACT

➤ Lancelot Hogben, the original inventor of Glosa, was an Englishman and a secular humanist, as well as a member of both the Fabian Society and the Independent Labour Party. Concerning modern developments in language, he observed in his "Vocabulary of Science": The world-wide vocabulary of Science is the nearest thing to the lexicon of a truly global Language that Mankind has yet achieved. It derives its words from two dead languages— Greek and Latin.

IF YOU'RE INTERESTED IN LEARNING THE LANGUAGE

Go to the Glosa web page (*www.glosa.org/en*) to learn about Glosa.

FOR MORE INFORMATION

Review the works listed above, the resources listed in the bibliography, and the web page: Glosa (*www.glosa.org*).

SPEAKING OF LANGUAGES

There is no such thing as an ugly language. Today I hear every language as if it were the only one, and when I hear of one that is dying, it overwhelms me as though it were the death of the earth.

—Elias Canetti

Gnommish

SPOKEN BY

Gnommish is spoken by the fairies.

DOCUMENTED BY

Eoin Colfer (1965–) includes the world of the fairies in the Artemis Fowl series. The series starts with *Artemis Fowl* (2001) and continues with *Artemis Fowl: The Arctic Incident* (2002), *Artemis Fowl: The Eternity Code* (2003), *Artemis Fowl: The Opal Deception* (2005), *Artemis Fowl: The Lost Colony* (2006), *Artemis Fowl: The Time Paradox* (2008), and *Artemis Fowl: The Atlantis Complex* (2010). An eighth book is scheduled for 2012.

BEHIND THE WORDS

Artemis Fowl II is a twelve-year-old master criminal who kidnaps a fairy for ransom and, as a result, is gradually drawn into the complex political machinations of the fairy realm.

CHARACTERISTICS OF THE LANGUAGE

+ The Gnommish alphabet contains twenty-six symbols.
+ The letter e is placed under the letter that follows it.
+ The Gnommish alphabet does not differentiate between upper- and lowercase characters.

A TASTE OF THE LANGUAGE

Cowpog (adjective)—moron
D'Arvit (interjection)—Gnommish profanity
Ffurfor (verb)—to plunder

PHILOLOGICAL FACTS

➤ It is thought that Egyptian hieroglyphs were derived from the Gnommish alphabet. In actual fact, the Gnommish used in the books is a substitution code for English words. Gnommish was, at one time, written in spirals, but since these tend to give fairies migraines, the language is now written in horizontal lines.

➤ The books contain a quirky humor. Among the major characters is the fairy Captain Holly Short, a member of the Lower Elements Police, or LEP. She leads the reconnaissance unit of the police, naturally known as LEPrecon.

FOR MORE INFORMATION
Review the works listed above, the resources listed in the bibliography, and the web pages: "Artemis Fowl" (*www.artemisfowl.com*), "Artemis Fowl" (*http://artemisfowl.wikia.com/wiki /Artemis_Fowl_(book)*), and "Gnommish" (*http://artemisfowl.wikia.com/wiki/Gnommish*). To download the Gnommish font, go to *www.webcitation.org/query?url=http://www.geocities.com/thephlegmpot /index.html&date=2009-10-25+23:01:58*

SPEAKING OF LANGUAGES

I want a language that speaks the truth.

—Studs Terkel

Goa'uld

SPOKEN BY
Goa'uld is spoken by the Goa'uld, parasites from the planet P3X-888.

DOCUMENTED BY
The film *Stargate* (1994) introduced the story, which was continued in the television shows *Stargate SG-1* (1997–2007), *Stargate: Atlantis* (2004–2009), and *SGU Stargate Universe* (2009–2011). There have also been Stargate games, Stargate comics, Stargate books, and two direct-to-DVD films as well as an animated series, *Stargate Infinity* (2002–2003).

BEHIND THE WORDS
The Goa'uld are serpent parasites that infect humans, using their hosts as tools to conquer and dominate. Infected humans become healthier, stronger, and quicker to heal.

A TASTE OF THE LANGUAGE
a'roush (noun)—village
cal mah (noun)—sanctuary
chappa'ai (noun)—Stargate
Dis'tra (noun)—master
Kal'ma (noun)—child
Krenol (verb)—to attack
Nema (noun)—priest
Ni'ya (verb)—to listen

Rai (noun)—star
rin nok! (interjection)—silence!
shol'va (noun)—traitor
tak (noun)—trick
tal'lak (adjective)—lifeless
Tau'ri (noun)—Earth
teltac (noun)—cargo ship
Tuat (noun)—the underworld

SOME USEFUL PHRASES
Dal Shakka Mel. (I die Free.)
Harek rel kree lo'mak onak rak shel'na. (I know everything. There is nothing you can do to help.)
Sejem secher hereh, neswet. Hekat irt kaping at weben taa. Weya set se rech reshwet weben. Shiak hanweysun, herew. Herew. (I will speak the words of power and do the rites. You will be returned to Egypt and buried with honor. You will pass through the seven gates and see your wife and children again, and rejoice with them forever.)
Mol kek! (Kill them all!)

PHILOLOGICAL FACT

➤ The Goa'uld evolved on planet P3X-888 and gradually migrated through the galaxy in search of hosts. They eventually found them on ancient Earth, and as a result they ruled the planet for many thousands of years. The Goa'uld, in other words, are simply the originals of the gods of ancient religions, which explains the extensive serpent worship that is found in many old systems of belief.

FOR MORE INFORMATION

Review the works listed above, the resources listed in the bibliography, and the web pages: "Goa'uld Dictionary" (*www.tokraresistance.com/dictionary.html*) and "Goa'uld Dictionary" (*http://rdanderson.com/stargate/dictionary/goauld.htm*).

SPEAKING OF LANGUAGES

I ascribe a basic importance to the phenomenon of language. . . . To speak means to be in a position to use a certain syntax, to grasp the morphology of this or that language, but it means above all to assume a culture, to support the weight of a civilization.

—Frantz Fanon

Gobbledegook

SPOKEN BY

Gobbledegook is spoken by the goblins in the Harry Potter series.

DOCUMENTED BY

J. K. Rowling (1965–) chronicles the story of Harry Potter in the bestselling Harry Potter series: *Harry Potter and the Philosopher's Stone* (1997), *Harry Potter and the Chamber of Secrets* (1998), *Harry Potter and the Prisoner of Azkaban* (1999), *Harry Potter and the Goblet of Fire* (2000), *Harry Potter and the Order of the Phoenix* (2003), *Harry Potter and the Half-Blood Prince* (2005), and *Harry Potter and the Deathly Hallows* (2007).

PHILOLOGICAL FACTS

➤ The word *gobbledygook* (sometimes spelled *gobbledegook*) was made up by U. S. Representative Maury Maverick (1895–1954) to describe the "convoluted language of bureaucrats" and was used in a memo dated March 30, 1944. Maverick's grandfather, Samuel Maverick (1803–1870), was the inspiration for using the word *maverick* to describe an independent thinker. *Gobbledygook* was derived from the sound turkeys make, a process of word formation called onomatopoeia (a term made up by Edgar Allan Poe [1809–1849], hence the *poe* towards the end of word).

➤ Gobbledygook and Parseltongue (the language of snakes) are the only two languages mentioned in Rowling's Harry Potter novels (aside, of course, from the natural languages spoken by various inhabitants of the wizarding world). It seems odd that goblins should have their own language, though perhaps not as much when Bill Weasley explains to Harry in *Harry Potter and the Deathly Hallows* that goblins have a substantially different outlook on life (particularly on ownership) than humans.

FOR MORE INFORMATION

Review the works listed above, the resources listed in the bibliography, and the web pages: "Gobbledygook" (*http://en.wikipedia.org/wiki/Gobbledegook*), "Harry Potter" (*http://en.wikipedia.org/wiki/Harry_Potter*), "J. K. Rowling" (*http://en.wikipedia.org/wiki/J._K._Rowling*), and "Samuel Maverick" (*http://en.wikipedia.org/wiki/Samuel_Maverick*).

Goldogrin

SPOKEN BY

Goldogrin was spoken by the Second Clan of Elves, the Gnomes, and thus the language is often called Gnommish. The Gnomes were later called the Ñoldor.

DOCUMENTED BY

J. R. R. Tolkien (1892–1973) explored many languages and cultures as he told the stories of Middle-earth: *The Hobbit* (1937), *The Fellowship of the Ring* (1954), *The Two Towers* (1954), and *The Return of the King* (1955). (The last three are collectively called *The Lord of the Rings*.) After his death, his son Christopher Tolkien (1924–) edited *The Silmarillion* (1977) with the help of Guy Gavriel Kay (1954–). Christopher Tolkien then deeply analyzed his father's notebooks, letters, and drafts to produce an extended study of Middle-earth and its creation: *The Book of Lost Tales, Part One* (1983), *The Book of Lost Tales, Part Two* (1984), *The Lays of Beleriand* (1985), *The Shaping of Middle-earth* (1986), *The Lost Road and Other Writings* (1987), *The Return of the Shadow (The History of The Lord of the Rings, Part One)* (1988), *The Treason of Isengard (The History of The Lord of the Rings, Part Two)* (1989), *The War of the Ring (The History of The Lord of the Rings, Part Three)* (1990), *Sauron Defeated (The History of The Lord of the Rings, Part Four)* (1992), *Morgoth's Ring (The Later Silmarillion, Part One)* (1993), *The War of the Jewels (The Later Silmarillion, Part Two)* (1994), and *The Peoples of Middle-earth* (1996).

BEHIND THE WORDS

The Ñoldor were originally called the Tatyar, meaning *second ones*. They were also referred to as Deep Elves and Gnomes. In Middle-earth, they were renowned as smiths, and Fëanor was their greatest craftsman. He created the *palantíri*, or seeing stones, one of which came into the possession of the wizard Sauruman the White and another of which was held by the Stewards of Gondor until the reign of the last steward, Denethor II.

DERIVATION OF THE LANGUAGE

Goldogrin was less influenced by Welsh phonology than were the later Noldorin and Sindarin. In some respects—for example in the formation of the past tense—it is grammatically similar to English.

CHARACTERISTICS OF THE LANGUAGE

+ Nouns have three cases (inessive or nominative, genitive, and allative or dative).

A TASTE OF THE LANGUAGE

agra (adjective)—extreme
ailion (noun)—lake
bothli (noun)—oven
crî (noun)—knife
dulwen (noun)—a feast
ectha (noun)—sword
finthi (noun)—idea
godra (adjective)—joined
heloth (noun)—frost
indos (noun)—house

leptha (noun)—finger
madri (noun)—food
nandor (noun)—farmer
octha (noun)—knee
porogwil (noun)—hen
rodrin (noun)—cavern
saig (adjective)—hungry
tavros (noun)—forest
ubri (noun)—rain

PHILOLOGICAL FACT

➤ Goldogrin is sometimes called I-Lam na-Ngoldathon, or the language of the Noldoli. Some consider it an early form of Sindarin; Tolkien seems to have come to this point of view while writing *The Lord of the Rings* trilogy. However, he had been working on Goldogrin as early as 1917, when he wrote the first drafts of the *Legendarium*.

FOR MORE INFORMATION

Review the works listed above, the resources listed in the bibliography, and the web pages: "Ardalambion" (*www.folk.uib.no/hnohf/*), "Cirth" (*www.omniglot.com/writing/cirth.htm*), "How many languages did J.R.R. Tolkien make?" (*www.folk.uib.no/hnohf/howmany.htm*), "J. R. R. Tolkien: A Biographical Sketch" (*www.tolkiensociety.org/tolkien/biography.html*), "Sarati alphabet" (*www.omniglot.com/writing/sarati.htm*), and "Tengwar" (*www.omniglot.com/writing/tengwar.htm*).

SPEAKING OF LANGUAGES

England and America are two countries separated by a common language.

—George Bernard Shaw

Goodenuf English

SPOKEN BY

Goodenuf English is spoken by people in a future set twenty-five years after the publication of the book *Rainbow's End* by Vernor Vinge (1944–).

DOCUMENTED BY

Vernor Vinge tells the story of Robert Gu, who is trying to recover from Alzheimer's disease in a future where augmented reality is the norm. Reality, in other words, is created and networked, so the line between what is real and what is merely perceived has become frighteningly vague. The novel also contains a plot concerning a high-level conspiracy and an anthropomorphic rabbit.

FOR MORE INFORMATION

Review the work listed above, the resources listed in the bibliography, and the web page: "A Scientist's Art: Computer Fiction" (*www.nytimes.com/2001/08/02/technology/a-scientist-s-art-computer-fiction.html*).

SPEAKING OF LANGUAGES

Actually, language wasn't a problem. They'd get together on his beach or hers—depending on which side of the world was daylight or had the nicest weather—and chatter away in Goodenuf English, the air around them filled with translation guesstimates and picture substitutions. Their little clique had contributed lots to the answerboards; it was the most "socially responsible" of Miri's hobbies.

—Rainbow's End

Genuine poetry can communicate before it is understood.

—T. S. Eliot

Groilish

SPOKEN BY
Groilish is spoken by Jumbeelia and the other giants who live in Groil. When Jumbeelia climbs down to the land of the miniature people, the iggly pops, she brings back three of them (Collette, Stephen, and baby Poppy) as playthings.

DOCUMENTED BY
Julia Donaldson (1948–) introduces younger readers to constructed languages in *The Giants and The Joneses* (2004). She includes a dictionary to explain what the giants are saying, although much of the meaning of their speech can be inferred by context.

A TASTE OF THE LANGUAGE
aheesh (verb)—to help
blebber (noun)—sheep
gloosh (verb)—to drink
jum (noun)—home

kraggle (verb)—to kill
lolshly (adjective)—white
niffle (verb)—to give
oggle (verb)—to look

NUMBERING SYSTEM
wunk—one
twunk—two
thrink—three

PHILOLOGICAL FACT

➤ *The Gruffalo*, based on Julia Donaldson's book, was made into a 2009 animated movie, starring Helena Bonham Carter, James Corden, and Tom Wilkinson. Robbie Coltrane played the Gruffalo.

FOR MORE INFORMATION
Review the works listed above, the resources listed in the bibliography, and the web pages: "The Giants and the Joneses" (*www.amazon.com/Giants-Joneses-Julia-Donaldson/dp/0805078053*) and "Julia Donaldson Talks Groilish" (*www.britishcouncil.org/arts-literature-matters-3-donaldson.htm*).

SPEAKING OF LANGUAGES

I have always been fascinated by the sound of words and enjoy playing around with them, which is partly why many of my picture-book texts, such as The Snail and the Whale *and* The Gruffalo, *are in rhyme.*

—Julia Donaldson

Most of the fundamental ideas of science are essentially simple, and may, as a rule, be expressed in a language comprehensible to everyone.

—Albert Einstein

Hani

SPOKEN BY

Hani is spoken by the Hani, a maned and bearded species that's covered by fur and lives on the planet Anuurn.

DOCUMENTED BY

C. J. Cherryh (1942–) writes of the Hani in the Chanur series: *The Pride of Chanur* (1981), *Chanur's Venture* (1981), *The Kif Strike Back* (1985), *Chanur's Homecoming* (1986), and *Chanur's Legacy* (1992).

BEHIND THE WORDS

The Hani are one of the species that are part of the Compact, a trade organization that facilitates interstellar economies. They use a pictograph machine to communicate with other species. Hani look something like large, bearded cats, with red or tawny fur and thick manes.

THE BABEL TEXT

Fai-shukh-aarn nai-Terra lin-aarn hen-fhaif chuch hen-fhaan.

Viarr, ri nai-neg shaih-hiuman-aa-im fai-rrach-haur hen-bek, ri nai-hen-aa fai-kah-gfaan Shinar-im hen-chuj-m'ha shiah-nab chuch hen-mosh-m'ha chai-nup.

Ri nai-hen-aa hen-rukh-m'ha kha chai-laam, "Re nai-mur m'chaun-m'ha chai-shir-aa chuch shaohsh-aarn mur-khaumsam'ha chai-hen-aa." Nai-hen-aa chai-turr-aa-viarr hen-shiarr-m'ha chai-shir-aa chuch chai-orr-chup-viarr hen-shiarr-m'ha chai-ull.

Ri nai-hen-aa hen-rukh-m'ha chai-laam, "Re nai-mur mur-chi mur-chaul-m'ha chai-jiahn chuch chai-naukh tai-faat hauitia nai-mur fai-kuut-aa-khe hen-bog-m'ha; re nai-mur mur-chi mur-gaif-m'ha chai-llauhn uukh haatia khai-mur-aa kurr-aarn fai-nekhrhof fai-terra-im mur'rrib.

Ri Na nai-Rraohm hen-raos uukh nai-hen h'-gfirr-m'ha chai-jiahn chuch chai-naukh, chai-faat ri-rait fai-hiuman-im nai-chaach-aa hen-chauul-m'ha.

Ri na nai-Rraohm hen-rukh-m'ha chai-laam, "fai-shukh-aarn nai-hiuman-aa hen-chan chuch hen-fhiaf; haa-hau-ro-tia khai-haamrhaohch, chai-faat ri-rait nai-hen-aa h'-siaj-m'ha, hen-haurr h'-mia-naohs-m'ha.

"Re nai-mur-aa m'-raos chuch nu-paarn mur-kaf-m'ha tai-hen chai-fhiaf, uukh haa-hau-ro-tia nai-hen-aa h'-rhaarn-m'ha tai-ges chai-fhaan."

Uukh, ri Na nai-Rraohm kurr-aarn fai-nekhrh-of fai-terra-im mur-'-rrib-m'ha chai-hen-aa: chuch ri nai-hen-aa h'-llaig-m'ha fai-jiahn-im chai-chaul.

Rhau, ri khai-Babel, nai-faat hen'-sem-m'ha chai-kaf, nai-hen h'-pukh-m'ha; rrum ri Na nai-Rraohm shukh-aarn fai-terra-im hem-kaf-m'ha chai-fhiat: chuch ri Na nai-Rraom kurr-aarn fai-nekhrh-of fai-terra-im hem'-rrib-m'ha chai-hen-aa.

PHILOLOGICAL FACTS

➤ The Hani language later developed into a pidgin for the Compact since it was grammatically simple and easy to pick up.

➤ The violent and aggressive male Hani are relegated to the homeworld rather than allowed into space to cause problems at the interplanetary level.

➤ There is, in fact, a real Hani language, which is spoken in areas of China, Laos, Myanmar (Burma), and Vietnam by the Hani people. Until the 1950s, there was no written version, but in 1957 the Chinese government developed one based on the language's phonetics.

FOR MORE INFORMATION

Review the works listed above, the resources listed in the bibliography, and the web page: "Hani Language and Culture Page" (*http://strengthofthehills.tripod.com/hanilanguageandculturepage/*).

SPEAKING OF LANGUAGES

If you talk to a man in a language he understands, that goes to his head. If you talk to him in his language, that goes to his heart.

—Nelson Mandela

Hardic

SPOKEN BY

Hardic, also known as the Common Tongue, is widely spoken in the lands of Earthsea with the exceptions of the Kargard Lands and Osskil.

DOCUMENTED BY

Ursula K. Le Guin (1929–) relates the tales of Earthsea in: *A Wizard of Earthsea* (1968), *The Tombs of Atuan* (1971), *The Farthest Shore* (1973), *Tehanu: The Last Book of Earthsea* (1990), *Tales from Earthsea* (2001), and *The Other Wind* (2001).

BEHIND THE WORDS

> *But magic, true magic, is worked only by those beings who speak the Hardic tongue of Earthsea, or the Old Speech from which it grew.*
>
> *That is the language dragons speak, and the language Segoy spoke who made the islands of the world, and the language of our lays and songs, spells, enchantments, and invocations.*

> —A Wizard of Earthsea

DERIVATION OF THE LANGUAGE

Hardic is derived from Old Speech, the Language of the Making.

A TASTE OF THE LANGUAGE

alath (noun)—people
arkemmi (verb)—give!
harrekki (noun)—tiny dragon

kabat (noun)—pebble
sukien (noun)—foam

PHILOLOGICAL FACT

➤ Le Guin indicates in her books that Hardic runes are widely used for writing throughout Earthsea. They are nonmagical in character, different from The Six Hundred Runes of Hardic, which are "true runes" and used for magic.

FOR MORE INFORMATION

Review the works listed above, the resources listed in the bibliography, and the web pages: "Characters in Earthsea" (*http://en.wikipedia.org/wiki/Characters_in_Earthsea*), "The Isolate Tower" (*http://tavia.co.uk/earthsea/index.htm*), "Ursula K. Le Guin" (*www.ursulakleguin.com/*), and "Ursula LeGuin's Magical World of Earthsea" (*http://scholar.lib.vt.edu/ejournals/ALAN/spring96/griffin.html*).

SPEAKING OF LANGUAGES

The language of friendship is not words but meanings.

—Henry David Thoreau

High D'Haran

High D'Haran is spoken by those who live in the D'Haran Empire, ruled by Darken Rahl.

DOCUMENTED BY
Terry Goodkind (1948–) developed High D'Haran in *The Sword of Truth* series: *Wizard's First Rule* (1994), *Stone of Tears* (1995), *Blood of the Fold* (1996), *Temple of the Winds* (1997), *Soul of the Fire* (1999), *Faith of the Fallen* (2000), *Debt of Bones* (2001), *The Pillars of Creation* (2002), *Naked Empire* (2003), *Chainfire* (2005), *Phantom* (2006), and *Confessor* (2007).

BEHIND THE WORDS
D'Hara was, in the past, a loose confederation of kingdoms that were united by Panis Rahl. This led to a prolonged war between D'Hara and the Central Council of the Midlands, one that ended in a stalemate. Panis Rahl's son, Darken Rahl, inherited the throne from his father and continued his expansionist policies, albeit under the guise of wanting peace. Richard Cypher, a guide from Westland, became a Seeker of Truth, and when the D'Haran invaded the Midlands, Cypher traveled there to stop Darken Rahl from becoming all powerful.

A TASTE OF THE LANGUAGE
bandakar (noun)—the banished
grushdeva (noun)—vengeance
moss (noun)—wind
owbens (noun)—ovens
raug' (adjective)—divine

reechani (noun)—water
sentroshi (noun)—fire
surangie (verb)—to surrender
vasi (noun)—air

A USEFUL PHRASE
Grushdeva du kalt misht. (Vengeance is through me.)

FOR MORE INFORMATION
Review the works listed above, the resources listed in the bibliography, and the web page: "High D'Haran Dictionary" (*http://aydindril.5.forumer.com/a/high-d39haran-dictionary_post809.html*).

High Speech

SPOKEN BY

Roland Deschain of Gilead begins *The Dark Tower* series as the primary speaker of High Speech, a language that is all but dead.

DOCUMENTED BY

Stephen King (1947–) describes Roland Deschain's quest in the fantastical world of *The Dark Tower: The Gunslinger* (1982), *The Dark Tower II: The Drawing of the Three* (1987), *The Dark Tower III: The Waste Lands* (1991), *The Dark Tower IV: Wizard and Glass* (1997), *The Dark Tower V: Wolves of the Calla* (2003), *The Dark Tower VI: Song of Susannah* (2004), *The Dark Tower VII: The Dark Tower* (2004), and *The Dark Tower: The Wind Through the Keyhole* (2012).

BEHIND THE WORDS

In the *Dark Tower* universe, High Speech is the formal language, as opposed to Calla-Speak, Crunk, or Plain, spoken regularly by most people.

CHARACTERISTICS OF THE LANGUAGE

+ High Speech is written in all capitals.

A TASTE OF THE LANGUAGE

CHAR (noun)—death
DINH (noun)—leader
KA (noun)—fate

MIA (noun)—mother
POPKIN (noun)—sandwich

PHILOLOGICAL FACT

➤ Bestselling-author Stephen King wrote the *Dark Tower* series over twenty-two years. It comprises seven novels and a short story. King himself regards the series as his most important fictional work.

FOR MORE INFORMATION

Review the works listed above, the resources listed in the bibliography, and the web page: "The Dark Tower (series)" (*http://en.wikipedia.org/wiki/The_Dark_Tower_%28series%29*).

Houyhnhnm

Houyhnhnm is spoken by the Houyhnhnm of *Gulliver's Travels* (1726).

DOCUMENTED BY
Jonathan Swift (1667–1745) was a satirist who wrote about imaginary places and creatures in order to ridicule the failings of his own time.

BEHIND THE WORDS
The Houyhnhnm were civilized horses who shared an island with Yahoos, base and brute human beings. After being stranded ashore by his crew, Gulliver discovers both groups, turns his back on the Yahoos, and aligns himself with the Houyhnhnm, so impressed is he with their noble and idyllic society.

DERIVATION OF THE LANGUAGE
The name Houyhnhnm and the rest of the words sound close to a horse's whinny.

A TASTE OF THE LANGUAGE
Gnnauyh (noun)—bird of prey
Houyhnhnm (noun)—their race, literally "the perfection of nature"

PHILOLOGICAL FACT

➤ Although Swift is chiefly remembered today for *Gulliver's Travels,* in his own time he was also notorious for the short pamphlet *A Modest Proposal* (1729). In this biting satire, he recommended to the English that they solve the problem of Ireland's poverty by killing and eating Irish babies. He went so far as to include recommendations on how to prepare the children for cooking.

FOR MORE INFORMATION
Review the works listed above and the resources listed in the bibliography.

SPEAKING OF LANGUAGES

In speaking, they pronounce through the Nose and Throat, and their Language approaches nearest to the High Dutch or German, of any I know in Europe; but is much more graceful and significant.

—Gulliver's Travels

It put me to the Pains of many Circumlocutions to give my Master a right idea of what I spoke; for their Language doth not abound in a Variety of Words, because their Wants and Passions are fewer than among us.

—Gulliver's Travels

My principal Endeavor was to learn the Language, which my Master (for so I shall henceforth call him) and his Children, and every Servant of his house were desirous to teach me. For they looked upon it as a Prodigy, that a brute Animal should discover such Marks of a rational Creature. I pointed to every thing, and enquired the Name of it, which I wrote down in my Journal Book when I was alone, and corrected my bad Accent, by desiring those of the Family to pronounce it often.

—Gulliver's Travels

Language is wine upon the lips.

—Virginia Woolf

Ido

SPOKEN BY

Ido is spoken by those who wish to learn a constructed language as an aide to better world communication.

DOCUMENTED BY

In 1907, a group of professors and linguists created Ido as a reform of Esperanto.

BEHIND THE WORDS

Ido was developed from Esperanto as a result of disagreements within the Esperanto community. While the leaders of the Esperantist movement were seeking to gain wider international support for their language, some—in particular, Louis Couturat and Louis de Beaufort—argued for further changes to Esperanto before it was presented to the world as *the* auxiliary language. This disagreement escalated into a split in the Esperantist movement, and the supporters of Ido went their own way. Couturat was killed in an automobile accident in 1914; this, together with World War I, substantially weakened the movement.

Like Esperanto, the roots used in Ido were like those found in English, French, Spanish, German, Russian, and Italian. The estimated number of speakers of Ido at present ranges from 2,000 to 5,000.

CHARACTERISTICS OF THE LANGUAGE

+ Ido uses the twenty-six-letter Latin alphabet with the addition of two extra characters, *ch* and *sh*.
+ Rules in Ido are regular.
+ The language follows a subject-verb-object structure.

A TASTE OF THE LANGUAGE

amiko (noun)—friend
atakis (verb)—to attack
brava (adjective)—brave
dineo (noun)—dinner

dormar (verb)—to sleep
fisho (noun)—fish
incendio (noun)—fire
kavalo (noun)—horse

manjar (verb)—to eat
matro (noun)—mother
navo (noun)—ship
nigra (adjective)—black
patro (noun)—father
pluvo (noun)—rain

prenez (verb)—to take
rivero (noun)—river
somero (noun)—summer
suno (noun)—sun
ucelo (noun)—bird
vintro (noun)—winter

SOME USEFUL PHRASES

Quale vu standas? (How are you?)
La hundo ne parolas Ido. (The dog doesn't speak Ido.)
Querigez la mediko. (Send for the doctor.)

NUMBERING SYSTEM

un—one
du—two
tri—three
quar—four
kin—five

sis—six
sep—seven
ok—eight
non—nine
dek—ten

THE LORD'S PRAYER

Patro nia, qua esas en la cielo,
tua nomo santigesez;
tua regno advenez;
tua volo facesez quale en la cielo
tale anke sur la tero.
Donez a ni cadie la omnadiala pano,
e pardonez a ni nia ofensi,
quale anke ni pardonas a nia ofensanti,
e ne duktez ni aden la tento,
ma liberigez ni del malajo.

PHILOLOGICAL FACT

➤ There have been international Ido conventions every year since 2001.

IF YOU'RE INTERESTED IN LEARNING THE LANGUAGE

From the Ido web page (*http://idolinguo.org.uk/*), you can learn about Ido and locate additional resources.

FOR MORE INFORMATION

Review the work listed above, the resources listed in the bibliography, and the web pages: "Ido World" (*www.idomondo.org*) and "Patro nia (Our Father / The Lord's Prayer in Ido)" (*www.pagef30 .com/2008/11/patro-nia-our-father-lords-prayer-in.html*).

SPEAKING OF LANGUAGES

Finality is not the language of politics.

—Benjamin Disraeli

Ingliss

SPOKEN BY
Ingliss is spoken by the people in the Maurai Federation, which is located in the Pacific.

DOCUMENTED BY
Poul Anderson (1926–2001) made up three languages in *Orion Shall Rise* (1983): Angley, Ingliss, and Unglish. While each of the languages is rooted in English, each is nearly indecipherable to the speakers of the other two languages, owing to ways the languages developed over centuries of separation.

BEHIND THE WORDS
Several hundred years after a nuclear war, people—and nations—still have to find ways to deal with each other.

DERIVATION OF THE LANGUAGE
Ingliss is derived from English and Polynesian.

PHILOLOGICAL FACT

➤ Although Anderson began as a liberal, he moved steadily to the right and concluded by embracing libertarianism. Throughout this evolution, though, he was a strong advocate for space travel and exploration, arguing that to abandon this meant that humanity was doomed to a future in which resources and cultural advancement would steadily shrink.

FOR MORE INFORMATION
Review the work listed above, the resources listed in the bibliography, and the web pages: "Maurai" (*http://en.wikipedia.org/wiki/Maurai*) and "Thoughts on Poul Anderson" (*www.scifibookspot .com/markley/?p=48*).

Interlac

SPOKEN BY
Interlac is a constructed universal language allowing different species to communicate before learning to speak each other's language.

DOCUMENTED BY
The use of Interlac in the future was documented in the television series *Babylon 5* (1993–2007) and six television movies: *The Gathering* (February 22, 1993), *In the Beginning* (January 4, 1998), *Thirdspace* (July 19, 1998) *The River of Souls* (November 8, 1998), *A Call to Arms* (January 3, 1999), and *The Legend of the Rangers (To Live and Die in Starlight)* (January 19, 2002).

BEHIND THE WORDS
Babylon 5 was created by J. Michael Straczynski, who wanted to explore themes of technology, alien interaction, and how humans would evolve. English is the official language within the Babylon 5 space station, but Interlac is used when the species interact elsewhere, until they learn a common language.

PHILOLOGICAL FACTS

➤ Humans on Babylon 5 use English to communicate with one another and, occasionally, with some of the other alien races that inhabit the space station. However, some races, in particular the Gain, pak'ma'ra, and the Vorlons, refuse to speak or are incapable of speaking English and use translators.

➤ Interlac was also the name of a universal language used by DC Comics, appearing for the first time in *Adventure Comics* #379 (March, 1969).

FOR MORE INFORMATION
Review the works listed above, the resources listed in the bibliography, and the web page: "Interlac" (*www.firstones.com/wiki/Interlac*).

Interlingua

SPOKEN BY

Interlingua is spoken by those who wish to learn the constructed language.

DOCUMENTED BY

The International Auxiliary Language Association (IALA) developed Interlingua between 1935 and 1951, and then promoted the language as something that would allow scientists who spoke different languages to communicate their theories and findings.

BEHIND THE WORDS

Several large organizations provided the financing for the development of Interlingua, including the Rockefeller Foundation and the Carnegie Corporation. William E. Collinson, a professor at the University of Liverpool and an experienced Esperantist, began compiling the vocabulary of the language between 1936 and 1939. He drew for words on Europe's major Romance languages; thus Interlingua does not have a *constructed* vocabulary but an *extracted* one. During World War II, the work on the language moved to New York and was completed in 1951 with the publication of the *Interlingua-English Dictionary*, containing more than 27,000 words. Today that compilation has expanded to more than 60,000 words.

DERIVATION OF THE LANGUAGE

The language has no grammar rule that doesn't also appear in Spanish, Portuguese, Italian, French, and English. If even one of those languages does not address the grammatical issue, Interlingua does not include the rule.

CHARACTERISTICS OF THE LANGUAGE

+ Nouns have no gender.
+ Plurals are formed by adding -s or -es to the end of the noun.
+ Word order is generally subject-verb-object.

A TASTE OF THE LANGUAGE

annello (noun)—ring
aqua (noun)—water
attaccar (verb)—to attack
ave (noun)—bird
campana (noun)—bell
coragiose (adjective)—brave
dinar (noun)—dinner
estate (noun)—summer
gamba (noun)—leg
hiberno (noun)—winter

incendio (noun)—fire
mangiar (verb)—to eat
nigre (adjective)—black
ovo (noun)—egg
patre (noun)—father
prender (verb)—to take
riviera (noun)—river
serpente (noun)—serpent
sol (noun)—sun
verde (adjective)—green

SOME USEFUL PHRASES

Como sta vos? (How are you?)
Parla plus lentemente, per favor.
(Please speak more slowly.)

Ubi es le lavatorio? (Where is the bathroom?)
Qunto costa isto? (How much is this?)

NUMBERING SYSTEM

un—one
duo—two
tres—three
quatro—four
cinque—five

sex—six
septe—seven
octo—eight
nove—nine
dece—ten

THE LORD'S PRAYER

Patre nostre, qui es in le celos,
que sia sanctificate tu nomine;
que veni tu regno;
in le celo como etiam super le terra
Da nos pan nostre quotidian hodie,
e pardona a nos nostre debitas
como nos pardona los a nostre debitores
e non duce nos in tentation,
sed libera nos del mal.

PHILOLOGICAL FACT

➤ Alice Vanderbilt Morris (1874–1950) of the Vanderbilt family and her husband Dave Hennen Morris founded the International Auxiliary Language Association in 1924.

IF YOU'RE INTERESTING IN LEARNING THE LANGUAGE

The Societate American pro Interlingua (*www.interlingua.us*) is presented in Interlingua, although there is a link, "An Overview of Interlingua for English Speakers," that leads to an essay that covers the basics of the language.

FOR MORE INFORMATION

Review the works listed above, the resources listed in the bibliography, and the web page: "Concise English-Interlingua Dictionary" (*www.interlingua.com/an/ceid*).

SPEAKING OF LANGUAGES

"A language is a dialect with an army and a navy."

—Linguist Max Weinreich, quoting someone who audited of one of his courses

---

Iotic

SPOKEN BY
The residents of A-Io on the planet Urras speak Iotic.

DOCUMENTED BY
Ursula Le Guin (1929–) uses Iotic in *The Dispossessed: An Ambiguous Utopia* (1974), the fifth book in the Hainish Cycle: *Rocannon's World* (1964), *Planet of Exile* (1966), *City of Illusions* (1967), *The Left Hand of Darkness* (1969), *The Dispossessed* (1974), *The Word for World is Forest* (1976), and *The Telling* (2000).

BEHIND THE WORDS
The Dispossessed takes place on Urras, a planet divided between two major societies: A-Io (generally similar in social structure to the United States) and Thu (resembling the Soviet Union). To prevent a rebellion, both states offered anarcho-syndicalist revolutionaries the chance to live on Anarres, the planet's moon. The revolutionaries constructed a society on Anarres that included Pravic, a constructed language. The setting for the novel gives Le Guin the opportunity to explore themes of social change and the challenges of utopianism.

CHARACTERISTICS OF THE LANGUAGE
+ Formal Iotic is used by the upper class and respected media.
+ Lower Iotic is used by the lower class, the Niotic.

PHILOLOGICAL FACTS
➤ In *The Dispossessed* (1974), Ursula Le Guin describes the process of inventing the ansible, a device she mentioned in *Rocannon's World* (1966) that allows instantaneous communication across any distance.

➤ Le Guin has noted that her depiction of an anarchic society was influenced by the writings of the Russian anarchist Peter Kropotkin (1842–1921), particularly his *Mutual Aid: A Factor of Evolution* and *The Conquest of Bread*.

FOR MORE INFORMATION
Review the works listed above, the resources listed in the bibliography, and the web page: Ursula K. Le Guin (*www.ursulakleguin.com*).

Ithkuil

SPOKEN BY

Ithkuil is spoken by those who wish to learn the constructed language.

DOCUMENTED BY

As stated on his website (*www.ithkuil.net*), John Quijada created Ithkuil (2004) in hopes of developing "an idealized language whose aim is the highest possible degree of logic, efficiency, detail, and accuracy in cognitive expression via spoken human language, while minimizing the ambiguity, vagueness, illogic, redundancy, polysemy (multiple meanings) and overall arbitrariness that is seemingly ubiquitous in natural human language."

CHARACTERISTICS OF THE LANGUAGE

+ Ithkuil uses roots and stems to pack more meaning into fewer syllables.
+ The language takes advantage of every fricative, alveolar, alveolar-retroflex, postalveolar, palatal, velar, and uvular position to create the largest possible number of unique sounds.

A TASTE OF THE LANGUAGE

Let's suppose that English is similar to Ithkuil and that the root of the word for automobile is c-r. Let's further suppose that:

- The middle vowel will signify color (a equals *red*, e equals *blue*, and i equals *white*)
- The vowel prefix indicates ownership (*a* equals *mine*, *e* equals *your*, and *i* equals *belonging to my mother*)
- A doubling of the vowel prefix indicates permanency (doubled equals *owned* and not doubled equals *rented*)
- The vowel suffix indicates the shape of the vehicle (a equals *runs well and looks good*; e equals *runs better than it looks*; and i equals *looks better than it runs*)
- A doubling of the vowel suffix indicates how the speaker feels about the car (doubled equals *positive* and not doubled equals *negative*).

Given what we've supposed, the single word *iicaree* equals *My mother's red car may look better than it runs, but I like it.*

If the root of the word for domicile is *h-s* and it happens to fall into the same root grouping as *c-r* so that prefix and suffix rules are the same, then the single word *ehisa* equals *that lousy white house you rented.*

Furthermore, let's suppose that *höte* equals *struck by accident and I'm sorry.*

The three-word sentence *iicaree höte ehisa* equals *My mother's red car may look better than it runs now that it slammed into that lousy white house you rented. Sorry.*

NUMBERING SYSTEM

las—one	*tas*—six
kas—two	*nas*—seven
šas—three	*xas*—eight
pas—four	*fas*—nine
ṭas—five	*mas*—ten

PHILOLOGICAL FACTS

➤ In a Russian popular-science magazine, *Computerra,* Stanislav Kozlovsky suggested that Ithkuil would allow people to think "about five or six times as fast." He compared it to Robert Heinlein's Speedtalk and George Orwell's Newspeak, both of which aim at more concise communication.

➤ Ithkuil has eighty-one noun cases (ways in which nouns can be modified to change meaning). When people suggested that the language was too difficult to pronounce, John Quijada redesigned the morphology to create Ilaksh, which boasts ninety-six noun cases.

IF YOU'RE INTERESTED IN LEARNING THE LANGUAGE

To learn Ithkuil, head on over to the website *www.ithkuil.net/*. Be forewarned, however, as even John Quijada has never learned to speak the language.

FOR MORE INFORMATION

Review the works listed above, the resources listed in the bibliography, and the web pages: "Ithkuil" (*www.frathwiki.com/Ithkuil*), "A Philosophical Grammar of Ithkuil, a Constructed Language" (*www.ithkuil.net*), and "John Quijada interview" (*http://library.conlang.org/articles/Ithkuil_Q_A.pdf*).

Kargish

SPOKEN BY
Kargish is spoken by the barbarian Kargs from the Kargard Lands.

DOCUMENTED BY
Ursula K. Le Guin (1929–) relates the tales of Earthsea in: *A Wizard of Earthsea* (1968), *The Tombs of Atuan* (1971), *The Farthest Shore* (1973), *Tehanu: The Last Book of Earthsea* (1990), *Tales from Earthsea* (short stories, 2001), and *The Other Wind* (2001).

BEHIND THE WORDS
Magic and writing are banned in the Kargard Lands, four islands in the northeast of Earthsea. The inhabitants pride themselves on their militaristic culture and regard reading as one of the Black Arts. Despite this, and despite the hatred of most Kargs for magic, some few Kargs study magic and are described in Le Guin's books.

A TASTE OF THE LANGUAGE
edran (noun)—leader of an army; dragon
feyagat (adjective)—veiled

gadda (noun)—firstborn child
gaínha (noun)—queen
ganaí (noun)—princess

FOR MORE INFORMATION
Review the works listed above, the resources listed in the bibliography, and the web pages: "Characters in Earthsea" (*http://en.wikipedia.org/wiki/Characters_in_Earthsea*), "The Isolate Tower" (*www.tavia.co.uk/earthsea/index.htm*), "Ursula K. Le Guin" (*www.ursulakleguin.com*), and "Ursula LeGuin's Magical World of Earthsea" (*http://scholar.lib.vt.edu/ejournals/ALAN/spring96/griffin.html*).

SPEAKING OF LANGUAGES

Man acts as though he were the shaper and master of language, while in fact language remains the master of man.

—Martin Heidegger

Kēlen

SPOKEN BY
Kēlen is spoken by those who wish to learn the constructed language.

DOCUMENTED BY
Kēlen was developed by Sylvia Sotomayor.

BEHIND THE WORDS
Sotomayor began creating Kēlen in high school under the influence of Tolkien's *Lord of the Rings*. Later, when she majored in linguistics in college, she began to experiment with the language to test various linguistic theories.

CHARACTERISTICS OF THE LANGUAGE

+ The chief defining characteristic of Kēlen is that it contains no verbs.
+ Nouns consist of a stem, a prefix, and a suffix. They are divided into animate nouns, inanimate nouns, and possessed nouns.
+ Sentences in Kēlen can be in one of six different moods: declarative, emphatic, interrogative, hortatory, imperative, and prohibitive.

A TASTE OF THE LANGUAGE

anākexa (adjective)—agile
anākiwa (adjective)—clumsy
ancāra (adjective)—brave
ancīlri (noun)—frost
anmēxa (adjective)—soft
anōlñe (adjective)—white
anūlmi (noun)—lava
jahōha (noun)—food
jalōnen (noun)—star
jamāonre (noun)—city
jamēþa (noun)—tree
jamāla jīstelon (noun)—birthday
janāola (noun)—fire
janāma (noun)—egg
jatāna (noun)—river
jaxāela (noun)—night
jīlcīlre (noun)—winter
malīcīñ (noun)—a female child
malō (noun)—sun
masāltanen (noun)—someone who sings

A USEFUL PHRASE

kexien tele jekīþa to jāo; (Of course I knew that.)

NUMBERING SYSTEM

án—one	*té*—six
énne—two	*ónne*—seven
wíjté—three	*ánór*—eight
wíór—four	*aríw*—nine
ámme—five	*énnen*—ten

THE BABEL TEXT:

iēlte la anmārwi pa antaxōni ān tēna;

il ñatta jarēþa rūānnie il ñatta jamāesa japōññe sū jekiēn xīnār il aþ ñatta āke jamāramma;

ē teteñ ien hēja ñanna jacālmi jajūti nā aþ te sāim nīkan jacālmi ñe jakīþi aþ te sāim nīkan ancēwri ñe anhērmi;

ē teteñ ien hēja ñanna jamāonre nīkan jakōnōr ja ñi jōl rā anīstīli;

ē teteñ ien hēja ñanna lewēra tō tūaþ wā ñi ñēim makkepōlien rā anmārwi āñ pēxa;

il aþ ñi λi ārōn rā āke tō sema mo sarōña jamāonre nīkan jakōnōr ja ōrra ñatta;

il tamma ien ē pa mēli anānīke ī pa sāim antaxōni ān tēna ī la ankāe ancēji ja ñatta rēha pa jāo jānne;

il tamma ien rēha ñatta janahan ja se jaþēnne jacē lā;

il tamma ien ē ñi liēn rā āke aþ ñalla anwaxāon tō tūaþ ñi anxiēna nīkamma sāim ankewōra cī;

ē ñamma jāo ā i ārōn ī ñamma sāim makkepōlien rā anmārwi āñ pēxa ī sū jamāonre ñamma jalāīke jahūwīke;

tō jāo sete sawēra λi waxāon tō sū āke ōrra ñamma anwaxāon tō antaxōni tēna ā λi ārōn;

IN THEIR OWN WORDS

From Sotomayor's website:

> *In college, I happened to take a Linguistics course. This proved to be a major turning point in my life, as I ended up majoring in linguistics and completely revising my language at least a dozen times. Kēlen went through*

so many revisions during those four years that I lost track of them. Linguistics was also responsible for showing me the sheer diversity of language and getting me interested in those underlying patterns that go by the name of linguistic universals.

IF YOU'RE INTERESTED IN LEARNING THE LANGUAGE

If you want to learn Kēlen, visit *www.terjemar.net/kelen.php* for information and an introduction to the language.

FOR MORE INFORMATION

Review the works listed above, the resources listed in the bibliography, and the web pages: "An Introduction to Kēlen" (*www.terjemar.net/kelen.php*), "Kēlen" (*www.frathwiki.com/K%C4%93len*), and "Kēlen" (*http://en.wikipedia.org/wiki/K%C4%93len*).

SPEAKING OF LANGUAGES

Never resist a sentence you like, in which language takes its own pleasure and in which, after having abused it for so long, you are stupefied by its innocence.

—Jean Baudrillard

Kesh

SPOKEN BY

The language Kesh is spoken by the Kesh people in *Always Coming Home* (1985).

DOCUMENTED BY

Ursula K. Le Guin (1929–) writes about the Kesh, a post-apocalyptic society living in what is now Northern California.

BEHIND THE WORDS

The narrator of *Always Coming Home*, Pandora, describes the Kesh, focusing on one in particular: a woman named Stone Telling. The Kesh, it has been suggested, strongly resemble Native Americans, just as the Valley of Na where they live resembles the Napa Valley in California. As in her other works, in *Always Coming Home* Le Guin focuses on the theme of the contrast between an acquisitive, materialistic society and an anarchic society that attempts to cast off material things.

A TASTE OF THE LANGUAGE

adre (noun)—moon
ansai (noun)—rainbow
arba (noun)—hand
arrakush (noun)—poet

dagga (noun)—leg
dest (noun)—snake
dót (noun)—sheep
drevi (adjective)—green

NUMBERING SYSTEM

ap—zero
dai—one
hú—two
íde—three
kle—four
chem—five

díde—six
dúse—seven
bekel—eight
gahó—nine
chúm—ten

PHILOLOGICAL FACT

➤ A boxed set of the novel *Always Coming Home* included an audiocassette containing performances of ten pieces of Kesh music and three pieces of Kesh poetry.

FOR MORE INFORMATION

Review the works listed above, the resources listed in the bibliography, and the web pages: "LeGuin: Songs and Poetry of the Kesh" (*http://archives.conlang.info/ga/sueldau/vhopuedhian.html*) and "Ursula K. Le Guin" (*www.ursulakleguin.com*).

SPEAKING OF LANGUAGES

Great literature is simply language charged with meaning to the utmost possible degree.

—Ezra Pound

Khuzdul

SPOKEN BY
Khuzdul is spoken by the Dwarves.

DOCUMENTED BY
J. R. R. Tolkien used Khuzdul in *The Silmarillion, The Hobbit,* and *The Lord of the Rings.*
Tolkien (1892–1973) explored many languages and cultures as he told the stories of Middle-earth: *The Hobbit* (1937), *The Fellowship of the Ring* (1954), *The Two Towers* (1954), and *The Return of the King* (1955). (The last three are collectively called *The Lord of the Rings.*) After his death, his son Christopher Tolkien (1924–) edited *The Silmarillion* (1977) with the help of Guy Gavriel Kay (1954–). Christopher Tolkien then deeply analyzed his father's notebooks, letters, and drafts to produce an extended study of Middle-earth and its creation: *The Book of Lost Tales, Part One* (1983), *The Book of Lost Tales, Part Two* (1984), *The Lays of Beleriand* (1985), *The Shaping of Middle-earth* (1986), *The Lost Road and Other Writings* (1987), *The Return of the Shadow (The History of The Lord of the Rings, Part One)* (1988), *The Treason of Isengard (The History of The Lord of the Rings, Part Two)* (1989), *The War of the Ring (The History of The Lord of the Rings, Part Three)* (1990), *Sauron Defeated (The History of The Lord of the Rings, Part Four)* (1992), *Morgoth's Ring (The Later Silmarillion, Part One)* (1993), *The War of the Jewels (The Later Silmarillion, Part Two)* (1994), and *The Peoples of Middle-earth* (1996).

BEHIND THE WORDS
Tolkien's Dwarves are a private race who keep much of their culture secret from outsiders. His view of them was much influenced by Germanic mythology; the names of the dwarves who appear in *The Hobbit* come from the epic work *The Poetic Edda*. In *The Hobbit*, Tolkien remarked that Dwarves were generally commercially minded with a great notion of the value of things.

DERIVATION OF THE LANGUAGE
Khuzdul was created for the Dwarves by Aulë.

CHARACTERISTICS OF THE LANGUAGE

+ Khuzdul shares many traits with Arabic and Hebrew.
+ The language differed from other languages in the West and was considered difficult.

- Words in Khuzdul begin with a vowel or one consonant, never two (*kh* is a single unit).

A TASTE OF THE LANGUAGE

bund (noun)—head
gathol (noun)—fortress
inbar (noun)—horn
Khazâd (noun)—Dwarves

kheled (noun)—glass
sigin (adjective)—long
zâram (noun)—lake

A USEFUL PHRASE

Baruk Khazâd! Khazâd ai-mênu! (Axes of the Dwarves! The Dwarves are upon you!)

PHILOLOGICAL FACTS

➤ Concurrently with Khuzdul, young Dwarves learned Iglishmêk, a sign language.

➤ Khuzdul was made for the Dwarves by Aulë, a god of skill and craftsmanship—traits much associated with Dwarves. Because of this, Khuzdul is not connected to Elvish. Dwarves rarely spoke it to outsiders. In *The Fellowship of the Ring*, when the Company of the Ring is preparing to enter Moria, Gandalf the wizard remarks that he will not need Gimili the Dwarf to tell him any of the secret Dwarvish words. Later Gimili is astonished when Galadriel, an Elf, speaks to him using Khuzdulish words for some of the Dwarves' sacred places.

FOR MORE INFORMATION

Review the works listed above, the resources listed in the bibliography, and the web pages: "Ardalambion" (*www.folk.uib.no/hnohf/*), "Cirth" (*www.omniglot.com/writing/cirth.htm*), "How many languages did J.R.R. Tolkien make?" (*www.folk.uib.no/hnohf/howmany.htm*), "J. R. R. Tolkien: A Biographical Sketch" (*www.tolkiensociety.org/tolkien/biography.html*), "Khuzdul—the secret tongue of the Dwarves" (*http://folk.uib.no/hnohf/khuzdul.htm*), "Sarati alphabet" (*www.omniglot.com/writing/sarati.htm*), and "Tengwar" (*www.omniglot.com/writing/tengwar.htm*).

SPEAKING OF LANGUAGES

War is what happens when language fails.

—Margaret Atwood

SPOKEN BY

Kiffish is spoken by the Kif, bare-skinned, long-snouted predators from the planet Akkht.

DOCUMENTED BY

C. J. Cherryh (1942–) writes of the Kif in the Chanur series: *The Pride of Chanur* (1981), *Chanur's Venture* (1981), *The Kif Strike Back* (1985), *Chanur's Homecoming* (1986), and *Chanur's Legacy* (1992).

BEHIND THE WORDS

The Kif are one of the species that are part of the Compact, a trade organization that facilitates interstellar economies. They are highly aggressive predators. Because of their constant forays into piracy and cannibalism, they are greatly disliked by other species in the books.

NUMBERING SYSTEM

rukt—one
ktum—two
ruskk—three
nikh—four
ktkhng—five

kteng—six
ruk—seven
paikht—eight
ghinkt—nine

THE BABEL TEXT

Ginkt-ku umankt-kkt Tera-kta kkisf-ok ruk-ku kkoiskk-otk ruk-ku trakk-ska, tha.

Sgat kktokht-ok sothog-otk naigh-lit gukkt ktokkkt aim-otk gekk-ku rekt sfig-lit Shinar-kta khtosf-ok khtan ktaip-ok.

Skku-ok nokikkt shkhskk kkak: "Kkko-i sgigh-kkt-otk khtan noki-kkt ktoth-i." Rekkt, ktokkkt ufik-ok sgigh-kkt-otk roikt-ing khtan khtoir-otk skkoi-ku nkhn-ing.

Skku-ok sgonkt-thu nokikkt shkhskk kkak: "kkko-i nkhf-otk khtan gesg-otk makkt skthi gakt skth-os ktatr-otk; khtan sfik-chu-i makkt-uk nokkkt hukk-rok poilit sgakk Tera-ud."

Kig-ok Treskk-ku Haikkt-otk makkt-uk ktk ta-sfo nkht-nktain-otk khtan gesg-nktain-otk makkt umankt-kkt ktaikkt-zik, mak.

Treskk-ku Haikkt tinkt-ok, "Kktkktkkt! Umankt-kkt-otk ktkhtr-o khtan ktokkkt ginkt-ku kkisf-o ruk-ku kkoiskk-otk; kktunkt-ska, hakkaip-otk pok-os nokikkt-lit ktokk skthikkt trek-nkte-lit gukkt.

Ktkkkt sgkhkt-os pigh khtan sgaskk-esg-os skthikkt kkoiskk-otk makkt-uk ktokkkt sgaskk-i hukk nokikkt-esg," tha.

Rekkt, rok-ok Treskk-ku Haikkt nokikkt pigh-lit gukkt poi-lit sgakk Tera-ud, tha.

Rekkt-chu, taikkt skthi Papel-otk, ktokk sgaskk-esg-gu-otk; kkkotok Treskk-ku Haikkt pigh-tok sgaskk-esg-ok ginkt-ku umankt-kkt-otk: khtan rok-ok nokikkt pigh-lit gukkt poi-lit sgakk Tera-ud, na.

FOR MORE INFORMATION

Review the works listed above, the resources listed in the bibliography, and the web page: "Babel Text for the Kiffish language" (*http://strengthofthehills.tripod.com/hanilanguageandculturepage/id11 .html*).

SPEAKING OF LANGUAGES

The problems of language here are really serious. We wish to speak in some way about the structure of the atoms. . . . But we cannot speak about atoms in ordinary language.

—Werner Heisenberg

Klingon

SPOKEN BY

Klingon is spoken by Klingons in the Star Trek universe: in the television series (Gene Roddenberry's *Star Trek: The Original Series* [1966–1969], *Star Trek: The Animated Series* [1973–1974], *Star Trek: The Next Generation* [1987–1994], *Star Trek: Deep Space Nine* [1993–1999], *Star Trek: Voyager* [1995–2001], and *Star Trek: Enterprise* [2001–2005]) and the film series (*Star Trek: The Motion Picture* [1979], *Star Trek II: The Wrath of Khan* [1982], *Star Trek III: The Search for Spock* [1984], *Star Trek IV: The Voyage Home* [1986], *Star Trek V: The Final Frontier* [1989], *Star Trek VI: The Undiscovered Country* [1991], *Star Trek Generations* [1994], *Star Trek: First Contact* [1996], *Star Trek: Insurrection* [1999], *Star Trek Nemesis* [2002], and *Star Trek* [2009]).

DOCUMENTED BY

Klingons spoke English or gibberish until Marc Okrand was hired to develop the Klingon language for *Star Trek III: The Search for Spock* (1984). The language proved so popular with viewers that he documented the grammar and vocabulary in *The Klingon Dictionary*.

BEHIND THE WORDS

The Klingons are a warrior race that progresses from enemy (in the original television series) to more or less neutral (in *Star Trek VI: The Undiscovered Country*) to ally of the United Federation of Planets (in *Star Trek: The Next Generation* and *Star Trek: Deep Space Nine*). Interestingly, the original depiction of Klingons in *Star Trek* presented them as looking and speaking more or less like dark-skinned Russians. By the time *Star Trek: The Next Generation* came along, Klingons had morphed both physically and culturally. They became tall with bumpy foreheads, dark skin, and long hair. Their culture was largely based on the values of medieval Samurai Japan, with an emphasis on honor and tradition.

DERIVATION OF THE LANGUAGE

Klingon is derived from language spoken by Kahless the Unforgettable.

Marc Okrand designed an aggressive, guttural sound for Klingon by not including the softer phonemes found in most languages on Earth.

CHARACTERISTICS OF THE LANGUAGE

+ Klingon has twenty-one consonants and five vowels.
+ A syllable always starts with a consonant (or consonant cluster) that is followed by a vowel.
+ Nouns have twenty-five possible suffixes in Klingon.

A TASTE OF THE LANGUAGE

bach (verb)—to shoot
chargh (verb)—to conquer
DIr (noun)—skin
ghargh (noun)—serpent
Ha'DIbaH (noun)—animal
jab (verb)—to serve food
leng (verb)—to roam
maghwI' (noun)—traitor
nIQ (noun)—breakfast

peng (noun)—torpedo
qach (noun)—building
ramjep (noun)—midnight
SIS (noun)—rain
tlhutlh (verb)—to drink
'uS (noun)—leg
vub (noun)—hostage
wIj (verb)—to farm
yay (noun)—victory

SOME USEFUL PHRASES

tlhIngan Hol Dajatlh'a' (Do you speak Klingon?)
bIjeghbe'chugh vaj bIHegh (Surrender or die!)
nuqDaq 'oH puchpa"e' (Where is the bathroom?)

NUMBERING SYSTEM

wa'—one
cha'—two
wej—three
loS—four
vagh—five

jav—six
Soch—seven
chorgh—eight
Hut—nine
wa'maH—ten

PHILOLOGICAL FACTS

➤ *Star Trek: The Motion Picture* was the first time Klingon was heard by audiences, and what was heard was developed by James Doohan, the actor who played Scotty.

➤ In 2010, a Chicago Theatre company presented a Klingon version of *A Christmas Carol* and the Washington Shakespeare Company performed selections in Klingon from *Hamlet* and *Much Ado About Nothing*.

► One of the biggest topics of discussion among Star Trek fans was the reason for the discrepancy between the Klingons of the original series and those appearing in the movies and the later series. The explanation finally came in a two-part episode of *Star Trek: Enterprise*, which aired in early 2005. Suffice it to say that the reason had to do with a plague that spread throughout the Klingon empire, causing physical changes to Klingons.

IF YOU'RE INTERESTED IN LEARNING THE LANGUAGE

Pity the fictional language student who wants to learn anything other than Klingon. Not only does the Klingon language have its own school, the Klingon Language Institute (*www.kli.org*), it also has *The Klingon Dictionary*, written by none other than Marc Okrand, the person who constructed the Klingon language and culture.

FOR MORE INFORMATION

Review the works listed above, the resources listed in the bibliography, and the web pages: "Klingon Language Institute" (*http://en.wikipedia.org/wiki/Klingon_Language_Institute*), "Lawrence M. Schoen" (*http://en.wikipedia.org/wiki/Lawrence_M._Schoen*), and "Star Trek" (*http://en.wikipedia.org/wiki/Star_Trek*).

SPEAKING OF LANGUAGES

While a people preserves its language, it preserves the marks of liberty.

—Jose Rizal

Krakish

SPOKEN BY

The ancient language of Krakish is spoken by the owls from the Northern Kingdoms.

DOCUMENTED BY

Kathryn Lasky (1944–) wrote about the owl civilizations in the *Guardians of Ga'Hoole* series: *Guardians of Ga'Hoole Book 1: The Capture* (2003), *Guardians of Ga'Hoole Book 2: The Journey* (2003), *Guardians of Ga'Hoole Book 3: The Rescue* (2004), *Guardians of Ga'Hoole Book 4: The Siege* (2004), *Guardians of Ga'Hoole Book 5: The Shattering* (2004), *Guardians of Ga'Hoole Book 6: The Burning* (2004), *Guardians of Ga'Hoole Book 7: The Hatchling* (2005), *Guardians of Ga'Hoole Book 8: The Outcast* (2005), *Guardians of Ga'Hoole Book 9: The First Collier* (2006), *Guardians of Ga'Hoole Book 10: The Coming of Hoole* (2006), *Guardians of Ga'Hoole Book 11: To Be a King* (2006), *Guardians of Ga'Hoole Book 12: The Golden Tree* (2007), *Guardians of Ga'Hoole Book 13: The River of Wind* (2007), *Guardians of Ga'Hoole Book 14: Exile* (2008), and *Guardians of Ga'Hoole Book 15: The War of the Ember* (2008).

BEHIND THE WORDS

The fifteen novels that are part of the series tell the story of a conflict between the guardians of the Great Ga'Hoole Tree and a group of evil owls, called The Pure Ones, who seek to take over all owldom with the aid of strange particles called flecks. The owls in the Southern Kingdoms (S'rythgar) speak Hoolian, and the owls in the Northern Kingdoms speak Krakish, an unpleasant-sounding language.

CHARACTERISTICS OF THE LANGUAGE

+ Verbs are conjugated into six forms in Krakish.

A TASTE OF THE LANGUAGE

blaue (adjective)—blue
frisen (noun)—friend
frissah (noun)—fires
hordo (noun)—snake

issen (noun)—ice
plurrh (noun)—blood
yoicks (adjective)—crazy

FOR MORE INFORMATION

Review the works listed above, the resources listed in the bibliography, and the web pages: "Guardians of Ga'Hoole" (*http://en.wikipedia.org/wiki/Guardians_of_Ga%27Hoole*) and "Krakish" (*http://guardiansofgahoole.wikia.com/wiki/Krakish*).

SPEAKING OF LANGUAGES

Nothing exists except through language.

—Hans-Georg Gadamer

Krakozhian

SPOKEN BY

Viktor Navorski, played by Tom Hanks, speaks his home language of Krakozhian when he flies to New York and finds himself trapped in *The Terminal* (2004).

DOCUMENTED BY

The film *The Terminal* was directed by Steven Spielberg.

BEHIND THE WORDS

While Victor Navorski is flying to the United States, a civil war erupts in his country, causing the borders to be closed. He can't return home, but since the new Krakozhian government is not recognized by the United States, Homeland Security won't allow Navorski to enter the United States. He's a man without a country. As a result he remains in the terminal, where he gradually makes friends with the staff and becomes involved in their lives.

DERIVATION OF THE LANGUAGE

Krakozhia is a fictional country, with all indicators pointing to an Eastern European setting. A map that appears on a television screen shows Krakozhia overlying the Republic of Macedonia, although there are several references in the film to Krakozhia bordering Russia and its language being Russian-like. In fact, Krakozhian is derived from Bulgarian, and Tom Hanks was coached by his wife's father, who came from that region.

CHARACTERISTICS OF THE LANGUAGE

+ Krakozhian sounds the way one imagines a person from the Eastern bloc speaks.

PHILOLOGICAL FACTS

➤ During the course of his stay in the terminal, Viktor Navorski learns English as a second language.

➤ Mehran Karimi Nasseri, an Iranian refugee, lived at the Charles de Gaulle Airport in Paris from 1988 to 2006. After being expelled from Iran, he was awarded refugee status in Britain, but en route to Britain his papers were stolen in Paris. When he arrived in Britain he was returned to France, but the French refused him permission to enter that country. Eventually he was hospitalized for an unknown illness and after his release, remained in Paris.

FOR MORE INFORMATION

Review the work listed above, the resources listed in the bibliography, and the web page: "The Terminal" (*www.imdb.com/title/tt0362227/*).

SPEAKING OF LANGUAGES

Speech happens to not be his language.

—Madame de Staël

Kryptonian

SPOKEN BY

Kryptonian was spoken by the inhabitants of Krypton, the planet from where Superman hails.

DOCUMENTED BY

The adventures of Superman have been chronicled in the *Superman* comics, the television series [*Adventures of Superman* (1952–1958), *Lois & Clark: The New Adventures of Superman* (1993–1997), and *Smallville* (2001–2011)], and the films *Superman* (1978), *Superman II* (1980), *Superman III* (1983), *Supergirl* (1984), *Superman IV: The Quest for Peace* (1987), *Superman Returns* (2006), and the animated *Superman/Batman: Apocalypse* (2010).

BEHIND THE WORDS

Although Superman first appeared in *Action Comics #1* (1938), his native language was only represented by random squiggles until Edward Nelson Bridwell (1931–1987) decided to turn these squiggles into the 118-letter Kryptonese alphabet while he was editor. This became canon until DC Comics redefined Superman in 1986. In 2000, DC Comics introduced a new alphabet and changed the name of the language to Kryptonian. This new and current language simply replaces Kryptonian symbols one-for-one with characters from the language spoken by the buying public in each market country.

PHILOLOGICAL FACTS

➤ Kryptonian is heard for the first time in *Smallville* episode 141, "Gemini" (December 13, 2007), when a woman in the hospital is thought to be muttering incoherently.

➤ Linguist Darren Doyle is constructing an unofficial version of Kryptonian (*www.kryptonian.info*). According to him, the languages spoken on Krypton were descended from a single protolanguage, which eventually evolved into five Father Languages: Kandorian, Vath, Twenx, Urrikan, and Lurvanish. When the various nations of the planet united, Kandor was dominant among them, and thus Kandorian became the official language of the planet.

FOR MORE INFORMATION

Review the works listed above, the resources listed in the bibliography, and the web pages: "Kryptonian" (*www.kryptonian.info*), "Kryptonian" (*www.omniglot.com/writing/kryptonian.php*), and "Kryptonian" (*http://smallville.wikia.com/wiki/Kryptonian*).

SPEAKING OF LANGUAGES

Very early in life I became fascinated with the wonders language can achieve. And I began playing with words.

—Gwendolyn Brooks

Ku

SPOKEN BY

Ku is spoken by the inhabitants of the Democratic Republic of Matobo, a fictional African country, and understood by United Nations interpreter Silvia Broome, who overhears two people conspiring to assassinate Matoban president Edmond Zuwanie.

DOCUMENTED BY

Said el-Gheithy was hired by Sydney Pollack to develop the Ku language heard in the film *The Interpreter* (2005).

DERIVATION OF THE LANGUAGE

Said el-Gheithy based Ku on the Bantu languages Swahili and Shona.

CHARACTERISTICS OF THE LANGUAGE

+ Although based on Swahili and Shona, Ku uses suffixes rather than prefixes.
+ Said el-Gheithy (as quoted in the *Los Angeles Times*, April 30, 2005):
  "Then I created tenses and so on. Throughout the process the speech emerged."

A TASTE OF THE LANGUAGE

We're kepéla. It means standing on opposite sides of the river.

—Silvia Broome, character in *The Interpreter*

FOR MORE INFORMATION

Review the work listed above, the resources listed in the bibliography, and the web pages: "Ku made up" (*http://watchmesleep.blogspot.com/2005/05/ku-made-up.html*), "KU?" (*http://itre.cis.upenn.edu/~myl/languagelog/archives/002083.html*), "KU TWO" (*http://itre.cis.upenn.edu/~myl/languagelog/archives/002085.html*), and "A New Word Order" (*www.azcentral.com/ent/movies/articles/0430ku30.html?&wired*).

SPEAKING OF LANGUAGES

Angota ho ne njumata.

(The truth needs no translation.)

—The tagline *of The Interpreter*

Ms. Kawasaki [After a long speech in Japanese]: He want you to turn and look in camera. Okay?

Bob: Is that all he said?

—Bob Harris, character in *Lost in Translation* (2003)

Láadan

SPOKEN BY

Láadan is developed and spoken by the oppressed women of a dystopian future in *Native Tongue* (1984), *The Judas Rose* (1987), and *Earthsong* (1993), written by Suzette Haden Elgin.

DOCUMENTED BY

Suzette Haden Elgin (1936–) constructed Láadan in 1982 both as an element in her fiction and as an experiment: She wanted to know what would happen if women banded together to construct a language that reflected their perceptions (a test of the Sapir-Whorf Hypothesis). She also writes nonfiction on the uses and abuses of language and is the founder of the Science Fiction Poetry Association.

BEHIND THE WORDS

Suzette Haden Elgin on constructing Láadan:

> *First, much of the plot for* Native Tongue *revolved around a group of women, all linguists, engaged in constructing a language specifically designed to express the perceptions of human women; because I'm a linguist and linguistics is the science in my novels, I felt obligated actually to construct the language before I wrote about it.*

The stories take place in a future where women have lost all their rights. These women, skilled as linguists, are kept to breed and raise future linguists to facilitate trade with alien races.

CHARACTERISTICS OF THE LANGUAGE

+ Láadan doesn't use articles (such as *the* or *a*).
+ Nouns can be used as verbs, and verbs can be used as nouns.
+ The language uses two distinct tones: a short tone, either medium or low; and a short, high tone.
+ Láadan includes evidentials, which must appear as the last word in the sentence and describe why the preceding statement is believed.

A TASTE OF THE LANGUAGE

babí (noun)—bird
bel (verb)—to take
beth (noun)—home
ezha (noun)—snake
héeya (verb)—to fear
loyo (adjective)—black
máa (noun)—egg
miwith (noun)—city
náal (noun)—night
óoba (noun)—leg

óoha (adjective)—tired
óowa (noun)—fire
rosh (noun)—sun
shebasheb (noun)—death
thade (noun)—birthday
weman (noun)—winter
wili (noun)—river
wuman (noun)—summer
yod (verb)—to eat
zhub (noun)—insect

NUMBERING SYSTEM

nede—one
shin—two
boó—three
bim—four
sham—five

bath—six
um—seven
nib—eight
bud—nine
thab—ten

PHILOLOGICAL FACT

➤ Láadan includes words defined as what they're not and vowels used to define specific meaning to a root word:

ramína—callousness for no reason [ra=non- + mína=compassion for no reason]

ramúna—callousness for bad reasons [ra=non- + múna=compassion for bad reasons]

ramóna—callousness for foolish reasons [ra=non- + móna=compassion for foolish reasons]

raména—callousness for good reasons [ra=non- + ména=compassion for good reasons]

IN THEIR OWN WORDS

Láadan was described as a language designed to express the perceptions of women. I had to find out what that meant; I had to find out what design elements could plausibly be included in such a project.

—Suzette Haden Elgin

IF YOU'RE INTERESTED IN LEARNING THE LANGUAGE

LáadanLanguage.org (*www.laadanlanguage.org/pages/*) is the official site of the language, complete with lessons, reference materials, and notes by Elgin. There's also a dictionary that's currently out of print: *A First Dictionary and Grammar of Láadan* (1985, 2nd ed. 1988).

FOR MORE INFORMATION

Review the works listed above, the resources listed in the bibliography, and the web pages: "The Láadan Language" (*www.sfwa.org/members/elgin/NativeTongue/Laadan_FAQ.html*), "LáadanLanguage.org" (*www.laadanlanguage.org/pages/*), and "Native Tongue (Suzette Haden Elgin novel)" (*http://en.wikipedia.org/wiki/Native_Tongue_%28Suzette_Haden_Elgin_novel%29*).

SPEAKING OF LANGUAGES

It is difficult for a woman to define her feelings in a language which is chiefly made by men to express theirs.

—Thomas Hardy

Language of the Making

SPOKEN BY

The Language of the Making (or Old Speech) is spoken by dragons and sometimes by wizards.

DOCUMENTED BY

Ursula K. Le Guin (1929–) relates the tales of Earthsea in: *A Wizard of Earthsea* (1968), *The Tombs of Atuan* (1971), *The Farthest Shore* (1973), *Tehanu: The Last Book of Earthsea* (1990), *Tales from Earthsea* (short stories, 2001), and *The Other Wind* (2001).

A TASTE OF THE LANGUAGE

agni (noun)—king
ahm (noun)—the beginning, long ago
emenn (verb)—to open
essa (noun)—foam
essiri (noun)—willow
gorbardon (noun)—crown
haath (noun)—dragon
inien (noun)—sea

kebbo (noun)—rabbit
kest (noun)—minnow
medeu (noun)—sibling
siasa (noun)—eyelash
sobriost (verb)—to mount
suk (noun)—feather
tolk (noun)—rock, pebble

SOME USEFUL PHRASES

Aissadan verw nadannan. (What was divided is divided.)
Anvassa mane harw pennodathe! (I break the bond that holds you!)
Memeas. (I will come.)

FOR MORE INFORMATION

Review the works listed above, the resources listed in the bibliography, and the web pages: "Characters in Earthsea" (*http://en.wikipedia.org/wiki/Characters_in_Earthsea*), "The Isolate Tower" (*www.tavia.co.uk/earthsea/index.htm*), "Ursula K. Le Guin" (*www.ursulakleguin.com*), and "Ursula LeGuin's Magical World of Earthsea" (*http://scholar.lib.vt.edu/ejournals/ALAN/spring96/griffin.html*).

SPEAKING OF LANGUAGES

By degrees I made a discovery of still greater moment. I found that these people possessed a method of communicating their experience and feelings to one another by articulate sounds. I perceived that the words they spoke sometimes produced pleasure or pain, smiles or sadness, in the minds and countenances of the hearers. This was indeed a godlike science, and I ardently desired to become acquainted with it. But I was baffled in every attempt I made for this purpose. Their pronunciation was quick, and the words they uttered, not having any apparent connection with visible objects, I was unable to discover any clue by which I could unravel the mystery of their reference.

—The Creature, *Frankenstein*

Lapine

SPOKEN BY

The rabbits in *Watership Down* (1972) speak Lapine.

DOCUMENTED BY

Richard Adams (1920–) wrote *Watership Down*, the tale of a heroic band of rabbits seeking a new home. The novel, published in 1972, has been a perennial favorite and was adapted into an animated film.

BEHIND THE WORDS

The rabbits are the only creatures in Adams's world who speak Lapine. The other animals speak Hedgerow. The story follows the progress of a small group of rabbits, led by the mystic Fiver and his brother Hazel, as they search for a new home. When they establish themselves on the hillside of Watership Down, they must then grapple with the problem that without female rabbits, the colony is doomed to extinction.

DERIVATION OF THE LANGUAGE

The Lapine language sounds related to Welsh, Irish, Scottish, and Gaelic, as if the rabbits based their language on the human sounds they heard.

The name of the language itself is derived from the French word for rabbit, *lapin*.

CHARACTERISTICS OF THE LANGUAGE

+ In the introduction to the 2005 edition, Richard Adams said he wanted Lapine to sound "wuffy, fluffy."

A TASTE OF THE LANGUAGE

elil (noun)—enemies of the rabbits
embleer (adjective)—stinking, smelling like a predator
flay (noun)—food
Frith (noun)—the Sun
homba (noun)—fox

hraka (noun)—droppings
tharn (adjective)—stupefied
thlay (noun)—fur
zorn (adjective)—suffered a catastrophe

PHILOLOGICAL FACTS

➤ Multiplying like rabbits, more than 50 million copies of *Watership Down* have made their way into the world.

➤ The rabbits worship Lord Frith, who is the sun god and creator of the universe, and El-ahrairah, a trickster god (whose name, with clear Arabic roots, is a contraction of *Elil-Hrair-Rah*, or *prince with a thousand enemies*, a rather good description of rabbits).

FOR MORE INFORMATION

Review the work listed above, the resources listed in the bibliography, and the web page: "Lapine: The Language of Watership Down" (*www.langmaker.com/featured/lapine.htm*).

SPEAKING OF LANGUAGES

Every quotation contributes something to the stability or enlargement of the language.

—Samuel Johnson

Lingua Ignota

SPOKEN BY

Even if Lingua Ignota contains enough words to effectively communicate, and most of what is known are nouns, the glossary has never been used as the basis for actual speech.

DOCUMENTED BY

Hildegard of Bingen (1098–1179), abbess of Rupertsberg, wrote down one of the earliest constructed languages, for her personal use.

BEHIND THE WORDS

Hildegard was placed by her parents with the church when she was eight years old. She was known for her visions, which she believed were revelations from God. As well as the Lingua Ignota, Hildegard wrote on a variety of subjects, including theology, botany, and medicine. Only two manuscripts of Hildegard's book on her invented language, *Lingua Ignota per simplicem hominem Hildegardem prolata*, have survived, both produced not that long after her death, and it is unknown whether Hildegard wrote further on the subject.

DERIVATION OF THE LANGUAGE

The language came to Hildegard through divine revelation.

CHARACTERISTICS OF THE LANGUAGE

+ As best as can be known, Lingua Ignota consisted of twenty-three letters.

A TASTE OF THE LANGUAGE

Aigonz (noun)—God
Maiz (noun)—mother
Peueriz (noun)—father

FOR MORE INFORMATION

Review the resources listed in the bibliography and the web page: "The Wiesbaden ('Giant') Codex (Hildegard of Bingen)" (*www.hlb-wiesbaden.de/index.php?p=202*).

SPEAKING OF LANGUAGES

Ubi tunc vox inauditae melodiae? Et vox inauditae linguae?

(Where, then, the voice of the unheard melody? And the voice of the unheard language?)

—Hildegard's friend Wolmarus, on hearing that Hildegard might be dying

I trade both the living and the dead, for the enrichment of our native language.

—John Dryden

Linyaari

SPOKEN BY

Linyaari is spoken by the Linyaari people of the planet Vhiliinyar.

DOCUMENTED BY

Anne McCaffrey (1926–), best known for her Pern novels, tells of the Linyaari people in two series. The Acorna series includes: *Acorna the Unicorn Girl* (1997), *Acorna's Quest* (1998), *Acorna's People* (1999), *Acorna's World* (2000), *Acorna's Search* (2001), *Acorna's Rebels* (2003), and *Acorna's Triumph* (2004). The Acorna's Children series includes: *First Warning* (2005), *Second Wave* (2006), and *Third Watch* (2007). (The first two books were co-written with Margaret Ball, and the other eight, with Elizabeth Ann Scarborough.)

BEHIND THE WORDS

The Linyaari are a peaceful race whose home planet was invaded by the evil Khleevii. Acorna is orphaned when her parents sacrifice themselves to save her from the Khleevii. Acorna's daughter, Khorii, is the main character in the second series.

CHARACTERISTICS OF THE LANGUAGE

- The double vowel indicates stress.
- Stress indicates whether the word is a verb (stress on the first syllable), noun (stress on the next to last syllable), or adjective (stress on the last syllable).
- Adding an *-ii* to the end of a noun creates an adjective.

A TASTE OF THE LANGUAGE

khleevii (adjective)—barbarous
linyaarii (adjective)—civilized

PHILOLOGICAL FACTS

➤ Anne McCaffrey and Margaret Ball wrote two books. Thinking they were done with Acorna, Margaret Ball went off to start something new. By the time the publishers told McCaffrey that they wanted to extend the series with more books, Margaret Ball was already committed elsewhere, and McCaffrey asked Elizabeth Ann Scarborough if she had any ideas.

➤ In McCaffrey's most famous creation, the world of Pern, apparently everyone on the planet speaks the same language. In addition, dragonriders are psychically linked to their dragons.

FOR MORE INFORMATION

Review the works listed above, the resources listed in the bibliography, and the website: The Worlds of Anne McCaffrey (*http://pernhome.com/aim/*).

SPEAKING OF LANGUAGES

Death stands above me, whispering low
I know not what into my ear;
Of his strange language all I know
Is, there is not a word of fear.

—Walter Savage Landor

Loglan

SPOKEN BY
Loglan is spoken by those who wish to learn the constructed language.

DOCUMENTED BY
Dr. James Cooke Brown (1921–2000) wanted to create a logical language (hence, Loglan) that contained no ambiguities, in order to release people from the constraints imposed by lesser languages. A believer in the Sapir-Whorf Hypothesis, Brown started in 1955 to construct a culturally neutral language that would be simple and clear enough to act as an interface between people and computers.

BEHIND THE WORDS
Brown created the Loglan Institute as a laboratory to develop and study the language. He kept a very tight rein on Loglan, believing it a work in progress that should be kept from entering the general realm of common speech. Others disagreed with his approach and started their own logical language, Lojban.

DERIVATION OF THE LANGUAGE
Brown developed the basic vocabulary: some 1,000 words that would seem familiar to speakers of English, Chinese, Hindi, Russian, Spanish, French, Japanese, and German.

CHARACTERISTICS OF THE LANGUAGE

+ Words in Loglan are pronounced the way they're spelled.
+ The language is designed such that you have to say what you mean.
+ Loglan consists of little words (numbers, pronouns, conjunctions), predicates (content words such as nouns, verbs, and adjectives), and names (particular people, places, and things).

A TASTE OF THE LANGUAGE

bekli (noun)—bell
blonajda (noun)—dagger
dotra (noun)—winter

filcea (adjective)—moody
la Lun (noun)—moon
la Sol (noun)—sun

lo cimra (noun)—summer
lo fagro (noun)—fire
marmao (verb)—to mark (to make a)
negda (noun)—egg
nigro (adjective)—black
nirdu (noun)—bird
po morto (noun)—death
rajmra (noun)—mark (scratch)

recmra (noun)—mark (distinguishing)
rigsii (adjective)—brave
stomarmao (verb)—to mark (intentionally and permanently)
titci (verb)—eat
tugle (noun)—leg
vrici (noun)—river

SOME USEFUL PHRASES

Oa no durzo ta. (You must not do that.)
Mi na takna. (I am now talking.)
Ei ba gleca cutse vi? (Does anyone speak English here?)

NUMBERING SYSTEM

ne—one
to—two
te—three
fo—four
fe—five

so—six
se—seven
vo—eight
ve—nine
neni—ten

PHILOLOGICAL FACTS

➤ The United States Patent and Trademark Office refuses to allow Loglan to be trademarked. Trademark was sought to keep Loglan (the word for "logical languages") from being applied to logical languages other than Loglan.

Although James Cooke Brown used Loglan in his novel *The Troika Incident* (1970), he called the language Panlan.

Robert Heinlein was sufficiently impressed with the logical qualities of Loglan that he mentioned it in his novels *The Moon Is a Harsh Mistress* (1966) and *The Number of the Beast* (1980).

➤ Although the supporters of Lojban broke from Brown over his restrictions on Loglan, they adopted the term "loglan" for any constructed language seeking to build on purely logical principles. Needless to say, supporters of Loglan find this usage insulting and deny its validity. However, a court ruled that the term "loglan" cannot be trademarked.

IF YOU'RE INTERESTED IN LEARNING THE LANGUAGE

Loglan's official website (*www.loglan.org*) is the place to learn all about Loglan.

FOR MORE INFORMATION

Review the works listed above, the resources listed in the bibliography, and the web pages: "The Job Market of the Future—About the author—James Cooke Brown" (*www.jobmarketbook.com/About.html*), "Loglan" (*http://en.wikipedia.org/wiki/Loglan*), and "Welcome to Loglan.org" (*www.loglan.org*).

SPEAKING OF LANGUAGES

The great thing about human language is that it prevents us from sticking to the matter at hand.

—Lewis Thomas

Lojban

SPOKEN BY

Lojban is spoken by those who wish to learn the constructed language. As of 1997, 300 people on the 1,200-person Lojban mailing list identified themselves as actively learning the language.

DOCUMENTED BY

The people who left the Loglan project in 1987 started their own logical language under the name of the Logical Language Group.

BEHIND THE WORDS

While Loglan was thought of as a laboratory experiment, those who switched to Lojban did so in part to allow the language to grow "in the wild," as it were. They concluded that any language must have an organic component and must be permitted to develop without restriction. In 1988, the Logical Language Group, the organization behind Lojban, published *The Complete Lojban Language*.

DERIVATION OF THE LANGUAGE

Lojban started out being very similar to Loglan in theory but used a different vocabulary, making words that would seem familiar to speakers of Mandarin, English, Hindi, Spanish, Russian, and Arabic. As the Loglan people and the Lojban people continued to work on their projects separately, the two languages have drifted apart.

CHARACTERISTICS OF THE LANGUAGE

+ Words in Lojban are pronounced the way they're spelled.
+ The 1,300 root words can be combined to form millions of other words.
+ Punctuation is spoken as words.

A TASTE OF THE LANGUAGE

cipni (noun)—bird

citka (verb)—to eat

crisa (noun)—summer

djacu (noun)—water

djine (noun)—ring
dunra (noun)—winter
fagri (noun)—fire
gunta (verb)—to attack
mamta (noun)—mother
palta (noun)—plate
patfu (noun)—father
pendo (noun)—friend

rirxe (noun)—river
since (noun)—serpent
solri (noun)—sun
sovda (noun)—egg
tavla (verb)—to talk
tuple (noun)—leg
virnu (adjective)—brave
xekri (adjective)— black

SOME USEFUL PHRASES

.i .e'o ko skusno zenba (Could you talk more slowly please?)
ma stuzi le djacu kumfa (Where is the bathroom?)
mi se bangu le glibau (I speak English.)

NUMBERING SYSTEM

no—zero
pa—one
re—two
ci—three
vo—four
mu—five

xa—six
ze—seven
bi—eight
so—nine
pano—ten

PHILOLOGICAL FACTS

➤ The use of attitudinal and emotional indicators in Lojban was borrowed from Suzette Haden Elgin's Láadan.

➤ Both Lojban and Loglan are based on mathematical logic. However, aspiring speakers of either language don't have to be mathematicians. Nonetheless, supporters of both languages argue that this basis makes the languages useful for talking to computers.

THE LORD'S PRAYER

doi cevrirni.iu noi zvati le do cevzda do'u fu'e .aicai .e'ecai lo do cmene ru'i censa
.i le do nobli turni be la ter. ku se cfari
.i loi do se djica ba snada mulno vi'e le cevzda .e .a'o la ter.
.i fu'e .e'o ko dunda ca le cabdei le ri nanba mi'a
.i ko fraxu mi loi ri zu'o palci
.ijo mi fraxu roda poi pacyzu'e xrani mi

.i ko lidne mi fa'anai loi pacyxlu
.i ko sepri'a mi loi palci
.i .uicai ni'i loi se turni .e loi vlipa .e loi mi'orselsi'a cu me le do romei
fa'o

IF YOU'RE INTERESTED IN LEARNING THE LANGUAGE

Information on learning Lojban can be found at the web page *www.lojban.org/
tiki/la+lojban.+mo*.

FOR MORE INFORMATION

Review the work listed above, the resources listed in the bibliography, and the web pages: "Lojban" (*www.lojban.org/tiki/la+lojban.+mo*) and "Lojban: The Logical Language" (*www.omniglot.com/
writing/lojban.htm*).

SPEAKING OF LANGUAGES

*The language of the age is never the language of poetry, except among
the French, whose verse, where the thought or image does not support it,
differs in nothing from prose.*

—Thomas Gray

Marain

SPOKEN BY

Marain is spoken by members of the Culture, an alien society where there is more than enough wealth and comfort for everybody.

DOCUMENTED BY

Iain M. Banks (1954–) writes of the Culture in the novels *Consider Phlebas* (1987), *The Player of Games* (1988), *Use of Weapons* (1990), *Excession* (1996), *Inversions* (1998), *Look to Windward* (2000), *Matter* (2008), and *Surface Detail* (2010). The short-story collection *The State of the Art* (1991) contains three Culture short stories.

BEHIND THE WORDS

Since there's little conflict if everybody has what they need, the stories tend to focus on the people at the fringes of the culture and those who deal with beings outside the Culture.

DERIVATION OF THE LANGUAGE

Marain was constructed by the Minds, computerized systems that became self-aware and decided that the key to peace was a universal language.

CHARACTERISTICS OF THE LANGUAGE

- The Marain alphabet contains thirty-two symbols.
- Various versions of the language exist in a hierarchy of increasing complexity. The most complicated, designated "M32," is used only for highly secret information.
- The symbols making up the alphabet represent a nine-bit binary code arranged three bits high and three bits deep.

PHILOLOGICAL FACT

➤ Iain M. Banks's first novel, *The Wasp Factory*, excited controversy by its detailed depiction of violence and its suggestion that the reader was intended to sympathize with the psychopathic hero. However, a 1997 poll listed it as one of the top 100 books of the twentieth century.

FOR MORE INFORMATION

Review the works listed above, the resources listed in the bibliography, and the web pages: "A few Notes on Marain" (*www.pcplayer.de/~ps/iainbanks/artikel/marain.html*), "Marain alphabet" (*www .omniglot.com/writing/marain.htm*), and "Welcome to the Culture, the Galactic Civilization That Iain M. Banks Built" (*http://io9.com/354739/welcome-to-the-culture-the-galactic-civilization-that-iain-m-bank*).

SPEAKING OF LANGUAGES

I have laboured to refine our language to grammatical purity, and to clear it from colloquial barbarisms, licentious idioms, and irregular combinations.

—Samuel Johnson

Martian

SPOKEN BY

Martian was spoken by the Martians in *Across the Zodiac: The Story of a Wrecked Record* (1880), the forerunner of the sword-and-planet subgenre.

DOCUMENTED BY

Percy Greg (1836–1889) tells the story of an anonymous narrator who travels in his "Astronaut" to Mars, where he encounters an intelligent race.

BEHIND THE WORDS

Percy Greg may well be the first author to fully develop an alien language and grammar.

DERIVATION OF THE LANGUAGE

Greg suggests that it was constructed from an earlier natural language or languages.

CHARACTERISTICS OF THE LANGUAGE

+ The Martian language has twelve vowels and perhaps twenty-seven or so consonants.
+ There are two words for *I*, one masculine and one feminine.
+ Meanings are altered by adding prefixes and suffixes.

A TASTE OF THE LANGUAGE

âfi (verb)—to breathe
asfe-l (noun)—city
crâv (verb)—to kill
dâca (noun)—anvil

mepi (verb)—to rule
zefoo (noun)—female child
zevleen (noun)—stars

PHILOLOGICAL FACTS

➤ Percy Greg includes only a single Martian adjective in the novel. It is unknown whether that scarcity was representative of the language.

➤ In 1892 a French spiritualist named Hélène Smith declared that she had been transported, while in a trance, to the planet Mars and had spoken to the planet's inhabitants. She spoke for long periods, while in a trance, in what sounded like a genuine language and afterwards explained in great detail the appearance, conversation, and society of the Martians. Not especially surprising was the fact that "Martian" proved remarkably similar to French.

FOR MORE INFORMATION
Review the work listed above, the resources listed in the bibliography, and the web pages: "Across the Zodiac by Percy Greg" (*www.gutenberg.org/ebooks/10165*) and "Percy Greg" (*http://en.wikipedia.org/wiki/Percy_Greg*).

SPEAKING OF LANGUAGES

The language I have learn'd these forty years,
My native English, now I must forego:
And now my tongue's use is to me no more
Than an unstringed viol or a harp.

—Thomas Mobray, William Shakespeare's character in *Richard II*

Matoran

SPOKEN BY

Matoran is spoken by the Matoran race, small humanoids who all wear Kanohi masks that give them various powers.

DOCUMENTED BY

The Bionicle universe and the Matoran language were presented by the LEGO Group from 2001–2010. The story was developed through the *Bionicle Chronicles* story arc (four books, fifteen issues of the comic book, a direct-to-video movie and novelization, the *Matu Nui* online game, and the *Lego Bionicle* video game), the *Bionicle Adventures* story arc (ten books, eleven issues of the comic book, and two direct-to-video movies), and the *Bionicle Legends* story arc (eight books, fifteen issues of the comic book, and four Young Reader Bionicle books), all of which was aggregated on LEGO Group's Bionicle web page (*http://bionicle.lego.com/en-us/default.aspx?domainredir=www.bionicle.lego.com*).

BEHIND THE WORDS

Six heroes are summoned to the island of Mata Nui in order to awaken a great spirit that's been put to sleep by the evil Master of Shadows, Makuta. The heroes, called the Toa, are protectors of the Matoran race, and they must pass through many dangers before their quest will be successful.

A TASTE OF THE LANGUAGE

garai (noun)—gravity
ignika (noun)—life
kanohi (noun)—mask
koro (noun)—village
kraahkan (noun)—shadows

manas (noun)—monster
nui (adjective)—great
rua (noun)—wisdom
voya (noun)—journey
zya (verb)—to attack

PHILOLOGICAL FACTS

➤ Māori groups threatened legal action if LEGO Group did not stop using Māori words as product names in the Bionicle line. An executive from LEGO Group met with Māori representatives, and the naming convention was changed.

► The Bionicle line received the Toy of the Year Award (2001) from the Toy Industry Association and was LEGO Group's top-performing product in 2003.

FOR MORE INFORMATION

Review the works listed above, the resources listed in the bibliography, and the web pages: "Bionicle" (*http://bionicle.lego.com/en-us/default.aspx?domainredir=www.bionicle.lego.com*) and "BIONICLEstory.com (*www.bioniclestory.com*).

SPEAKING OF LANGUAGES

Language is called the garment of thought: however, it should rather be, language is the flesh-garment, the body, of thought.

—Thomas Carlyle

Miramish

SPOKEN BY
Miramish is spoken by the women on the planet Eho Miriam, in the Damiriak solar system.

DOCUMENTED BY
K Gerard Martin explored their world in *The Carreña series: Carreña 1: The Fall of Evanita*, *Carreña 2: Lamina*, and *Carreña 3: Imperative Birth*. The language is further described in *Cerafina's Damiriak Language Handbook*.

BEHIND THE WORDS
The Damiriak solar system is home to a race of women who live on three of the planets: Eho Miriam, Eho Dahma, and Nimsant. Eho Miriam was the home world, where people spoke Old Damiriak until the men died off because of emissions from the sun, Seris. The women left behind slowly switched from Old Damiriak to Miramish, which they had always used in their religious ceremonies. They then developed Mirsua as the language of the high priestesses.

DERIVATION OF THE LANGUAGE
Miramish was derived from Old Damiriak.

CHARACTERISTICS OF THE LANGUAGE

+ Miramish words almost always contain a vowel between every two consonants.
+ Miramish uses a root-word construct.
+ Sentences follow a subject-verb-object structure.

A TASTE OF THE LANGUAGE
arilushiato (verb)—to interrogate
beilebaka (noun)—dagger
falima (noun)—stream
giata (noun)—boss

hauthu (adjective)—healthy
igalifa (noun)—incursion
iteliko (verb)—to insist
kaifopo (noun)—jail

liauko (verb)—to raid
mioripalitu (adjective)—radioactive
olafeshalita (noun)—apartment
pelipa (noun)—mail
perinelitu (adjective)—faithful
rena (noun)—sun

sharlt (adjective)—heroic
taluna (noun)—memory
uferitha (noun)—identity
vaifopa (noun)—dinner
volaisho (verb)—to enjoy
wiena (noun)—home

PHILOLOGICAL FACTS

➤ Miramish words always end in a vowel, and the verbs always end with an *o*.
➤ Miramish uses the characters of the Marfi language, which contains twenty-seven symbols, each with an upper- and lowercase.

IF YOU'RE INTERESTED IN LEARNING THE LANGUAGE

Pick up a copy of *Cerafina's Damiriak Language Handbook*, by K Gerard Martin, to learn more about Miramish than you probably know about your native tongue.

SPEAKING OF LANGUAGES

Words may be false and full of art,

Sighs are the language of the heart.

—Thomas Shadwell

Mirsua

SPOKEN BY
Mirsua is spoken by the high priestesses on the planet Eho Miriam, in the Damiriak solar system.

DOCUMENTED BY
K Gerard Martin explored their world in *The Carreña series: Carreña 1: The Fall of Evanita*, *Carreña 2: Lamina*, and *Carreña 3: Imperative Birth*. The language is further described in *Cerafina's Damiriak Language Handbook*.

BEHIND THE WORDS
The Damiriak solar system is home to a race of women who live on three of the planets: Eho Miriam, Eho Dahma, and Nimsant. Eho Miriam was the home world, where people spoke Old Damiriak until the men died off because of emissions from the sun, Seris. The women left behind slowly switched from Old Damiriak to Miramish, which they had always used in their religious ceremonies. They then developed Mirsua as the language of the high priestesses.

DERIVATION OF THE LANGUAGE
Mirsua is descended from Old Damiriak by way of Miramish.

CHARACTERISTICS OF THE LANGUAGE

+ Mirsua uses different personal pronouns from the other languages descended from Old Damiriak.
+ Mirsua differs from Miramish, as Mirsua uses *s/z* where Miramish uses *sh/zh*.
+ The language is invoked only during religious ceremonies.

PHILOLOGICAL FACTS

➤ Mirsua replaced Miramish as the holy language when Miramish came into standard use.

> Mirsua uses the characters of the Marfi language, which contains twenty-seven symbols, each with an upper- and lowercase.

IF YOU'RE INTERESTED IN LEARNING THE LANGUAGE
Pick up a copy of *Cerafina's Damiriak Language Handbook*, by K Gerard Martin, to learn more about Mirsua than you probably know about your native tongue.

SPEAKING OF LANGUAGES

By such innovations are languages enriched, when the words are adopted by the multitude, and naturalized by custom.

—Miguel de Cervantes Saavedra

Molvanian

SPOKEN BY
The inhabitants of the fictional country of Molvania speak Molvanian.

DOCUMENTED BY
The Molvanians will live forever, according to the travel guide *Molvania: A Land Untouched by Modern Dentistry* (2004), by Santo Cilauro, Tom Gleisner, and Rob Sitch. They also wrote *Traditional Molvanian Baby Names: With Meanings, Derivations, and Probable Pronunciations* (2011).

BEHIND THE WORDS
The faux travel guide was so successful that sequels were quickly produced. These include *San Sombrero: A Land of Carnivals, Cocktails and Coups* (2006) and *Phaic Tan: Sunstroke on a Shoestring* (2006).

CHARACTERISTICS OF THE LANGUAGE

+ Molvanian uses four genders: male, female, neutral, and the collective noun for cheeses.
+ The language includes a high percentage of silent characters.

SOME USEFUL PHRASES
Erkjo ne szlepp statsik ne var ne vladrobzko ne? (Can I drink the water?)
Dyuszkiya trappokski drovko? (What is that smell?)

PHILOLOGICAL FACTS

➤ Molvania, for most of its existence, has been a wasteland. It was allied with Germany in World War II and then occupied by the Soviet Union, after which it became even more of a wasteland. Currently it is run by the Molvanian Mafia.

➤ It takes, on average, sixteen years to learn Molvanian; tourists are not encouraged to try.

FOR MORE INFORMATION

Review the works listed above, the resources listed in the bibliography, and the web page: "Language" (*www.jetlagtravel.com/molvania/useful.html*).

SPEAKING OF LANGUAGES

He that travelleth into a country before he hath some entrance into the language, goeth to school, and not to travel.

—Francis Bacon

Nadsat

SPOKEN BY

Nadsat is spoken by the nadsat, a teen subculture in the dystopian future of *A Clockwork Orange* (1962).

DOCUMENTED BY

Anthony Burgess (1917–1993) developed Nadsat so that Alex, the novel's antihero, and the other teenage characters could speak an alienating slang that wouldn't become dated.

BEHIND THE WORDS

Anthony Burgess was later dismissive of *A Clockwork Orange*, characterizing it as "a *jeu d'esprit* knocked off for money in three weeks." In fact, the novel deals with serious themes that Burgess returned to in later work: the threat of a powerful state, the increasing alienation of young people, and the peculiarities of language. Burgess thought the 1971 Stanley Kubrick movie misrepresented the book by emphasizing the sex and violence, missing the point the author was trying to make.

DERIVATION OF THE LANGUAGE

Nadsat is derived from Russian, British, and Cockney rhyming slang. Burgess said that elements of the language were inspired by the Edwardian Strutters, British teenagers in the later 1950s who carried out violent attacks on innocent people. Rhyming slang is characteristic of London's East End, where speakers substitute random rhyming words for others: for example, "nasty" becomes "Cornish pasty"; "key" becomes "Bruce Lee"; and so on. A dictionary of Cockney rhyming slang can be found at *www.cockneyrhymingslang.co.uk*.

A TASTE OF THE LANGUAGE

bezoomy (adjective)—mad
bugatty (adjective)—rich
collocol (noun)—bell
cutter (noun)—money
domy (noun)—house
drat (verb)—to fight

glazz (noun)—eye
govoreet (verb)—to talk
hound-and-horny (adjective)—corny
jeezny (noun)—life
oobivat (verb)—to kill
pishcha (noun)—food

pooshka (noun)—gun
razrez (verb)—to rip
sinny (noun)—movies
skvat (verb)—to take

smot (verb)—to look
spoogy (adjective)—terrified
tass (noun)—cup
warble (noun)—song

NUMBERING SYSTEM
odin—one
dva—two
tree—three

PHILOLOGICAL FACTS

➤ Since much of Nadsat was derived from Russian, translating *A Clockwork Orange* for the Russian market has proven problematic. How can publishers maintain the impenetrability of Nadsat if the roots were based on the native tongue of the readers, spiced with a British slang the Russians knew?

➤ In constructing Nadsat, Burgess eschewed abstract terms, focusing instead on concrete nouns, verbs, and adjectives. Also, many terms were shortened, leading to greater economy of speech.

FOR MORE INFORMATION
Review the works listed above, the resources listed in the bibliography, and the web pages: "Anthony Burgess on the English Language" (*http://grammar.about.com/od/writersonwriting/a/burgesslang07.htm*) and "A Nadsat Glossary" (*www.visual-memory.co.uk/amk/doc/nadsat.html*).

■ TXT MSGS ■

Does text messaging qualify as a language?

The 140-character limit and awkward-to-use keyboards have resulted in a stream of messages (a raging river?) containing acronyms (*lol* equals *laugh out loud*), symbol mash-ups (*gr8* equals *great*), and ungrammatical sentences (to say the least). Foreign speakers borrow these English textisms and spell native words with Latin characters that are quicker to send.

In 2006, high school students in New Zealand were given permission to use "text-speak" in their national tests. While this author has been unable to update the story by searching through the website of the New Zealand Qualifications Authority (*www.nzqa.govt.nz*), it might just be that he's not fluent enough in txt.

Nandorin

SPOKEN BY

The Elves in Tolkien's works who refused to cross the Misty Mountains and were later called the Nandor ("Those who go back") became separated from the others and eventually developed their own language, Nandorin—also called the Green-elven tongue, Danian, and Silven Elvish.

DOCUMENTED BY

J. R. R. Tolkien (1892–1973) explored many languages and cultures as he told the stories of Middle-earth: *The Hobbit* (1937), *The Fellowship of the Ring* (1954), *The Two Towers* (1954), and *The Return of the King* (1955). (The last three are collectively called *The Lord of the Rings*.) After his death, his son Christopher Tolkien (1924–) edited *The Silmarillion* (1977) with the help of Guy Gavriel Kay (1954–). Christopher Tolkien then deeply analyzed his father's notebooks, letters, and drafts to produce an extended study of Middle-earth and its creation: *The Book of Lost Tales, Part One* (1983), *The Book of Lost Tales, Part Two* (1984), *The Lays of Beleriand* (1985), *The Shaping of Middle-earth* (1986), *The Lost Road and Other Writings* (1987), *The Return of the Shadow (The History of The Lord of the Rings, Part One)* (1988), *The Treason of Isengard (The History of The Lord of the Rings, Part Two)* (1989), *The War of the Ring (The History of The Lord of the Rings, Part Three)* (1990), *Sauron Defeated (The History of The Lord of the Rings, Part Four)* (1992), *Morgoth's Ring (The Later Silmarillion, Part One)* (1993), *The War of the Jewels (The Later Silmarillion, Part Two)* (1994), and *The Peoples of Middle-earth* (1996).

BEHIND THE WORDS

When the Elves first awakened, the Valar decided to summon them to Valinor where they would be safe from harm. Most of the Elves made this journey, though some (the Avari) were unwilling to leave their homes. The others united under three leaders: Ingwë, Finwë, and Elwë. Some of those following Elwë refused to cross the Misty Mountains and became the Nandor. They eventually settled in Ossiriand, which they called Lindon.

DERIVATION OF THE LANGUAGE

Nandorin derived from Common Telerin.

CHARACTERISTICS OF THE LANGUAGE

+ Nandorin uses the -*î* to indicate plurality.

A TASTE OF THE LANGUAGE

beorn (noun)—man

cogn (noun)—bow

dunna (adjective)—black

ealc (noun)—swan

galad (noun)—tree

lygn (adjective)—pale

spenna (noun)—cloud

urc (noun)—Orc

PHILOLOGICAL FACT

➤ The name *Nimrodel* is probably of Nandorin origin. In *The Fellowship of the Ring*, as the company rests on the borders of Lothlórien, Legolas sings them a ballad of an Elvish maiden named Nimrodel.

FOR MORE INFORMATION

Review the works listed above, the resources listed in the bibliography, and the web pages: "Ardalambion" (*www.folk.uib.no/hnohf/*), "Cirth" (*www.omniglot.com/writing/cirth.htm*), "How many languages did J.R.R. Tolkien make?" (*www.folk.uib.no/hnohf/howmany.htm*), "J. R. R. Tolkien: A Biographical Sketch" (*www.tolkiensociety.org/tolkien/biography.html*), "Nandorin—the Green-elven tongue" (*http://folk.uib.no/hnohf/nandorin.htm*), "Sarati alphabet" (*www.omniglot.com/writing/sarati .htm*), and "Tengwar" (*www.omniglot.com/writing/tengwar.htm*).

SPEAKING OF LANGUAGES

You taught me language; and my profit on't
Is, I know how to curse. The red plague rid you,
For learning me your language!

—Caliban, *The Tempest,* Shakespeare

Nautilus Language

SPOKEN BY

The Nautilus language was spoken by the captain and crew of the submarine, *Nautilus*.

DOCUMENTED BY

Jules Verne (1828–1905) introduced the Nautilus language in *Twenty Thousand Leagues Under the Sea* (1870).

BEHIND THE WORDS

In Verne's classic, a French professor and his two companions are accidentally taken aboard the secret submarine *Nautilus*, skippered by the mysterious Captain Nemo (*Nemo*, of course, means *no one*). After traveling under the sea, wrestling with a giant squid, and observing the destruction of a ship chasing the *Nautilus*, the professor and his friends escape when Nemo's ship is accidentally caught in a giant maelstrom. Perhaps, just as a universal nautical language (a *rope* is a *line* whether you speak English, French, or Spanish) developed to cope with the diverse nationalities aboard sailing ships, the mixed crew on the *Nautilus* spoke a made-up neutral tongue.

A TASTE OF THE LANGUAGE

The narrator, Professor Aronnax, observes the second officer repeat: "*Nautron respoc lorni virch.*"

PHILOLOGICAL FACT

➤ In *Walk the Plank* (2003), a play adapted from *Twenty Thousand Leagues Under the Sea*, the Nautilus language was a mix of Polish and Persian.

FOR MORE INFORMATION

Review the works listed above and the resources listed in the bibliography.

Na'vi

SPOKEN BY

Na'vi is spoken by the Na'vi, a native tribe on the planet Pandora. Now that humans are mining Pandora for unobtainium, the Na'vi and their human visitors are spending more time together than ever before.

DOCUMENTED BY

Na'vi is heard in James Cameron's *Avatar* (2009) and *James Cameron's Avatar: The Game* (2009).

BEHIND THE WORDS

Desiring a complete alien language for the film, James Cameron hired communications professor and linguist Paul Frommer to create the Na'vi language with three criteria in mind: Na'vi should sound alien but pleasing to audiences, Na'vi should be learnable by the humans on Pandora, and Na'vi must be able to be spoken by the actors. Cameron gave Frommer the vocabulary he'd developed, and Frommer came back with three different sound schemes. Once Cameron chose one of the three designs, Frommer started developing the language in earnest, a process that took six months.

DERIVATION OF THE LANGUAGE

The vocabulary that James Cameron created, combined with the sounds he wanted, gave Paul Frommer direction on where to take the language. Knowing the desired end result, he chose a phonology and orthography that met Cameron's needs. Frommer then assisted during filming, making changes to the Na'vi language and its vocabulary as needed. Errors by the actors were corrected or absorbed into the canon, a process that was repeated when working on the *Avatar* video game.

CHARACTERISTICS OF THE LANGUAGE

+ Pronoun forms indicate whether *we* includes the listener and whether *we* means *two*, *three*, or more.

- Nouns in Na'vi have singular, plural, dual, and trial forms.
- Verbs in Na'vi do not reflect number.

A TASTE OF THE LANGUAGE

hangham (verb)—to laugh
kelku (noun)—home
kilvan (noun)—river
kinam (noun)—leg
kxitx (noun)—death
layon (adjective)—black
payoyang (noun)—fish
sa"nok (noun)—mother
sempul (noun)—father
skxawng (noun)—idiot

syuve (noun)—food
taronhunt (verb)—to hunt
ting nari (verb)—to look
tirey (noun)—life
tsawke (noun)—sun
tsray (noun)—village
tstal (noun)—knife
tstew (adjective)—brave
yayo (noun)—bird
yom (verb)—to eat

SOME USEFUL PHRASES

Tsun oe nga-hu nì-Na'vi p‹iv›ängkxo a fì-'u oe-ru prrte' lu. (It's a pleasure to be able to chat with you in Na'vi.)

Fì-skxawng-ìri tsap'alute sengi oe. (I apologize for this moron.)

Oe-ri ta peyä fahew a-kewong ontu teya l‹äng›u. (My nose is full of his alien smell.)

NUMBERING SYSTEM

Na'vi uses a base-eight numbering system rather than the base-ten numbering system used in English.

'aw—one
mune—two
pxey—three
tsìng—four

mrr—five
pukap—six
kinä—seven
vol—eight

PHILOLOGICAL FACT

➤ While James Cameron started writing the screenplay in 2006, work on the Na'vi language had been started the previous year.

IF YOU'RE INTERESTED IN LEARNING THE LANGUAGE

Being a language born during the Internet age, Na'vi has better online representation than most other made-up languages. "Learn Na'vi" (*www.learnnavi.org*) is where you go to learn the basics (and not so basics). But go to "Na'viteri" (*http://*

naviteri.org/), and you'll watch the language actually develop, as that is the Na'vi blog of Dr. Paul Frommer, the creator of the language.

FOR MORE INFORMATION
Review the works listed above, the resources listed in the bibliography, and the web pages: "Avatar (2009)" (*www.imdb.com/title/tt0499549/*), "Do You Speak Na'vi? Giving Voice To 'Avatar' Aliens" (*www.npr.org/templates/story/story.php?storyId=121350582*), "Fictional Languages in Film: The Linguists Behind Na'vi, Sindarin, Klingon And Ulam" (*www.altalang.com/beyond-words/2010/03/05/fictional-languages-in-film*), "Learn Navi" (*www.learnnavi.org*), and "USC professor creates an entire alien language for 'Avatar'" (*http://herocomplex.latimes.com/2009/11/21/usc-professor-creates-alien-language-for-avatar/*).

SPEAKING OF LANGUAGES

But it is assuredly an error to speak of any language as an art, in the sense of its having been elaborately and methodically formed.

—Charles Darwin

Newspeak

SPOKEN BY

The inhabitants of the totalitarian country of Oceania are having their native language changed from Oldspeak (English) to Newspeak, a change the state desires because Newspeak, with its reduced vocabulary and removed shades of meaning, will force citizens to think in a limited way.

DOCUMENTED BY

George Orwell describes Newspeak in the dystopian future of *Nineteen Eighty-Four* (1949). The language is then heard again in the 1956 and 1984 films of the same name (sometimes "*1984*").

BEHIND THE WORDS

George Orwell had praised the constructed language Basic English in the early 1940s. Seeing what was lost in the process and how English was being altered for the worse, however, he changed his point of view, publishing his thoughts in the essay "Politics and the English Language" (*Horizon*, 1946). In *1984* he takes the Sapir-Whorf Hypothesis to its logical conclusion: The government controls thought by controlling language. In the totalitarian future, according to Orwell, thoughtcrime will eventually become impossible because there will be no words with which to express it.

DERIVATION OF THE LANGUAGE

Newspeak is derived from English, condensing and reducing it in order to remove choice, which suggests free will.

CHARACTERISTICS OF THE LANGUAGE

- Many of the words in Newspeak are combinations of contradictory ideas.
- Newspeak features short, punchy words and syllables.

A TASTE OF THE LANGUAGE

bellyfeel (noun)—an idea that has become internalized into a gut instinct
blackwhite (noun)—the concept of being able to replace black with white without believing the color was ever different

duckspeak (noun)—the ability to speak without considering the content, and to repeat rote phrases, statements, and arguments

thoughtcrime (noun)—when one thinks of something one shouldn't

unperson (noun)—a person who has been removed from the public record and personal memories (note that memory is not considered private)

SOME USEFUL PHRASES

For examples of Newspeak in action, study any available political speech or corporate position paper. As to usefulness, that's a matter of perspective.

PHILOLOGICAL FACTS

➤ George Orwell's *Nineteen Eighty-Four* is often incorrectly credited with creating the words *doublespeak* (coined in the 1950s) and *groupthink* (first used by William H. Whyte in *Fortune Magazine* in 1952).

➤ The character Syme in the novel is at work on a new dictionary of Newspeak. "It's a beautiful thing, the destruction of words," he tells Winston Smith, the novel's protagonist. Shortly after, Syme vanishes; he has become an *unperson*.

FOR MORE INFORMATION

Review the works listed above and the resources listed in the bibliography. and the web page: "Doublespeak" (*www.etymonline.com/index.php?term=doublespeak*).

SPEAKING OF LANGUAGES

None of your live languages for Miss Blimber. They must be dead—stone dead—and then Miss Blimber dug them up like a Ghoul.

—Charles Dickens

Nimiash

SPOKEN BY

Nimiash is spoken by the women on the planet Nimsant, in the Damiriak solar system. Men don't speak something else; they don't exist.

DOCUMENTED BY

K Gerard Martin chronicles his world in *The Carreña series: Carreña 1: The Fall of Evanita*, *Carreña 2: Lamina*, and *Carreña 3: Imperative Birth*. The language is further described in *Cerafina's Damiriak Language Handbook*.

BEHIND THE WORDS

The Damiriak solar system is home to a race of women who live on three of the planets: Eho Miriam, Eho Dahma, and Nimsant. Eho Miriam was the home world, and people spoke Old Damiriak until the men died off because of emissions from the sun, Seris. The planet Nimsant is used as a prison, and those there speak Nimiash.

DERIVATION OF THE LANGUAGE

Nimiash is descended from Old Damiriak.

CHARACTERISTICS OF THE LANGUAGE

+ Nimiash words tend to be short.
+ Nimiash verbs always end with an *o*.

A TASTE OF THE LANGUAGE

arilushiato (verb)—to interrogate
beilebak (noun)—dagger
falm (noun)—stream
giat (noun)—boss
hauthu (adjective)—healthy
igalf (noun)—incursion
itelko (verb)—to insist
kairfpo (noun)—jail

liako (verb)—to raid
miorpaltu (adjective)—radioactive
olfeshalt (noun)—apartment
pelp (noun)—mail
prineltu (adjective)—faithful
ren (noun)—sun
sharolita (adjective)—heroic
taln (noun)—memory

uferth (noun)—identity

vaifp (noun)—dinner

volaisho (verb)—to enjoy

wien (noun)—home

PHILOLOGICAL FACTS

➤ Nimiash uses the Noimil alphabet, which contains twenty-seven symbols, each with an upper- and lowercase.

➤ All three of the languages spoken in the Damiriak solar system use the same words for numbers.

IF YOU'RE INTERESTED IN LEARNING THE LANGUAGE

Pick up a copy of *Cerafina's Damiriak Language Handbook*, by K Gerard Martin, to learn more about Nimiash than you probably know about your native tongue.

SPEAKING OF LANGUAGES

A different language is a different vision of life.

—Federico Fellini

Occidental

SPOKEN BY
Occidental is spoken by those who wish to learn the constructed language.

DOCUMENTED BY
Edgar de Wahl (1867–1948) created Occidental as an international auxiliary language.

BEHIND THE WORDS
Edgar de Wahl had been a fan of Volapük before switching his allegiance to Esperanto, advising L. L. Zamenhof on grammar and vocabulary. Discouraged with both experiences, de Wahl started creating his own language, which he publicized in 1922. Occidental went on to become one of the four most popular auxiliary languages in Europe, but with the outbreak of World War II, de Wahl drifted away from those working on Occidental to join the Committee of Linguistic Advisors to the International Auxiliary Language Association.

The International Auxiliary Language Association would release Interlingua three years after de Wahl's death, and speakers of Occidental switched to the new language.

DERIVATION OF THE LANGUAGE
Occidental was derived from Western European languages. Edgar de Wahl developed de Wahl's Rule, which was used to create new forms of words originally derived from Romance languages.

CHARACTERISTICS OF THE LANGUAGE
+ Occidental uses the twenty-six letters of the Latin alphabet: A (a), B (be), C (ce), D (de), E (e), F (ef), G (ge), H (ha), I (i), J (jot), K (ka), L (el), M (em), N (en), O (o), P (pe), Q (qu), R (er), S (es), T (te), U (u), V (ve), W (duplic ve), X (ix), Y (ypsilon), and Z (zet).

A TASTE OF THE LANGUAGE

al (noun)—air
blu (adjective)—blue
davo (verb)—to give
foj (noun)—fire
fost (noun)—forest
gam (noun)—leg
glen (adjective)—green
has (noun)—house
jedo (verb)—to eat
klajo (verb)—to shout

kotèl (noun)—knife
mand (noun)—hand
mori (adjective)—dead
nar (adjective)—black
noc (noun)—night
ov (noun)—egg
pol (noun)—town
riv (noun)—river
soma (noun)—summer
vima (noun)—winter

NUMBERING SYSTEM

un—one
du—two
tri—three
kwer—four
pin—five

ses—six
sep—seven
oc—eight
nev—nine
des—ten

THE LORD'S PRAYER

Patre nor, qui es in li cieles.
Mey tui nómine esser sanctificat,
mey tui regnia venir.
Mey tui vole esser fat
qualmen in li cieles talmen anc sur li terre.
Da nos hodie nor pan omnidial,
e pardona nor débites,
qualmen anc noi pardona nor debitores.
E ne inducte nos in tentation,
ma libera nos de lu mal.
Amen.

PHILOLOGICAL FACT

➤ De Wahl's Rule is used for creating nouns from infinitives. In its simplest form:

1. If you remove the *-er* or *-r* from the end of an infinitive and the root ends in a vocal, add a *-t* and the word becomes a noun.
2. If you remove the *-er* or *-r* from the end of an infinitive and the root ends in *d* or *r*, change the end letter to an *s* to form a noun.
3. In all other cases (with six exceptions), remove the *-er* or *-r* from the infinitive, and you've got a noun.

Old Solar

Old Solar (or Hlab-Eribol-ef-Cordi) was spoken on all worlds of our solar system except Earth, which was cut off from the universal connection by the events of the Christian fall.

DOCUMENTED BY

C. S. Lewis (1898–1963) made a deal with his friend J. R. R. Tolkien. Lewis would write about space travel if Tolkien wrote about time travel. Tolkien never finished his story "The Lost Road," but Lewis wrote a three-book series alternately called the *Space Trilogy*, the *Ransom Trilogy*, and the *Cosmic Trilogy*. Whatever the name, the series consists of *Out of the Silent Planet* (1938), *Perelandra* (1943), and *That Hideous Strength* (1945).

BEHIND THE WORDS

Professor Ransom is kidnapped and taken to Malacandra (Mars) as a religious offering. Ransom escapes his kidnappers and adventures his way across Malacandra, meeting members of many different races and cultures. In *Perelandra*, the angelic ruler of Malacandra sends Ransom to Perelandra (Venus) to save the queen of that planet from the evil plans of the man who kidnapped Ransom in *Out of the Silent Planet*. In the third book, *That Hideous Strength*, Mark Studdock enlists the help of Dr. Ransom to defeat the evil forces behind The National Institute of Coordinated Experiments (N.I.C.E.), which intends to kill all life on Earth so that the planet can be ruled by newly engineered beings.

DERIVATION OF THE LANGUAGE

Old Solar was the original universal language.

CHARACTERISTICS OF THE LANGUAGE

+ Some Old Solar words are made plural by adding *-a* or *-i*, although other words are made more complex to indicate plurality.

A TASTE OF THE LANGUAGE

Arbol (noun)—the Sun
eldil (noun)—spirit or angel
Glund (noun)—Jupiter
handra (noun)—a planet or land
handramit (noun)—valley
harandra (noun)—plateau
hlab (noun)—language
hluntheline (verb)—to yearn for something
hnakra (noun)—a vicious sea creature
hnua (noun)—rational being with a soul
hru (noun)—blood

Lurga (noun)—Saturn
Malacandra (noun)—Mars
Maleldil (noun)—Jesus
Neruval (noun)—Uranus
Perelandra (noun)—Venus
Sulva (noun)—The Moon
Thulcandra (noun)—Earth, "The Silent Planet"
Viritrilbia (noun)—Mercury
wondelone (verb)—to miss something from the past

PHILOLOGICAL FACTS

➤ The title *That Hideous Strength* came from the poem *Ane Dialog betwix Experience and ane Courteour of the Miserabyll Estait of the World* by Sir David Lyndsay of the Mount (c. 1490–c. 1555). The lines "The shadow of that hyddeous strength / sax myle and more it is of length" refer to the Tower of Babel.

➤ Authors Larry Niven and Alan Moore both made use of Lewis's races of creatures. Niven included the hrossa, séroni, and pfifltriggi in his novel *Rainbow Mars*, while Moore used the séroni in the second volume of *The League of Extraordinary Gentlemen*.

FOR MORE INFORMATION

Review the works listed above, the resources listed in the bibliography, and the web pages: "C. S. Lewis" (*http://en.wikipedia.org/wiki/C._S._Lewis*), and "Out of the silent planet" (*www.bensfriends.com/whatnot/archives/001059.html*).

A SIGN LANGUAGE OF THE TIMES

Just as people developed regional languages, they developed regional sign languages. There are an estimated 200 sign languages used in the world today. Like any other language, sign languages come and go, fall in and out of favor.

The Old Tongue

SPOKEN BY

The Old Tongue is considered a dead language, spoken only by scholars. This, however, does not keep the language from being a pivotal component in the unfolding events of *The Wheel of Time*.

DOCUMENTED BY

Robert Jordan (1948–2007) relates the cycling ebb and flow of good and evil in his series *The Wheel of Time*: *The Eye of the World* (1990), *The Great Hunt* (1990), *The Dragon Reborn* (1991), *The Shadow Rising* (1992), *The Fires of Heaven* (1993), *Lord of Chaos* (1994), *A Crown of Swords* (1996), *The Path of Daggers* (1998), *Winter's Heart* (2000), *Crossroads of Twilight* (2003), *Knife of Dreams* (2005), *The Gathering Storm* (with Brandon Sanderson, 2009; Sanderson was chosen to complete the series after Jordan's death in 2007), *Towers of Midnight* (with Brandon Sanderson, 2010), and *A Memory of Light* (with Brandon Sanderson, to be published in 2012).

BEHIND THE WORDS

The Creator made the universe, imprisoned Shai'tan (Dark One), and set the Wheel of Time spinning. Unfortunately, someone mistakenly breached the Dark One's prison, allowing evil into the world. As The Dark One gathered allies, the Wheel of Time spawned a dragon named Lews Therin Telamon to defeat them. Thus began the never-ending battle between good and evil. The dragon failed to seal the Dark One's prison, and in his grief he killed his own kin and then, finally, himself. For 3,000 years, humanity endured the slow rise and fall of civilizations and wars spawned by the Dark One's agents. Then, as the dark powers were gathering once more, the allies of Good were searching for one who had been called the Dragon Reborn.

DERIVATION OF THE LANGUAGE

The Old Tongue was spoken during the Age of the Legends before The Breaking of the World. Although it passed out of common usage, it is still spoken by those few who are highly educated and knowledgeable about history.

A TASTE OF THE LANGUAGE

The most common examples of the Old Tongue are ancient words preserved as names:

Aldieb (noun)—West Wind
Atha"an Miere (noun)—Those Bound to the Sea (the Sea Folk)
Chalinda (noun)—Sweet Girl
Daishar (noun)—Glory
Faile (noun)—Falcon

Jeade"en (noun)—True Finder
Mageen (noun)—Daisy
Mandarb (noun)—Blade
Serenla (noun)—Stubborn Daughter
Siswai (noun)—Spear
Tai"daishar (noun)—True Glory

SOME USEFUL PHRASES

Dovie'andi se tovya sagain. (It's time to toss the dice.)
Sene sovya caba'donde ain dovienya. (Luck is a horse to ride like any other.)
Mia ayende, Aes Sedai! Caballein misain ye! Inde muagdhe Aes Sedai misain ye! Mia ayende! (Release me, Aes Sedai! I am a free man! I am no Aes Sedai meat! Release me!)

PHILOLOGICAL FACT

➤ Before *The Wheel of Time*, Robert Jordan wrote *Conan the Barbarian* novels.

FOR MORE INFORMATION

Review the works listed above, the resources listed in the bibliography, and the web page: "The Wheel of Time" (*http://en.wikipedia.org/wiki/The_Wheel_of_Time*).

SPEAKING OF LANGUAGES

Whoever controls the language, the images, controls the race.

—Allen Ginsberg

Orghast

SPOKEN BY

Orghast was spoken only once, and only by the actors on the stage when *Orghast* (1971) was performed.

DOCUMENTED BY

Filmmaker Peter Brook and poet Ted Hughes wrote the play *Orghast* entirely in the constructed language of Orghast. The play was performed at the Shiraz/Persepolis festival in 1971.

BEHIND THE WORDS

The play tells of a myth based on and around that of Prometheus.

DERIVATION OF THE LANGUAGE

In the words of Ted Hughes, documented by A. C. H. Smith in the book *Orghast At Persepolis*:

> *The deeper into language one goes, the less visual/conceptual its imagery, and the more audial/visceral/muscular its system of tensions. . . . In other words, the deeper into language one goes, the more dominated it becomes by purely musical modes, and the more dramatic it becomes—the more unified with total states of being and with the expressiveness of physical action. Visualization in language is at odds with immediately expressive dramatic action in that it is the conceptual substitute for physical action.*

CHARACTERISTICS OF THE LANGUAGE

+ Orghast is pure sound, primal and instinctual.

A TASTE OF THE LANGUAGE

bullorga (noun)—darkness

gr (verb)—to eat

kr (verb)—to devour

ull (verb)—to swallow

FOR MORE INFORMATION
Review the works listed above, the resources listed in the bibliography, and the web pages: "I See It Feelingly: Orghast At Persepolis" (*http://little-object-a.blogspot.com/2009/10/i-see-it-feelingly-orghast-at.html*), "On the Possibility of a Universal Language" in "Peter Brook and Traditional Thought" (*www.gurdjieff.org/nicolescu3.htm*), "Orghast" (*http://en.wikipedia.org/wiki/Orghast*), and "Orghast at Persepolis" (*www.complete-review.com/reviews/theater/orghast.htm*).

TRANSLATION ROCK STARS

The Cippi of Melquart (discovered in Malta, 1694) were inscribed with Ancient Greek and Carthaginian. The bilingual message allowed the first decipherings of the Carthaginian alphabet.

The Rosetta Stone (discovered in Egypt, 1799) was inscribed with Ancient Greek, Demotic, and Hieroglyphic texts. The trilingual messages allowed scholars to make sense of Egyptian hieroglyphic writing.

The Pyrgi Tablets (discovered in Italy, 1964) were inscribed with Phoenician and Etruscan. The bilingual message allowed researches to read Etruscan for the first time.

Osskili

SPOKEN BY
Osskili is spoken by the Osskilians from the northern island of Osskil in Earthsea.

DOCUMENTED BY
Ursula K. Le Guin (1929–) relates the tales of Earthsea in: *A Wizard of Earthsea* (1968), *The Tombs of Atuan* (1971), *The Farthest Shore* (1973), *Tehanu: The Last Book of Earthsea* (1990), *Tales from Earthsea* (short stories, 2001), and *The Other Wind* (2001).

DERIVATION OF THE LANGUAGE
Osskili is derived from Old Speech, the Language of the Making.

A TASTE OF THE LANGUAGE
akhad (noun)—firstborn child
kelub (noun)—the red one
serret (adjective)—silver

FOR MORE INFORMATION
Review the works listed above, the resources listed in the bibliography, and the web pages: "Characters in Earthsea" (*http://en.wikipedia.org/wiki/Characters_in_Earthsea*), "Islands of Earthsea" (*http://en.wikipedia.org/wiki/Islands_of_Earthsea*), "The Isolate Tower" (*www.tavia.co.uk/earthsea/index.htm*), "Ursula K. Le Guin" (*www.ursulakleguin.com*), and "Ursula LeGuin's Magical World of Earthsea" (*http://scholar.lib.vt.edu/ejournals/ALAN/spring96/griffin.html*).

SPEAKING OF LANGUAGES

Language is by its very nature a communal thing; that is, it expresses never the exact thing but a compromise—that which is common to you, me, and everybody.

—Thomas Ernest Hulme

Pakuni

SPOKEN BY

Pakuni is spoken by the primitive Pakuni in the television series *Land of the Lost* (1974–1977); the series remake, *Land of the Lost* (1991–1992); and again in the movie *Land of the Lost* (2009).

DOCUMENTED BY

Producers Sid and Marty Krofft hired linguist Victoria Fromkin to create the Pakuni language.

BEHIND THE WORDS

Park Ranger Rick Marshall and his two children, Will and Holly, are rafting down a river when an earthquake drops them through a tear in time. They find themselves in a world ruled by dinosaurs, ape-men, and the lizard-insect-humanoid Sleestak, who wish to sacrifice the Marshalls to the god of the Sleestaks.

DERIVATION OF THE LANGUAGE

Professor Victoria Fromkin turned to the Kwa languages of West Africa to develop the 300-word vocabulary, phonology, and grammar of Pakuni.

A TASTE OF THE LANGUAGE

amura (noun)—friend
dinda (verb)—to eat
echichi (noun)—egg
ejiri (noun)—house
eram (noun)—moon
fa (verb)—to take
fusachi (adverb)—quickly

kasa (adjective)—happy
ky (verb)—to go
onam (noun)—food
osu (noun)—water
pakuni (noun)—people
wu (verb)—to see
yuman (noun)—human

A USEFUL PHRASE

Me tobi ye. (I welcome you.)

PHILOLOGICAL FACT

➤ NBC censors demanded that all Pakuni dialogue in the script be translated so that they could be sure Professor Fromkin wasn't including inappropriate material.

FOR MORE INFORMATION

Review the works listed above, the resources listed in the bibliography, and the web pages: "Land of the Lost (TV Series 1974–1977)" (*www.imdb.com/title/tt0071005/*) and "Pakuni–English Dictionary" (*http://lotl.popapostle.com/html/nels/pakudict.html*).

SPEAKING OF LANGUAGES

Language has always been held to be man's richest art form, that which distinguishes him from the animal creation.

—Marshall McLuhan

Parseltongue

SPOKEN BY

Harry Potter is one of the few Parselmouths who can speak Parseltongue, the language of snakes.

DOCUMENTED BY

J. K. Rowling (1965–) chronicles the story of Harry Potter in the bestselling Harry Potter series: *Harry Potter and the Philosopher's Stone* (1997), *Harry Potter and the Chamber of Secrets* (1998), *Harry Potter and the Prisoner of Azkaban* (1999), *Harry Potter and the Goblet of Fire* (2000), *Harry Potter and the Order of the Phoenix* (2003), *Harry Potter and the Half-Blood Prince* (2005), and *Harry Potter and the Deathly Hallows* (2007).

BEHIND THE WORDS

Harry Potter and his friends Ron Weasley and Hermione Granger are students at the Hogwarts School of Witchcraft and Wizardry. While still learning how to use his powers, Harry goes on a quest to defeat the evil Lord Voldemort. During the course of this quest, Harry discovers that he can speak Parseltongue, a highly unusual attribute and one that was matched in the past by Lord Voldemort.

A TASTE OF THE LANGUAGE

From *Harry Potter and the Half-Blood Prince* (2005) comes this exchange between Tom Marvolo Riddle and Morfin:

"Psā!" — "You speak it?"

"Efe iska?" — "Yes, I speak it. Where is Marvolo?"

"Sā, skæ. Hút fis Marvolo?" — "Dead. Died years ago, didn't he?"

"Tæn. Suōs tænas, au?" — "Who are you, then?"

"Simī hí fú?" — "I'm Morfin, ain't I?"

"Dē Morfin, au?" — "Marvolo's son?"

"Tuva Marvolī?" — "Course I am, then . . . I thought you was that Muggle. You look mighty like that Muggle."

"Sasōl, ebei? Shēsin Muggle saum hwinæ. Tōr shēsin Muggle harisa."

"Stop."

PHILOLOGICAL FACTS

➤ When interviewed by Stephen Fry at the Royal Albert Hall (June 26, 2003), J. K. Rowling stated, "Parselmouth is an old word for someone who has a problem with the mouth, like a harelip."

➤ J. K. Rowling has said that the idea for the Harry Potter series came to her during a train trip from Manchester to London. She began writing the story immediately and wrote a great deal of it in cafes in Edinburgh, since, as she subsequently remarked, taking her child out for a walk helped the baby go to sleep.

FOR MORE INFORMATION

Review the works listed above, the resources listed in the bibliography, and the web pages: "Fry, Stephen, interviewer: J. K. Rowling at the Royal Albert Hall, 26 June 2003." (*www.accio-quote.org/articles/2003/0626-alberthall-fry.htm*), "J. K. Rowling" (*http://en.wikipedia.org/wiki/J._K._Rowling*), and "Parseltongue-inspired" (*www.frathwiki.com/Parseltongue-inspired*).

SPEAKING OF LANGUAGES

To handle a language skillfully is to practice a kind of evocative sorcery.

—Charles Baudelaire

Pastiche

SPOKEN BY

Pastiche is a language made up by a group of young linguists and learned by Beran Panasper who will later insist that all children are taught Pastiche.

DOCUMENTED BY

Jack Vance (1916–) wrote about the interplanetary intrigues of Pao in *The Languages of Pao* (1958), a novel-length exploration of the possibilities of the Sapir-Whorf Hypothesis.

BEHIND THE WORDS

The Pao speak Paonese, a language that reflects their passive state. In the imaginary book *The Languages of Pao* Vance writes:

"The Paonese sentence did not so much describe an act as it presented a picture of a situation. There were no verbs, no adjectives; no formal word comparison such as good, better, best. The typical Paonese saw himself as a cork on a sea of a million waves, lofted, lowered, thrust aside by incomprehensible forces—if he thought of himself as a discrete personality at all. He held his ruler in awe, gave unquestioning obedience, for on Pao nothing must vary, nothing must change.

"The ruler's brother, Bustamonte, must be atypical because he uses hypnosis to convince Beran Panasper to kill his father, the planet's ruler. Bustamonte takes control, and Beran is whisked away to another planet by Lord Palafox, a consultant who had been brought to Pao to assist in reforms. Bustamonte and Palafox set up a linguistic program to change Pao, creating three languages (Valiant, Technicant, and Cogitant) that will be force-fed to groups separated from the rest of the Paonese in order to form classes of warriors (speaking Valiant), technicians (speaking Technicant), and merchants (speaking Cogitant). A group of young linguists being trained to teach the constructed languages produce Pastiche, a well-rounded language that could serve as a universal language for Pao and would allow the Paonese to evolve from their passive state.

"Beran learns Pastiche and returns to Pao, where he takes his rightful place as ruler. After the warriors attempt a coup, Beran makes a deal: They can keep some control, but all children on the planet must be taught Pastiche, for Beran believes that the new language will reunite Paonese divided by the three constructed languages."

DERIVATION OF THE LANGUAGE
Pastiche is a blend of three constructed languages: Valiant, Technicant, and Cogitant. These three languages were engineered subsets of the native Paonese, which derived from Waydalic.

CHARACTERISTICS OF THE LANGUAGE

+ Paonese does not contain verbs, adjectives, or words that offer comparison.
+ Paonese is suitable for an agricultural society that offers blind obedience to the rulers.
+ Valiant uses a simple and direct grammar spoken with guttural vowels. Valiant invites contrast and comparisons of strength and prowess.
+ Technicant uses a complicated but logical grammar. Technicant is suitable for those developing engineering ideas.
+ Cogitant uses an elaborate grammar that highlights honorifics (for hypocrisy), homophones (for ambiguity), and alternation (for the give-and-take of bargaining). Cogitant is useful for those engaged in trade.
+ Pastiche combines the strengths of Paonese, Valiant, Technicant, and Cogitant to produce a language that will allow its speakers to cope with an ever-changing world.

FOR MORE INFORMATION
Review the work listed above, the resources listed in the bibliography, and the web page: "The Languages of Pao by Jack Vance" (*http://tenser.typepad.com/tenser_said_the_tensor/2005/01/ithe_languages__1.html*).

SPEAKING OF LANGUAGES

Our speech has its weaknesses and its defects, like all the rest. Most of the occasions for the troubles of the world are grammatical.

—Michel-Eyquen de Montaigne

Pravic

SPOKEN BY
Pravic is spoken by the inhabitants of the anarchist society on Anarres.

DOCUMENTED BY
Ursula K. Le Guin (1929–) uses Pravic in *The Dispossessed: An Ambiguous Utopia* (1974), the fifth book in the Hainish Cycle: *Rocannon's World* (1964), *Planet of Exile* (1966), *City of Illusions* (1967), *The Left Hand of Darkness* (1969), *The Dispossessed* (1974), *The Word for World is Forest* (1976), and *The Telling* (2000).

BEHIND THE WORDS
The Dispossessed (1974) takes place on Urras, where revolutionaries were offered the chance to live on Anarres, the planet's moon. Events on Urras are driven by the two superpowers, A-Io and Thu. Pravic is spoken on Anarres.

DERIVATION OF THE LANGUAGE
Farigv created the language Pravic for use on Anarres, fashioning the language to represent the anarchist beliefs of the society.

CHARACTERISTICS OF THE LANGUAGE

+ Since there is no private property on Anarres, possessive pronouns do not exist.
+ Shevek talking about Pravic with the ship's doctor:

"The vocabulary makes it difficult," Shevek said, pursuing his discovery. "In Pravic the word religion is seldom. No, what do you say—rare. Not often used. Of course, it is one of the Categories: the Fourth Mode. Few people learn to practice all the Modes. But the Modes are built of the natural capacities of the mind, you could not seriously believe that we had no religious capacity? That we could do physics while we were cut off from the profoundest relationship man has with the cosmos?"

A TASTE OF THE LANGUAGE

Since Pravic is translated into English in consideration of the readers, the primary examples of the language are names:

Farigv

Gvarab

Kadagv

Kvetur

Kvigot

PHILOLOGICAL FACT

➤ Le Guin was the daughter of an anthropologist, so it's perhaps not surprising that her novels deal with themes of interest to anthropology. She raises questions in her books about race, sexual identity, environmentalism, and political conflict.

FOR MORE INFORMATION

Review the works listed above, the resources listed in the bibliography, and the website: Ursula K. Le Guin (*www.ursulakleguin.com/*).

UNIVERSAL TRANSLATOR

In the Australian-American television series *Farscape* (1999–2003), John Crichton is injected with a bacteria that colonizes his brainstem and automatically translates most languages he hears.

SPEAKING OF LANGUAGES

Poetry should help, not only to refine the language of the time, but to prevent it from changing too rapidly.

—T. S. Eliot

Primitive Elvish

SPOKEN BY
Primitive Elvish was the language developed by the Quendi, the first Elves of Middle-earth.

DOCUMENTED BY
J. R. R. Tolkien (1892–1973) explored many languages and cultures as he told the stories of Middle-earth: *The Hobbit* (1937), *The Fellowship of the Ring* (1954), *The Two Towers* (1954), and *The Return of the King* (1955). (The last three are collectively called *The Lord of the Rings*.) After his death, his son Christopher Tolkien (1924–) edited *The Silmarillion* (1977) with the help of Guy Gavriel Kay (1954–). Christopher Tolkien then deeply analyzed his father's notebooks, letters, and drafts to produce an extended study of Middle-earth and its creation: *The Book of Lost Tales, Part One* (1983), *The Book of Lost Tales, Part Two* (1984), *The Lays of Beleriand* (1985), *The Shaping of Middle-earth* (1986), *The Lost Road and Other Writings* (1987), *The Return of the Shadow (The History of The Lord of the Rings, Part One)* (1988), *The Treason of Isengard (The History of The Lord of the Rings, Part Two)* (1989), *The War of the Ring (The History of The Lord of the Rings, Part Three)* (1990), *Sauron Defeated (The History of The Lord of the Rings, Part Four)* (1992), *Morgoth's Ring (The Later Silmarillion, Part One)* (1993), *The War of the Jewels (The Later Silmarillion, Part Two)* (1994), and *The Peoples of Middle-earth* (1996).

BEHIND THE WORDS
Primitive Elvish was the root of all languages, save those of Valarin and Khuzdul.

CHARACTERISTICS OF THE LANGUAGE

+ Most words had two or three vowels.
+ Many of the words in Primitive Elvish ended with long vowel sounds.

A TASTE OF THE LANGUAGE
lindâ (adjective)—sweet-sounding
ndorê (noun)—land

PHILOLOGICAL FACTS

➤ Primitive Elvish existed in two stages: Primitive Quendian, which was the origin language for all Elvish languages that subsequently developed; and Common Eldarin. The latter was the language spoken by those Elves who followed Oromë on his journey to Valinor. Common Eldarin is said to have arisen during the two and a half centuries of that journey. Common Eldarin eventually became Old Quenya; in Beleriand it evolved into Sindarin.

➤ Tolkien identified the origin of the Elves as having occurred at a particular place and time: when the Quendi were awakened near Cuiviénen. Thus, he was able to pinpoint the precise origins of Elvish as being the language spoken by the Quendi when they first became conscious.

FOR MORE INFORMATION

Review the works listed above, the resources listed in the bibliography, and the web pages: "Ardalambion" (*www.folk.uib.no/hnohf/*), "Cirth" (*www.omniglot.com/writing/cirth.htm*), "How many languages did J.R.R. Tolkien make?" (*www.folk.uib.no/hnohf/howmany.htm*), "J. R. R. Tolkien: A Biographical Sketch" (*www.tolkiensociety.org/tolkien/biography.html*), "Primitive Elvish—where it all began" (*www.folk.uib.no/hnohf/primelv.htm*), "Sarati alphabet" (*www.omniglot.com/writing/sarati.htm*), and "Tengwar" (*www.omniglot.com/writing/tengwar.htm*).

═══ THOU SHALT NOT LIE ═══

A purported feature of many constructed languages is that speakers are unable to lie.

People say that numbers don't lie, that mathematical formulas are based on accepted theories and proven truths. As demonstrated in *Nineteen Eighty-Four*, nothing stops anyone from writing two plus two equals five.

SPEAKING OF LANGUAGES

Learn a new language and get a new soul.

—Czech proverb

Ptydepe

Select members of an unnamed organization featured in Václav Havel's play *The Memorandum* (1966) use Ptydepe.

DOCUMENTED BY

Havel's play follows company director Josef Gross as he tries to determine the contents of a memo he's received. He doesn't understand Ptydepe, and the one person he finds who does, says that she lacks the necessary permit to conduct the translation.

BEHIND THE WORDS

Like many Russians and Eastern Europeans, Havel was frustrated by the bureaucratic inefficiency and corruption that were fostered by the leaders of the Soviet Union. His play intended to satirize this—hence the idea that the head of a company is sent a memorandum in a language he can't read, and the only person of his acquaintance who can read it, won't because she's not been given official permission to do so.

DERIVATION OF THE LANGUAGE

Ivan M. Havel, Václav Havel's brother, created the made-up language for the play.

CHARACTERISTICS OF THE LANGUAGE

+ In Ptydepe, the shorter the word, the more general its meaning. For example, the word for *whatever* is *gh*, as compared to the word for *wombat*, which would fill up most of this page.

A TASTE OF THE LANGUAGE

From the untranslated memorandum:
Ra ko hutu d dekotu ely trebomu emusohe, vdegar yd, stro reny er gryk kendy, alyv zvyde dezu, kvyndal fer teknu sely.

SOME USEFUL PHRASES
It is unlikely that Ptydepe, being a bureaucratic construct, would contain useful phrases.

FOR MORE INFORMATION
Review the work listed above, the resources listed in the bibliography, and the web page: "The Memorandum" (*http://en.wikipedia.org/wiki/The_Memorandum*).

SPEAKING OF LANGUAGES

In general, every country has the language it deserves.

—Jorge Luis Borges

Quenya

SPOKEN BY

Quenya is spoken by the Vanyar, Noldor, and Valar, as well as some in the Hither Lands and the Men of Gondor in Middle-earth.

DOCUMENTED BY

J. R. R. Tolkien (1892–1973) explored many languages and cultures as he told the stories of Middle-earth: *The Hobbit* (1937), *The Fellowship of the Ring* (1954), *The Two Towers* (1954), and *The Return of the King* (1955). (The last three are collectively called *The Lord of the Rings*.) After his death, his son Christopher Tolkien (1924–) edited *The Silmarillion* (1977) with the help of Guy Gavriel Kay (1954–). Christopher Tolkien then deeply analyzed his father's notebooks, letters, and drafts to produce an extended study of Middle-earth and its creation: *The Book of Lost Tales, Part One* (1983), *The Book of Lost Tales, Part Two* (1984), *The Lays of Beleriand* (1985), *The Shaping of Middle-earth* (1986), *The Lost Road and Other Writings* (1987), *The Return of the Shadow (The History of The Lord of the Rings, Part One)* (1988), *The Treason of Isengard (The History of The Lord of the Rings, Part Two)* (1989), *The War of the Ring (The History of The Lord of the Rings, Part Three)* (1990), *Sauron Defeated (The History of The Lord of the Rings, Part Four)* (1992), *Morgoth's Ring (The Later Silmarillion, Part One)* (1993), *The War of the Jewels (The Later Silmarillion, Part Two)* (1994), and *The Peoples of Middle-earth* (1996).

BEHIND THE WORDS

Quenya (High-elven) is similar to but not identical with Primitive Elvish, from which it evolved. By the time the stories of *The Lord of the Rings* unfold, the Elves speak variations of a different mother tongue, Sindarin. Nonetheless, it is occasionally still used, particularly by non-Elvish mortals, for formal occasions. Thus, when Aragorn declares that the name of his royal house will be Strider (the name by which he was first introduced to Frodo Baggins) he says, "In Elvish it will not sound so ill." Thus his house is known by the Quenyan translation of Strider: *Telcontar*.

CHARACTERISTICS OF THE LANGUAGE

+ Some nouns can have singular, dual, plural, and particular plural forms.
+ Nouns are declined, and Classic Quenya has ten forms.
+ Adding *ua-* before a verb makes the statement negative.

A TASTE OF THE LANGUAGE

amillë (noun)—mother
Anar (noun)—the sun
ango (noun)—snake
arta (adjective)—noble
coa (noun)—house
hoa (adjective)—large
hrívë (noun)—winter
imya (adjective)—identical
laivë (noun)—ointment
máma (noun)—sheep

mírë (noun)—jewel
morë (adjective)—black
oiolairë (noun)—summer
osto (noun)—city
qualmë (noun)—death
ruinë (noun)—fire
sangwa (noun)—poison
sicil (noun)—dagger
telco (noun)—leg
tyulma (noun)—mast

NUMBERING SYSTEM

mine—one
atta—two
nelde—three
canta—four
lempe—five

enque—six
otso—seven
tolto—eight
nerte—nine
cainen—ten

PHILOLOGICAL FACTS

➤ Tolkien first began to construct Quenya when he was a student at King Edward's School in Birmingham, England. Among the chief influences on it was the Finnish language, which Tolkien had discovered and fallen in love with.

➤ Quenya was the first language of Middle-earth to be written down.

IF YOU'RE INTERESTED IN LEARNING THE LANGUAGE

H. K. Fauskanger has developed a Quenya course (*http://folk.uib.no/hnohf/ qcourse.htm*) consisting of twenty lessons plus appendices.

FOR MORE INFORMATION

Review the works listed above, the resources listed in the bibliography, and the web pages: "Ardalambion" (*www.folk.uib.no/hnohf/*), "Cirth" (*www.omniglot.com/writing/cirth.htm*), "How many languages did J.R.R. Tolkien make?" (*www.folk.uib.no/hnohf/howmany.htm*), "J. R. R. Tolkien: A Biographical Sketch" (*www.tolkiensociety.org/tolkien/biography.html*), "Quenya—the Ancient Tongue" (*www.folk.uib.no/hnohf/quenya.htm*), "Quenya Wordlists" (*www.folk.uib.no/hnohf/wordlists .htm*), "Sarati alphabet" (*www.omniglot.com/writing/sarati.htm*), and "Tengwar" (*www.omniglot.com/ writing/tengwar.htm*).

SPEAKING OF LANGUAGES

But when the Elves learned it [the language Valar], they changed it from the first in the learning, and softened its sounds, and they added many words to it of their own liking and devices even from the beginning. For the Elves love the making of words, and this has ever been the chief cause of the change and variety of their tongues.

—J. R. R. Tolkien

Writing simply means no dependent clauses, no dangling things, no flashbacks, and keeping the subject near the predicate. We throw in as many fresh words as we can get away with. Simple, short sentences don't always work. You have to do tricks with pacing, alternate long sentences with short, to keep it vital and alive.

—Theodor Geisel (Dr. Seuss)

Quintaglio

SPOKEN BY

Quintaglio is spoken by the Quintaglio, dinosaurs that were transported from Earth to the moon of a gas giant some 65 million years ago. The Quintaglio have evolved into intelligent creatures and have since created a technological culture.

DOCUMENTED BY

Robert J. Sawyer (1960–) introduced the Quintaglio in the story "Uphill Climb" and then enlarged the tale over the course of the Quintaglio Ascension Trilogy: *Far-Seer* (1992), *Fossil Hunter* (1993), and *Foreigner* (1994).

BEHIND THE WORDS

In *Far-Seer*, Asfan must convince the rest of the Quintaglio of the truth about their place of origin before their natural propensity for territorial violence destroys them. Asfan's son, Toroca, fights to get across the radical idea of evolution in *Fossil Hunter*. While Toroca continues that work in *Foreigner*, Asfan starts a new treatment, psychoanalysis, learning truths about himself that have implications for all.

CHARACTERISTICS OF THE LANGUAGE

+ Quintaglios can not get away with lying, as their muzzles turn blue if they lie.

A TASTE OF THE LANGUAGE

calthat'ch (noun)—fraud
ca-tart (noun)—toys
far-seer (noun)—telescope

halpataars (noun)—bloodpriest
kev (adjective)—bright
latark (verb)—to giddyup

NUMBERING SYSTEM

semi-ten—five

PHILOLOGICAL FACTS

➤ Robert J. Sawyer wrote a stand-alone book about a sentient-dinosaur version of Galileo. His agent argued for a series. Sawyer relented but only if the series ran no more than three books. Book two would include a sentient-dinosaur version of Charles Darwin, and book three would include a sentient-dinosaur version of Sigmund Freud.

➤ Dinosaurs are a common theme in science fiction, though Sawyer's idea of making them sentient is an unusual approach. Most commonly, time travelers or explorers encounter them, as for instance in Arthur Conan Doyle's *The Lost World* and "A Sound of Thunder" by Ray Bradbury.

FOR MORE INFORMATION

Review the works listed above, the resources listed in the bibliography, and the web page: "Writing the Quintaglio Ascension" (*www.sfwriter.com/quintag.htm*).

■ UNIVERSAL TRANSLATOR ■

In the animated comedy series *Futurama* (1999–2003, 2008–), even though English is a nearly universal language, Professor Farnsworth invents a universal translator. Unfortunately, his device translates everything into a language that's become extinct, French (or German, in the French version of the series).

SPEAKING OF LANGUAGES

The chief virtue that language can have is clearness, and nothing detracts from it so much as the use of unfamiliar words.

—Hippocrates

Qwghlmian

SPOKEN BY

Qwghlmian is spoken by the inhabitants of Qwghlm, a fictitious small island off the northwest coast of England. Many of the Qwghlmians have emigrated to Australia, which is where one of them, Mary cCmndhd, is discovered by story protagonist Lawrence Waterhouse.

DOCUMENTED BY

Neal Stephenson (1959–) spins a convoluted tale of the present, past, and distant past in *Cryptonomicon* (1999) and the three volumes of *The Baroque Cycle*: *Quicksilver* (2003), *The Confusion* (2004), and *The System of the World* (2004). The three volumes of *The Baroque Cycle* actually represent eight individual titles: *Quicksilver*, *The King of the Vagabonds*, *Odalisque*, *Bonanza*, *The Juncto*, *Solomon's Gold*, *Currency*, and *The System of the World*.

BEHIND THE WORDS

Just as the United States used the Navajo speakers as code talkers to keep the Japanese from decoding transmissions, Neal Stephenson suggests that the British might have used the Qwghlmians, but not enough of them remembered the language to translate the messages they received.

DERIVATION OF THE LANGUAGE

Neal Stephenson describes Qwghlmian as pithy.

Qwghlmian seems influenced by German as well as by native British tongues, although Qwghlm itself generally seems to resemble Wales.

A TASTE OF THE LANGUAGE

As an example of Qwghlmian, following is an exchange between Lawrence Waterhouse and Rod as recorded in *Cryptonomicon*.

"So everyone hears it a little differently. Like just now—they heard your Outer Qwghlmian accent, and assumed you were delivering an insult. But I could tell you were saying that you believed, based on a rumor you heard last Tuesday in the meat market, that Mary was convalescing normally and would be back on her feet within a week."

"I was trying to say that she looked beautiful," Waterhouse protests.

"Ah!" Rod says. "Then you should have said, 'Gxnn bhldh sqrd m!'"

"That's what I said!"

"No, you confused the mid-glottal with the frontal glottal," Rod says.

PHILOLOGICAL FACT

➤ The title *Cryptonomicon* is a nod to the *Necronomicon*, the imaginary book referenced by H. P. Lovecraft. According to Lovecraft, the *Necronomicon*, written by "the mad Arab, Abdul Al-Hazrad," is filled with forbidden knowledge; a copy in the Latin translation by Olas Wormius is kept under lock and key in the library of Miskatonic University in Arkham, Massachusetts.

FOR MORE INFORMATION

Review the works listed above, the resources listed in the bibliography, and the web pages: "Cryptonomicon" (*www.harpercollins.com/books/Cryptonomicon-Neal-Stephenson/?isbn=9780060512804*), "Cryptonomicon cypher-FAQ" (*http://web.mac.com/nealstephenson/Neal_Stephensons_Site/cypherFAQ .html*), "Neal Stephenson: Cryptonomicon" (*www.nicholaswhyte.info/sf/stecry.htm*), and "The Baroque Cycle" (*http://en.wikipedia.org/wiki/The_Baroque_Cycle*).

UNIVERSAL TRANSLATOR

In the computer game *FreeSpace* (1998), a translator device allows the human player to understand the language of the Vasudan enemy.

SPEAKING OF LANGUAGES

To have another language is to possess a second soul.

—Charlemagne

Ragi

SPOKEN BY
Ragi is spoken by the atevi.

DOCUMENTED BY
C. J. Cherryh (1942–) writes of the atevi in a series alternately called the Foreigner series and the First Contact series: *Foreigner* (1994), *Invader* (1995), *Inheritor* (1996), *Precursor* (1999), *Defender* (2001), *Explorer* (2002), *Destroyer* (2005), *Pretender* (2006), *Deliverer* (2007), *Conspirator* (2009), *Deceiver* (2010), and *Betrayer* (2011).

BEHIND THE WORDS
Bren Cameron is one of the humans stranded on the planet of the atevi—dark-skinned humanoids who inhabit a far-distant world—when the humans' starship fails. A misunderstanding leads to war with the atevi, but afterward the atevi give the humans the use of an island. The atevi agree to communicate with one human, Bren Cameron, who will act as translator between the two species.

CHARACTERISTICS OF THE LANGUAGE

+ Ragi is a mathematical construct.
+ The number *two* sounds to the atevi like fingernails on a chalkboard.
+ The number *three*, however, is felicitous.

A TASTE OF THE LANGUAGE

buch (noun)—brick
chaid (noun)—person
dain (verb)—to speak
guf (verb)—to look
jeik (noun)—river
math (noun)—child
muhat (noun)—nothing
neib (noun)—city

peif (verb)—to say
sagh (verb)—to scatter
seg (noun)—language
sek (verb)—to reach
tegh (verb)—to find
thom (noun)—journey
ugh (verb)—to babble

THE BABEL TEXT

Shail, weiji chaidiin gathe segitas shail gathe dainitas fothasasu.

Chaith thu'a djoghitushi thomasama thu'a howati bushidi Shinaritush teghasasu shail hopafal

ghutasasu.

Shail, thu'a gaigiin peifasata, Bucheichatiin telasu, shal sha'ati keilu tobeishiin lunasu. Shail

thu'a buchatiin shaeichati dakasu shail idhation osheishion dakasu.

Shail, thu'a gaigiin peifasata, Telasu neibati shail farati, hanitush neiki dhailati sekuriepe,

shail dulati sha'aeishi telasu, trogh kosha'a asidi pathufon shail jeikufon saghiko.

Shail, Aija Dhailia chothasata in, neibati shail farati dheibeisha haneichati mathiin chaidisit

kelasu.

Shail, Aija Dhailia peifasata in, Gufasu. Mathiin chaidisit aishi'ima, shail thu'a segitusha

daine shail muhatati thuisit deiwuri in hanatiin thua hodasata.

Sha'a chotheghi, shail hopafal segati pareiseghi djage lap, han thu'a gaigna paikoulu.

Reb Aija Dhailia thuna saghasidi pathufon shail jeikufon saghisata in, shail thu'a neibati

tasaghi djaga kel.

Reb, Ughidan gagi fothasata in; theib Aija Dhailia segati pareisata djage lap in, shail

hopafalitas Aija Dhailia thuna pathufon shail jeikufon saghisata in.

PHILOLOGICAL FACT

➤ C. J. Cherryh's last name is pronounced "Cherry." She added the *h* to the end of it when editor Donald A. Wollheim warned her that "Cherry" made her sound too much like a romance writer.

FOR MORE INFORMATION

Review the works listed above, the resources listed in the bibliography, and the web pages: "Babel Text of the Ragi Language" (*http://strengthofthehills.tripod.com/hanilanguageandculturepage/id12.html*) and "Foreigner Guidebook" (*www.cherryh.com/WaveWithoutAShore/?page_id=1812*).

SPEAKING OF LANGUAGES

John Keating: Language was developed for one endeavor, and that is—
Mr. Anderson? Come on, are you a man or an amoeba?

[pause]

John Keating: Mr. Perry?

Neil: To communicate.

John Keating: No! To woo women!

—Dead Poets Society

Rihannsu

SPOKEN BY

Rihannsu is spoken by the Rihannsu (the name the Romulans use for themselves) in the Star Trek books of Diane Duane. Rihannsu is not considered canonical.

DOCUMENTED BY

Diane Duane (1952–) has written about the Rihannsu in *My Enemy, My Ally*—#18 (1984), *The Romulan Way*—#35 (with Peter Morwood, 1987), *Swordhunt*—#95 (2000), *Honor Blade*—#96 (2000), *The Empty Chair* (2006), and *Rihannsu: The Bloodwing Voyages* (an omnibus of the first four novels, 2006).

DERIVATION OF THE LANGUAGE

The Vulcans, contrary to some beliefs, are a deeply emotional race. Because of what they view as the destructive character of emotions, Surak, a Vulcan leader, taught them to live lives without emotion, ruled by pure logic. One of Surak's students, S'task, dissented. When the followers of S'task decided to leave Vulcan, they created a new language derived from Old High Vulcan to produce Rihannsu, which sounds a bit like Latin and Welsh. These new people became, in time, the Romulans.

BEHIND THE WORDS

Although the Romulans can be warlike when necessary, their society also includes artistic aspects such as sculpting and pottery, as well as Romulan literature, poetry, and drama.

A TASTE OF THE LANGUAGE

aedn"voi (noun)—information
eliu (verb)—to finish
haei"n (verb)—to signify
hre (adjective, adverb)—more
hveinu (noun)—border
hweithnaef (noun)—diversity
idh (adverb)—completely
ierra (adjective)—multiple

irrhaimehn (verb)—to settle a score
lai (noun)—premises
lh"hd (verb)—to proceed
lhiu (verb)—to stop
mrei (verb)—to approach
ra (adjective)—excellent
te (noun)—heading, course

SOME USEFUL PHRASES

aeh'lla'hnah. (Engage cloak.)
ta'khoi. (Screen off.)
Arhem oelh'ha. (I am most happy.)

NUMBERING SYSTEM

hwi—one
kre—two
sei—three
mne—four
rhi—five

fve—six
lli—seven
the—eight
lhi—nine
dha—ten

PHILOLOGICAL FACT

➤ Diane Duane has also written non-Rihannsu novels in the Star Trek universe: *The Wounded Sky*—#13 (1983), *Spock's World* (1988), and *Doctor's Orders*—#50 (1990) from the Original Series and *Dark Mirror* (1993) *and Intellivore*—#45 (1997) from the Next Generation.

FOR MORE INFORMATION

Review the works listed above, the resources listed in the bibliography, and the web page: "Rihannsu Encyclopedia" (*www.pfrpg.org/RH/*).

UNIVERSAL TRANSLATOR

In the long-running British television series *Doctor Who* (1963–89, 2005–), the TARDIS [Time and Relative Dimension(s) in Space] translates most languages using a telepathic field.

SPEAKING OF LANGUAGES

Language exerts hidden power, like the moon on the tides.

—Rita Mae Brown

R'lyehian

SPOKEN BY
Cthulhu and his adherents speak R'lyehian.

DOCUMENTED BY
H. P. Lovecraft (1890–1937) included fragments of the unnamed language in his various horror novels and short stories but did not produce a consistent dictionary, grammar, or pronunciation guide.

BEHIND THE WORDS
Lovecraft began writing about the horrific Cthulhu, a semi-aquatic monster-god, as early as 1925, but the key story, "The Call of Cthulhu," was not published until 1928, when it appeared in the magazine *Weird Tales*. It was followed by other classic stories and novels that elaborated on Lovecraft's basic premise: that in the incredibly remote past, Earth was ruled by powerful beings who came "from beyond the stars." These beings—including Cthulhu, Hastur, Yog-Sothoth, and Nyarlathotep—were, at some point, deposed from power and imprisoned, but they lay in waiting for the time when the stars would align and evil cults of men would free them from their prisons to once again rule this planet. Friends and colleagues of Lovecraft added to the mythology, both during his lifetime and after his death, and the mythos continues to grow even today.

CHARACTERISTICS OF THE LANGUAGE

+ Trying to understand R'lyehian has driven people mad.

A TASTE OF THE LANGUAGE
"The Call of Cthulhu" contains the following example of R'lyehian: "*ph'nglui mglw'nafh Cthulhu R'lyeh wgah'nagl fhtagn.*" (In his house at R'lyeh dead Cthulhu lies dreaming.)

PHILOLOGICAL FACT

➤ In *The Case of Charles Dexter Ward* (published posthumously in 1941), Lovecraft cites the following pair of invocations, which may or may not be linguistically related to R'lyehian:

Y'ai 'ng'ngah, Yog-Sothoth h'ee-l'geb f'ai throdog uaaah!

Ogthrod ai'f geb'l-ee'h Yog-Sothoth 'ngah'gn ai'y zhro!

FOR MORE INFORMATION

Review the works listed above, the resources listed in the bibliography, and the website: The H. P. Lovecraft Archive (*www.hplovecraft.com*).

UNIVERSAL TRANSLATOR

In Douglas Adams's *The Hitchhiker's Guide to the Galaxy* (1979), a Babel fish is placed in Arthur Dent's ear allowing him to understand alien languages.

SPEAKING OF LANGUAGES

In general, every country has the language it deserves.

—Jorge Luis Borges

Sandic

SPOKEN BY

Sandic is spoken by some 1.5 million people who live on the continent called Wytn on the planet Wadin.

DOCUMENTED BY

Aaron Wood constructed the Sandic language for his own pleasure. He has published a dictionary and plans to follow that with a collection of stories written in Sandic.

DERIVATION OF THE LANGUAGE

Sandic is derived from the language Weyr that Wood wrote half a dozen years ago.

CHARACTERISTICS OF THE LANGUAGE

+ Nouns have no separate endings to distinguish them from verbs.
+ Sandic is an inflected language.
+ There are two definite articles, *Ba* and *Ta*. The former is used for singular nouns, while the latter is used for plural nouns.

A TASTE OF THE LANGUAGE

bra (verb)—to hear
Dîo (noun)—book, scroll
Fel (noun)—plant
Fézu (verb)—to come
Jelēyu (noun)—cloud

kan (noun)—boy
laleg (noun)—worm
lēyar (noun)—sky
Talēl (verb)—to become different
Thîâ (noun)—bird

THE LORD'S PRAYER

Pé da aw pa leyar,
Daeyui obatara béenú pé,
Obafézu béno pé,
Obamectav wîc pé,
O ba imprîa obaahlto búra pa leyar.
Opétora wian pipab jémohni,
Wî opéfama ta lenadabin awin,

Wî opéfama ta opur wiab kémabin.
Wî opéneot mawîc wiab ân awma lenadabin,
A opéjjémz wiab dé akeno.
[Pa skra jébi- Ba imprîa bal pé, mé ba béno, mé ba auzeract,
Pa ba ivisrît, obatara,]
Leamian

FOR MORE INFORMATION
Review the resources listed in the bibliography and the web page: "Sandic" (*www.frathwiki.com/Sandic*).

UNIVERSAL TRANSLATOR

In William Gibson's *Neuromancer* (1984), computer chips called *microsofts* are inserted into a socket attached to the brain. These microsofts can be used when one needs to understand another language.

SPEAKING OF LANGUAGES

When there is a gap between one's real and one's declared aims, one turns, as it were, instructively to long words and exhausted idioms, like a cuttlefish squirting out ink.

—George Orwell

Simelan

SPOKEN BY

Simelan is spoken by the Simes, one of the two societies in the Sime~Gen universe.

DOCUMENTED BY

Jacqueline Lichtenberg (1942–) and Jean Lorrah (1938–) describe the Simes and the Gens in the books *House of Zeor* (1974), *Unto Zeor, Forever* (1978), *First Channel* [with Jean Lorrah] (1980), *Mahogany Trinrose* (1981), *Channel's Destiny* [with Jean Lorrah] (l982), *RenSime* (1984), *Zelerod's Doom* [with Jean Lorrah] (1986), *Ambrov Keon* [by Jean Lorrah] (1986), *To Kiss or to Kill* [by Jean Lorrah] (2011), *The Story Untold and Other Stories* [by Jean Lorrah] (2011), and *Personal Recognizance* (2011).

BEHIND THE WORDS

Jacqueline Lichtenberg introduced the Sime~Gen universe in "Operation High Time" (*If Magazine of Science Fiction,* January 1969). Her premise is that mankind has mutated and split into two factions, the Sime and the Gen. The Gens produce selyn, an energy source that the Simes require to live. The situation has led to Simes capturing Gens and keeping them like cattle.

A TASTE OF THE LANGUAGE

dynopter (noun)—a unit of measure

fosebine (noun)—an analgesic

Gen (noun)—a human who generates selyn

intil (adjective)—the desire for transfer

kerduvon (noun)—extract from the mahogany trinrose

lorsh (interjection)—an expletive

pilah (noun)—a plant

porstan (noun)—alcoholic beverage

prineridine (noun)—an antispasmodic

Reloc fever (noun)—a Gen illness

shedoni (interjection)—an expletive

shen (interjection)—an expletive

Sime (noun)—a human who requires selyn to live

trin (noun)—tea made from the leaves of the trin bush

PHILOLOGICAL FACT

➤ A child born into the Sime~Gen Universe has a chance of becoming either Gen or Sime. Thus a Sime child may be born of Gen parents and take selyn from them in order to live—though possibly killing them in the process, since if a Gen is frightened or resistant when selyn is taken, it dies.

FOR MORE INFORMATION

Review the works listed above, the resources listed in the bibliography, and the web pages: "Nivet Territory Accent Simelan Vocabulary Sound Files" (*www.simegen.com/jl/nivetsoundfiles/*) and "Sime – Gen Universe" (*http://en.wikipedia.org/wiki/Sime_%E2%80%93_Gen_Universe*).

UNIVERSAL TRANSLATOR

In the computer game *Galactic Civilizations* (2003), players must research and develop a universal translator to break down alien-language barriers.

SPEAKING OF LANGUAGES

We die. That may be the meaning of life. But we do language. That may be the measure of our lives.

—Toni Morrison

Sindarin

SPOKEN BY

Sindarin, or Grey-elven, is the primary language of the Sinder Elves, also called the Teleri.

DOCUMENTED BY

J. R. R. Tolkien (1892–1973) explored many languages and cultures as he told the stories of Middle-earth: *The Hobbit* (1937), *The Fellowship of the Ring* (1954), *The Two Towers* (1954), and *The Return of the King* (1955). (The last three are collectively called *The Lord of the Rings*.) After his death, his son Christopher Tolkien (1924–) edited *The Silmarillion* (1977) with the help of Guy Gavriel Kay (1954–). Christopher Tolkien then deeply analyzed his father's notebooks, letters, and drafts to produce an extended study of Middle-earth and its creation: *The Book of Lost Tales, Part One* (1983), *The Book of Lost Tales, Part Two* (1984), *The Lays of Beleriand* (1985), *The Shaping of Middle-earth* (1986), *The Lost Road and Other Writings* (1987), *The Return of the Shadow (The History of The Lord of the Rings, Part One)* (1988), *The Treason of Isengard (The History of The Lord of the Rings, Part Two)* (1989), *The War of the Ring (The History of The Lord of the Rings, Part Three)* (1990), *Sauron Defeated (The History of The Lord of the Rings, Part Four)* (1992), *Morgoth's Ring (The Later Silmarillion, Part One)* (1993), *The War of the Jewels (The Later Silmarillion, Part Two)* (1994), and *The Peoples of Middle-earth* (1996).

BEHIND THE WORDS

Sindarin was the most commonly spoken Elven tongue in the western part of Middle-earth.

Sindarin is the language most readers have in mind when they refer to Tolkien's Elvish language invention. It was extensively used in Númenor, although its use ceased when men and Elves were sundered after the fall of Númenor, though men still faithful to the Elves used various forms of Sindarin. Through their use, as well as that of the Elves, the language moved east; by the time of the War of the Ring, it was spoken by most of the Elves still living in Middle-earth, though there were regional variations of accents. Forms of Sindarin were spoken by men in Gondor during the Third Age; when Frodo and Sam met Faramir and his men in Ithilien, they were astonished to find that "it was the Elven-tongue that they spoke, or one but little different."

DERIVATION OF THE LANGUAGE

Sindarin evolved from Doriathrin and Old Noldorin.

CHARACTERISTICS OF THE LANGUAGE

+ Sindarin tends to not end words with vowels.
+ Sindarin has three forms of plurality: single (*êl*—star), plural (*elin*—stars), and 2nd plural (*elenath*—all the stars).
+ Sindarin carries many dialects, each with its own grammar.

A TASTE OF THE LANGUAGE

ada (noun)—father
amar (noun)—home
anor (noun)—sun
bein (adjective)—beautiful
cam (noun)—hand
cú (noun)—bow
duin (noun)—river
goth (noun)—enemy
ithil (noun)—moon
lalalith (noun)—laughter

lim (noun)—fish
lyg (noun)—snake
mîr (noun)—jewel
naneth (noun)—mother
nar (noun)—fire
nell (noun)—bell
nem (noun)—nose
ost (noun)—city
ross (noun)—rain
sigil (noun)—dagger

PHILOLOGICAL FACT

➤ Tolkien created Sindarin in 1944, though he had been at work on other Elvish languages much earlier. He had already created Noldorin, from which Sindarin was derived. He commented, "The changes worked on Sindarin [from Common Eldarin] very closely (and deliberately) resemble those which produced the modern and mediaeval Welsh from ancient Celtic, so that in the result Sindarin has a marked Welsh style."

FOR MORE INFORMATION

Review the works listed above, the resources listed in the bibliography, and the web pages: "Ardalambion" (*www.folk.uib.no/hnohf/*), "Cirth" (*www.omniglot.com/writing/cirth.htm*), "English to Elvish Dictionary" (*www.arwen-undomiel.com/elvish/eng_to_elv.html*), "How many languages did J.R.R. Tolkien make?" (*www.folk.uib.no/hnohf/howmany.htm*), "J. R. R. Tolkien: A Biographical Sketch" (*www.tolkiensociety.org/tolkien/biography.html*), "Sarati alphabet" (*www.omniglot.com/writing/sarati.htm*), "Sindarin" (*http://en.wikipedia.org/wiki/Sindarin*), "Sindarin—the Noble Tongue" (*www.folk.uib.no/hnohf/sindarin.htm*), and "Tengwar" (*www.omniglot.com/writing/tengwar.htm*).

Slovetzian

SPOKEN BY

Slovetzian is spoken by the people of Slovetzia, a small eastern-European country bordered by Hungary, Romania, and Ukraine.

DOCUMENTED BY

In the film *The Beautician and the Beast* (1997), Slovetzian is heard spoken by the children of President Pochenko and others.

DERIVATION OF THE LANGUAGE

Director Ken Kwapis hired dialect coach Francie Brown to help create a language for the film. Together, the two picked sounds from Czech, Russian, and Hungarian to fashion the Slovetzian language and accent.

FOR MORE INFORMATION

Review the work listed above, the resources listed in the bibliography, and the web pages: "The Beautician and the Beast" (*http://en.wikipedia.org/wiki/The_Beautician_and_the_Beast*) and "The Beautician and the Beast (1997)" (*www.imdb.com/title/tt0118691/*).

SPEAKING OF LANGUAGES

Language is the blood of the soul into which thoughts run and out of which they grow.

—Oliver Wendell Holmes

Solresol

SPOKEN BY

Solresol is spoken (communicated) by those who take the time to learn the language.

DOCUMENTED BY

François Sudre (1787–1864) started working on Solresol in 1817 and continued until his death.

BEHIND THE WORDS

Solresol was one of the first international languages to gain any popularity in the world. The last major reference to Solresol was Boleslas Gajewski's *Grammar of Solresol* (1902) (*https://webspace.utexas.edu/bighamds/LIN312/Files/SolReSol.pdf*).

DERIVATION OF THE LANGUAGE

François Sudre set out to create a simple language that anyone could learn, basing the language on the seven syllables of music: do, re, mi, fa, sol, la, si. (Note that the Western musical scale uses: do, re, mi, fa, so, la, ti.)

CHARACTERISTICS OF THE LANGUAGE

+ Words in Solresol are formed by combining the seven musical notes and thus can be spoken, written, sung, gestured, or even presented in visual patterns as each note is associated with a color.
+ The contradiction of any word is created by reversing the order of the syllables. (For example, *Misol* is good and *Solmi* is bad.)
+ Syllables (with the exception of *sol*, which drops the *l*) are often shortened by dropping the vowel. (For example, the word for *help*, *dosido*, is shorted to *dsd*.)

A TASTE OF THE LANGUAGE

ddf (noun)—winter
dlfr (noun)—food
dsds (noun)—egg
dsfso (noun)—coffee
dsor (verb)—to eat
dsos (noun)—water
fldr (verb)—to sail
frsod (noun)—horse
llrl (noun)—bookstore
lrmf (adjective)—green

lsof (verb)—to defeat
mds (noun)—friend
rfd (verb)—to look at
rfsod (noun)—fire
rfsso (noun)—knife
rmfl (noun)—house
sff (noun)—sun
sodrl (adjective)—black
sosf (verb)—to laugh
ssd (noun)—rain

NUMBERING SYSTEM

rdd—one
rmm—two
rff—three
rsoso—four
rll—five

rss—six
mmd—seven
mmr—eight
mmf—nine
mmso—ten

PHILOLOGICAL FACTS

➤ Solresol includes seven one-syllable words, forty-nine two-syllable words, 336 three-syllable words, and 2,268 four-syllable words, for a total of 2,660 words.

Syllables can be expressed using the following color chart:
do—red—*d*
re—orange—*r*
mi—yellow—*m*
fa—green—*f*
sol—blue—*so*
la—indigo—*l*
si—violet—*s*

The word for winter, *ddf*, would thus be represented by the pattern *red, red, green*.

A set of symbols has been designed, with a symbol representing each of the seven syllables—which as musical notes can also be sung, whistled, or played on an instrument. Seven notes? Represent them with numbers. Only seven notes? Represent them by touching seven points on your opposite hand.

➤ In addition to inventing Solresol, Sudre patented the Sudrophone, a brass musical instrument. It was held upright and played by means of four valves. Sudre intended it to sound like a cello or violin.

IF YOU'RE INTERESTED IN LEARNING THE LANGUAGE

There's the "Grammar of Solresol" (*www.mozai.com/writing/not_mine/solresol/*) and the "Solresol-English/French Mini-Dictionary" (*www.ifost.org.au/~gregb/ solresol/sorsolex.htm*). But I'm waiting for the site that takes full advantage of the color and music of the language to render Solresol as a thing of beauty.

FOR MORE INFORMATION

Review the works listed above, the resources listed in the bibliography, and the web pages: "Solresol" (*www.omniglot.com/writing/solresol.htm*), and "Solresol-English/French Mini-Dictionary" (*www.ifost.org.au/~gregb/solresol/sorsolex.htm*).

SPEAKING OF LANGUAGES

Now, children, do-re-mi-fa-so and so on are only the tools we use to build a song. Once you have these notes in your heads, you can sing a million different tunes by mixing them up. Like this.

—Maria, in *The Sound of Music*

The Speech

SPOKEN BY

The Speech is spoken by wizards when they are casting spells in novels by Diane Duane. While non-wizards can speak the language also, their spells are ineffective.

DOCUMENTED BY

Diane Duane (1952–) has written nine books about Nita and Kit, two young wizards who do battle with The Lone Power. Their struggle to use The Speech to defeat evil is chronicled in *So You Want to Be a Wizard* (1983), *Deep Wizardry* (1985), *High Wizardry* (1990), *A Wizard Abroad* (1993), *The Wizard's Dilemma* (2001), *A Wizard Alone* (2002), *Wizard's Holiday* (2003), *Wizards at War* (2005), and *A Wizard of Mars* (2010).

BEHIND THE WORDS

In the library, Nita Callahan finds a book called *So You Want to Be a Wizard*. That night, she takes the Wizard's Oath, and the next morning she finds her name in the book.

A TASTE OF THE LANGUAGE

afállonë (noun)—the lost city of Atlantis

asdurrafrith (noun)—a species that doesn't believe in aliens

hrasht (noun)—cousin; also what wizards call each other

hwatha-t (noun)—cavity

mathrára (noun)—fox

thelefeh (noun)—friend

PHILOLOGICAL FACT

➤ Diane Duane, besides writing a large number of science fiction and fantasy novels for adults and young readers, has worked extensively in television. She was the coauthor of one of the earliest scripts for *Star Trek: The Next Generation*—the episode titled "Where No One Has Gone Before," in which the *Enterprise* travels beyond the galaxy and back.

IN PRAISE OF AMBIGUITY

A goal of many constructed languages is to do away with ambiguity, to create a situation where speakers are forced to say what they mean and mean what they say.

Would you really want to bring home somebody to meet your parents in that situation?

"Mom, Dad, this is Janice, with whom I am sleeping, but whom I'd never actually marry. Janice, this is my mom, who wishes I'd get a real job, as if her secret drinking counts as one, and my dad, who will spend dinner trying to look down your shirt."

SPEAKING OF LANGUAGES

Language is a virus from outer space.

—William S. Burroughs

Spocanian

SPOKEN BY

Spocanian is a constructed language spoken by the inhabitants of the constructed island of Spocania, located between Ireland and the United States.

DOCUMENTED BY

Linguist Rolandt Tweehuysen has been working on Spocanian since 1962, compiling a vocabulary of 25,000 words. A Woordenboek *Dictio* (*www.spocania.com/dictio/index.htm*) translates Spocanian to and from Dutch, which—while inconvenient to many—makes sense since Tweehuysen is from the Netherlands.

BEHIND THE WORDS

Spocania is a parliamentary democracy, consisting of seven large islands, each having its own government. Languages include not only Spocanian but also Pegrevian and Garosh. The population of 7.6 million seem reasonably happy, despite the fact that Tweehuysen gave little indication of what economy keeps the country going.

DERIVATION OF THE LANGUAGE

Rolandt Tweehuysen constructed Spocanian with an Indo-Germanic influence.

CHARACTERISTICS OF THE LANGUAGE

+ Tense is indicated by word order. For example, compare the following three lines:

   Jân stinde eft letra. (John writes a letter.)
   Jân eft letra stinde. (John wrote a letter.)
   Stinde Jân eft letra. (John will write a letter.)

A TASTE OF THE LANGUAGE

aerunelira (adjective)—impressive
bas-šark (noun)—land forces
cralarder (noun)—omnivore
dânta (noun)—sparks

decadiy (noun)—decade
efrechbâlmerr (noun)—basketball player
falle (verb)—to stumble

gabanejeren (noun)—transport industry

geul (noun)—gully

henkos (noun)—disturbance

idereppe (verb)—to denounce

jalorsiy (noun)—jealousy

kafqummertos (noun)—concession

monârgétt (adjective)—regal

nylt (noun)—sleigh

omelechót (adjective)—windy

parinn (adjective)—thirst quenching

ralveldur (noun)—neighbor

šempiy (adjective)—hospitable

wârf (adjective)—poor

IF YOU'RE INTERESTED IN LEARNING THE LANGUAGE

First, learn Dutch, or wait until the project of translating the Spocanian website into English is completed. Then pay a visit to *www.spocanian.com* to learn how to communicate in Spocanian.

FOR MORE INFORMATION

Review the works listed above, the resources listed in the bibliography, and the web page: "Four Features Of Spocanian Grammar" (*www.spocania.com/archief/fourfeat.htm*).

■ UNIVERSAL TRANSLATOR ■

In the video game *Unreal* (1998), players can find a universal translator that allows them to read alien languages.

SPEAKING OF LANGUAGES

Poets are always ahead of things in a certain way, their sense of language and their vision.

—Jim Jarmusch

Stark

SPOKEN BY

Stark (Starways Common) is a universal language and the official language of the Starways Conference, which oversees the many planetary governments.

DOCUMENTED BY

Orson Scott Card (1951–) published the short story "Ender's Game" in 1977 and then spun that tale into the novel *Ender's Game* (1985) so that he could write the sequel *Speaker for the Dead* (1986). The complete series consists of ten short stories and these eleven books: *Ender's Game*, *Speaker for the Dead*, *Xenocide* (1991), *Children of the Mind* (1996), *Ender's Shadow* (1999), *Shadow of the Hegemon* (2001), *Shadow Puppets* (2002), *First Meetings* (a collection of short stories, 2002), *Shadow of the Giant* (2005), *A War of Gifts: An Ender Story* (2007), and *Ender in Exile* (2008).

BEHIND THE WORDS

Andrew "Ender" Wiggin is a child-warrior being trained at Battle School to fight the alien Formics. Only at the end of the novel does he realize that he has been tricked into committing genocide. The result sends him on a quest for meaning and redemption throughout the galaxy. Although the original short story and the first book are military science fiction, *Speaker for the Dead* and some of the other titles in the series focus more on philosophy, moral questions, and alien cultures.

DERIVATION OF THE LANGUAGE

Stark is said to derive from English but only because America was the most technologically advanced country when IF Common (the forerunner to Starways Common) was being developed.

CHARACTERISTICS OF THE LANGUAGE

+ As all the spoken Stark is translated into the native language of the reader, there is a scarcity of Stark examples to analyze. Several speakers mention that Stark is not English, and one points out that Stark does not include the word *whom*.

PHILOLOGICAL FACT

➤ Thanks to relativistic space travel, Ender ages only twenty-five years between *Ender's Game* and *Speaker for the Dead*, while 3,000 years pass between the events that occur in each book.

FOR MORE INFORMATION

Review the works listed above, the resources listed in the bibliography, and the web page: "Concepts in the Ender's Game series" (*http://en.wikipedia.org/wiki/Concepts_in_the_Ender%27s_Game_series*).

SPEAKING OF LANGUAGES

If language is not correct, then what is said is not what is meant; if what is said is not what is meant, then what must be done remains undone; if this remains undone, morals and art will deteriorate; if justice goes astray, the people will stand about in helpless confusion. Hence there must be no arbitrariness in what is said. This matters above everything.

—Confucius

Starsza Mowa

SPOKEN BY

Starsza Mowa is spoken by Geralt of Rivia, a witcher whose body has been modified so that he can hunt monsters and survive.

DOCUMENTED BY

Andrzej Sapkowski (1948–) first wrote about Geralt of Rivia in the short story "The Witcher," which was published in Poland's leading fantasy magazine, *Fantastyka*, in 1986. This was followed by a collection of five short stories called *The Witcher* (1990). When that book went out of print, the stories were sprinkled through later collections published by SuperNOWA: *Sword of Destiny* (1992), *The Last Wish* (1993), and *Something ends, Something begins* (2000). Geralt of Rivia also does his thing in the novels comprising the Witcher Saga: *Blood of Elves* (1994), *Times of Contempt* (1995), *Baptism of Fire* (1996), *The Swallow's Tower* (1997), and *Lady of the Lake* (1999). An unreleased thirteen-episode television series was edited to create a very confusing two-hour movie, *The Hexer* (2001); the television series was then released the following year but could not overcome the film's bad press.

BEHIND THE WORDS

Geralt of Rivia is a trained assassin who goes around killing monsters. His body has been specifically mutated in childhood to fit him for such a task. Working in such a morally ambiguous field, he's been compared to Raymond Chandler's Philip Marlowe. The world in which the stories take place is strongly influenced by Polish history and mythology.

DERIVATION OF THE LANGUAGE

Starsza Mowa (Polish for *Older Speech*) is based on English, French, Welsh, Irish, Latin, and other languages.

A TASTE OF THE LANGUAGE

aenya (noun)—fire
aveon (noun)—river
bleidd (noun)—wolf
caen (noun)—power
dhu (adjective)—black

Dice (verb)—to talk
eate (noun)—summer
evall (noun)—horse
feainne (noun)—sun
foil (adjective)—crazy

gloss (verb)—to look
gynvael (noun)—ice
Hav"caaren (adjective)—greedy
invaerne (noun)—winter
morvudd (noun)—enemies

raenn (verb)—to run
seidhe (noun)—elf
valo (adverb)—fast
woedd (noun)—forest
zireael (verb)—to swallow

SOME USEFUL PHRASES

elaine Tedd a'taeghane and va'en aesledde. (The weather today is beautiful. Let's go on a sled.)
ess'tuath esse. (It shall be.)
n'aen aespar and me. (Do not shoot me.)

PHILOLOGICAL FACTS

➤ An English edition of *Blood of Elves* (1994) was released in 2009.

➤ Geralt is also known as Gwynbleldd, which in Elder Speech means *the White Wolf*. This may have to do with his appearance, since he's depicted in comics and video games as having a shock of prematurely white hair. He's also sometimes called the Butcher of Blaviken because of his role in the death of a group of bandits.

FOR MORE INFORMATION

Review the works listed above, the resources listed in the bibliography, and the web pages: "Andrzej Sapkowski" (*http://en.wikipedia.org/wiki/Andrzej_Sapkowski*), "The Hexer (film)" (*http://en.wikipedia.org/wiki/The_Hexer*), "Starsza Mowa" (*http://en.wikipedia.org/wiki/Starsza_Mowa*), and "The Witcher" (*http://en.wikipedia.org/wiki/The_Witcher*).

SPEAKING OF LANGUAGES

Language is not an abstract construction of the learned, or of dictionary makers, but is something arising out of the work, needs, ties, joys, affections, tastes, of long generations of humanity, and has its bases broad and low, close to the ground.

—Noah Webster

Syldavian

SPOKEN BY

Syldavian is spoken by the inhabitants of Syldavia in *The Adventures of Tintin: King Ottokar's Sceptre*.

DOCUMENTED BY

Hergé (Georges Prosper Remi) (1907–1983) wrote and illustrated Tintin's adventures.

BEHIND THE WORDS

Tintin works to thwart a plot to steal the sceptre of Syldavia's King Ottokar IV. Because the story appeared in 1938, some interpreted it to be a commentary on Hitler's expansionist plans in Europe—particularly since the leader of the plot is named Müsstler, a combination of Hitler and Mussolini.

CHARACTERISTICS OF THE LANGUAGE

+ Syldavian resembles Dutch and German.
+ The language includes the *sz* and *cz* of Polish.
+ Syldavian is usually written using the Cyrillic alphabet.
+ While native words in Syldavian are made plural by adding *-en*, words of foreign origin are made plural by adding *-es*.

A TASTE OF THE LANGUAGE

blaveh (verb)—to stay
bûthsz (noun)—boat
döszt (noun)—thirst
fläsz (noun)—bottle
khôr (noun)—currency
kursaal (noun)—concert hall

kzommet (verb)—to come
muskh (noun)—courage
szlaszeck (noun)—type of meat
szprädj (noun)—type of red wine
Zrälùkz! (interjection)—Look!

SOME USEFUL PHRASES

Kzommetz pakkeho lapzâda. (Come seize the sceptre.)
Eih bennek, eih blavek. (Here I am, here I stay.)

Könikstz eszt güdd. (The king is good.)
Rapp! Noh dzem buthsz! (Quick! Into the boat!)

PHILOLOGICAL FACT

➤ While he was at work on the fifth Tintin adventure, *The Blue Lotus*, Hergé met a young Chinese art student who developed the author's interest in Chinese art and culture. Thereafter, Hergé sought to be extremely accurate in the cultures he depicted in the Tintin stories.

FOR MORE INFORMATION

Review the works listed above, the resources listed in the bibliography, and the web pages: "Hergé" (*http://en.wikipedia.org/wiki/Herge*) and "Hergé's Syldavian: A grammar" (*www.zompist .com/syldavian.html*).

SPEAKING OF LANGUAGES

Americans who travel abroad for the first time are often shocked to discover that, despite all the progress that has been made in the past thirty years, many foreign people still speak in foreign languages.

—Dave Barry

Talossan

SPOKEN BY
The inhabitants of Talossa (a micronation) speak Talossan.

DOCUMENTED BY
King Robert I (R. Ben Madison) invented the language Talossan as part of the fictional country he developed while spending time in his room. *Talossa* is the Finnish word for *inside the house*.

BEHIND THE WORDS
Talossa is a micronation—a complete society with government, culture, and language—that was created by R. Ben Madison in 1979 and that went online in November 1995. In fact, it is two micronations: the original Kingdom of Talossa, and the Republic of Talossa that was formed by a group of dissident Talossans. U.S. President Jimmy Carter failed to notice when Madison's bedroom broke off from the United States in 1979 and became a sovereign country.

Between 2005 and 2007, the Kingdom of Talossa was haunted by strife, and there are currently two factions claiming to be the official Kingdom of Talossa: *www.kingdomoftalossa.net/index.cgi* (representing the kingdom ruled by King John Whoolley) and the kingdom ruled by King Louis I.

DERIVATION OF THE LANGUAGE
Talossan is derived from Romance languages.

CHARACTERISTICS OF THE LANGUAGE

+ The alphabet consists of thirty-three symbols.
+ The infinitive form of verbs ends with *-arh* (or sometimes *-irh*).

A TASTE OF THE LANGUAGE

anel (noun)—ring	*carçer* (noun)—jail
apa (noun)—water	*çéu* (noun)—sky
canziun (noun)—song	*etéu* (noun)—summer

éu (pronoun)—I
eziun (noun)—food
fugla (noun)—bird
giatza (noun)—ice
moart (noun)—death
nic"ht (noun)—night
pà (noun)—bread

þivereu (noun)—winter
scaparh (verb)—to run
soleiglh (noun)—sun
tradidour (noun)—traitor
vaißal (noun)—ship
virt (adjective)—green
zestzinà (noun)—fate

PHILOLOGICAL FACTS

➤ There are more than 28,000 words in the "official" Talossan dictionary. In December 2007, a change in how stresses would be handled was issued. The change was accepted in the Kingdom of Talossa but not in the Talossan Republic. Following are two translations of John 3:16 showing the differences:

Talossan (Kingdom of Talossa): *Cair Díeu sa ameva el mundeu, qe O zoneva sieu Figlheu viensplet, qe qissensevol créa in Lo non pieriçarha, mas tischa la vida eternal.*

Talossan (Talossan Republic): *Cair Dïeu så ameva el mundeu, që O zoneva sieu Figlheu viensplet, qe qissensevol créa în Lo non pieriçarha, más tischa la vidâ eternál.*

➤ Other micronations include the Principality of Freedonia (based in Boston); the Republic of Minerva, which tried to create a man-made island on the Minerva Reefs near Fiji (they were turned out by troops from Tonga); and New Utopia (near the Cayman Islands).

IN THEIR OWN WORDS

The Kingdom of Talossa is an independent, sovereign nation in North America, which seceded peacefully from the United States in 1979 (but we're not sure the United States noticed). Our Kingdom is located on the western shore of La Mar Talossan (Lake Michigan), surrounded by the U.S. city of Milwaukee, Wisconsin, but today most of our active citizens live in other parts of the United States and Canada, Europe, South America, Asia, and Africa.

—The Kingdom of Talossa website

IF YOU'RE INTERESTING IN LEARNING THE LANGUAGE

Both Talossa sites have information on learning Talossan, but you might want to expend your energy learning some other language until the Talossan factions align.

FOR MORE INFORMATION

Review the works listed above, the resources listed in the bibliography, and the web pages: "The Kingdom of Talossa" (*www.kingdomoftalossa.net/index.cgi*) and "The Talossan Republic" (*http://talossa.org/*).

SPEAKING OF LANGUAGES

My language! Heavens!

I am the best of them that speak this speech,

Were I but where 'tis spoken.

—Ferdinand, *The Tempest*, Shakespeare

Telerin

There the Teleri abode as they wished under the stars of heaven, and yet within sight of Aman and the deathless shore; and by that long sojourn apart in the Lonely Isle was caused the sundering of their speech from that of the Vanyar and the Noldor.

—J. R. R. Tolkien

DOCUMENTED BY

J. R. R. Tolkien (1892–1973) explored many languages and cultures as he told the stories of Middle-earth: *The Hobbit* (1937), *The Fellowship of the Ring* (1954), *The Two Towers* (1954), and *The Return of the King* (1955). (The last three are collectively called *The Lord of the Rings*.) After his death, his son Christopher Tolkien (1924–) edited *The Silmarillion* (1977) with the help of Guy Gavriel Kay (1954–). Christopher Tolkien then deeply analyzed his father's notebooks, letters, and drafts to produce an extended study of Middle-earth and its creation: *The Book of Lost Tales, Part One* (1983), *The Book of Lost Tales, Part Two* (1984), *The Lays of Beleriand* (1985), *The Shaping of Middle-earth* (1986), *The Lost Road and Other Writings* (1987), *The Return of the Shadow (The History of The Lord of the Rings, Part One)* (1988), *The Treason of Isengard (The History of The Lord of the Rings, Part Two)* (1989), *The War of the Ring (The History of The Lord of the Rings, Part Three)* (1990), *Sauron Defeated (The History of The Lord of the Rings, Part Four)* (1992), *Morgoth's Ring (The Later Silmarillion, Part One)* (1993), *The War of the Jewels (The Later Silmarillion, Part Two)* (1994), and *The Peoples of Middle-earth* (1996).

BEHIND THE WORDS

Telerin, like most of Tolkien's Elvish tongues, diverged from Common Eldarin during the Great Journey when the Elves traveled to Valinor. There, one clan of Elves, the Lindar (so called because of their sweet singing), learned to love the sea. These were the Teleri. They were estranged from their fellow Elves and refused to take part in the war against the evil Morgoth, though they provided ships to those who did. Among the important members of the Teleri was Dior, son of Beren and Lúthien. He married Elwing and sired Eärendil, father of Elrond Half-Elven.

CHARACTERISTICS OF THE LANGUAGE

+ In Telerin, plurals are made by adding -i.
+ Adjectives can be formed in Telerin by adding -ia or -ima to nouns.

A TASTE OF THE LANGUAGE

alata (noun)—radiance
cáno (noun)—commander
népa (noun)—sister
níce (noun)—little finger
Óre (noun)—premonition
palta (verb)—to feel with the hand
páne (noun)—small gull
pen (noun)—person
ría (noun)—wreath
sila (verb)—to shine

spalasta (verb)—to foam
spanga (noun)—beard
spania (noun)—cloud
tolma (noun)—knob
trumbe (noun)—shield
vomentie (noun)—a meeting (of two)
ulgundo (noun)—monster
urus (noun)—copper
vilverin (noun)—butterfly
vola (noun)—a long wave

NUMBERING SYSTEM

tata—two
otoso—seven

toloth—eight
pai—ten

PHILOLOGICAL FACT

➤ Tolkien occasionally made reference to the Sea Elves in his stories, but they did not play an important role. Nonetheless, he worked on Telerin, though not with the same intensity as when he constructed such languages as Sindarin and Eldarin. It's been suggested by some that his primary influence in building the language was Italian. Tolkien said, "I remain in love with Italian and feel quite lorn without a chance of trying to speak it."

FOR MORE INFORMATION

Review the works listed above, the resources listed in the bibliography, and the web pages: "Ardalambion" (*www.folk.uib.no/hnohf/*), "Category: Telerin words" (*www.tolkiengateway.net/wiki/Category:Telerin_words*), "Cirth" (*www.omniglot.com/writing/cirth.htm*), "How many languages did J.R.R. Tolkien make?" (*www.folk.uib.no/hnohf/howmany.htm*), "J. R. R. Tolkien: A Biographical Sketch" (*www.tolkiensociety.org/tolkien/biography.html*), "Sarati alphabet" (*www.omniglot.com/writing/sarati.htm*), "Teleri" (*http://en.wikipedia.org/wiki/Teleri*), "Telerin—the language of the Sea-elves" (*www.folk.uib.no/hnohf/telerin.htm*), and "Tengwar" (*www.omniglot.com/writing/tengwar.htm*).

Tenctonese

SPOKEN BY

Tenctonese is spoken by the inhabitants of the planet Tencton, some of whom are currently living on Earth, mostly in the Los Angeles vicinity. They are called Newcomers, or Slags, by the people who fear and resent them.

DOCUMENTED BY

The story of the Tenctonese on Earth is explored in the film *Alien Nation* (1988), the television series *Alien Nation* (1989–1990), and the television movies *Alien Nation: Dark Horizon* (1994), *Alien Nation: Body and Soul* (1995), *Alien Nation: Millennium* (1996), *Alien Nation: The Enemy Within* (1996), and *Alien Nation: The Udara Legacy* (1997).

BEHIND THE WORDS

In the movie *Alien Nation*, "Sam" Francisco is a Tenctonese member of the LAPD (Los Angeles Police Department) who partners with human Detective Sergeant Matthew Sykes. When Francisco and Sykes investigate a murder that took place during a robbery and tie it back to the murder of Sykes's old partner, they uncover a conspiracy targeting the Newcomers.

PHILOLOGICAL FACTS

➤ Signs were created for the story and installed along Los Angeles streets; they consisted of Tenctonese characters replacing the English alphabet to spell out words in English. In the 1988 film, however, University of Southern California film school graduate Van Ling used sounds from Chinese, Samoan, and German to create an alien quality to spoken Tenctonese. Kenneth and Juliet Johnson used a different approach for the television show, scrambling English words or spelling them backwards to make the dialogue seem unearthly.

➤ Joe Hawthorne, a sign writer for Fox, created the Tenctonese alphabet, basing it on Pitman Shorthand. The latter was a system of shorthand writing created by Sir Isaac Pitman (1813–1897). Pitman was, for a time, widely popular until it was largely replaced by Gregg shorthand.

FOR MORE INFORMATION

Review the works listed above, the resources listed in the bibliography, and the web pages: "Tenctonese" (*http://en.wikipedia.org/wiki/Tenctonese*) and "Tenctonese alphabets" (*www.omniglot.com/writing/tencton.htm*).

Teonaht

SPOKEN BY

Teonaht is spoken by the Teonim, a race that live in a region that floats above or submerges below the Caspian and Black Seas. The Teonim have twelve fingers, twelve toes, and eyes that change color the way human skin reddens to blush.

DOCUMENTED BY

Sally Caves started developing Teonaht in 1962 when she was nine years old. The idea of constructing a language had come to her when she was given a kitten four years previously and she invented a winged feline race called the Feleonim. She was also impressed with Tolkien's work in creating the languages for his world.

BEHIND THE WORDS

Sally Caves kept her language secret for a long time. Finally she presented it on the Internet and discovered Conlang, a listserv devoted to constructed languages. In addition to a number of novels, she wrote the episode "Hollow Pursuits" for *Star Trek: The Next Generation*, Stardate 43807.4 (with a first air date of April 30, 1990). This was the episode that introduced the character of Reginald Barclay—the *Enterprise* crewman with an addiction to the holodeck and a crush on Counselor Troi.

DERIVATION OF THE LANGUAGE

Teonaht has traces of Latin, German, Welsh, Old Norse, Old Irish, Old English, Hebrew, Sumerian, and modern English.

CHARACTERISTICS OF THE LANGUAGE

+ Sentences in Teonaht are usually structured object-subject-verb.
+ That said, sentences are scrambled so that they sound best.
+ *The Law of Detachability* states that clitics used to indicate tense and aspect are typically detached from the verb and prefixed to a preceding noun.

A TASTE OF THE LANGUAGE

dendr (noun)—egg
dyron (adjective)—black
entom (noun)—monster
enyverem (verb)—to eat
fortmarem (verb)—to attack
frapia (noun)—dagger
fyaarlrem (verb)—to take
htesarem (verb)—to chase
larod (noun)—leg
pelnar (noun)—river

talaket (noun)—ring
tehsat (noun)—anger
tenuo (noun)—winter
tsōllai (noun)—sun
uor (adjective)—different
vaiua (noun)—bird
ve (noun)—sky
vyrm (adjective)—green
winnyf (noun)—food
ydonar (noun)—forest

PHILOLOGICAL FACT

➤ Sally Caves has posted Teonaht recipes in Teonaht on the web. An introductory excerpt:

To nimelevrod marrea:
Eyil nimelevrod MARREA hmaitso mal aija!
E nimelevrod hrelor hmaitso mal mareada!
(In Praise of Vegetables:
To the vegetables it is praise we must now offer!
To noble vegetables must we now deliver praise!)

IF YOU'RE INTERESTED IN LEARNING THE LANGUAGE

Learn Teonaht from the associate professor who invented it; her web page is *www.frontiernet.net/~scaves/teonaht.html.*

FOR MORE INFORMATION

Review the works listed above, the resources listed in the bibliography, and the web page: "The Teonaht Table Of Contents" (*www.frontiernet.net/~scaves/contents.html*).

Toki Pona

SPOKEN BY
Toki Pona is spoken by those who wish to learn the constructed language.

DOCUMENTED BY
Linguist and translator Sonja Elen Kisa (1978–) constructed Toki Pona to express the most by using the least.

BEHIND THE WORDS
Toki Pona consists of only fourteen phonemes and 123 root words. Kisa's goal was to create a minimalist language to test the Safir-Whorf Hypothesis as well as to see whether those who spoke it would achieve a zen-like simplicity of thought.

DERIVATION OF THE LANGUAGE
Toki Pona is a mixture of English, Tok Pisin, Finnish, Georgian, Dutch, Acadian French, Esperanto, Croatian, and Chinese. The bowl in which they were mixed was Taoist philosophy.

CHARACTERISTICS OF THE LANGUAGE

+ Toki Pona uses capital letters only to signify names and not to mark the beginning of a sentence.
+ There are only nine consonants and five vowels in the language.
+ Speaking or writing Toki Pona, you combine root words to create complex ideas.

A TASTE OF THE LANGUAGE

kute (verb)—to listen

mama (noun)—parent

moku (noun)—food

musi (verb)—to have fun

noka (noun)—leg

pali (noun)—work

pimeja (adjective)—black

pini (noun)—end

seli (noun)—fire

suno (noun)—sun

telo (noun)—water

waso (noun)—bird

SOME USEFUL PHRASES

sina kepeken ala kepeken e ni? (Are you using that?)
tenpo suno sin ale la sina moku e telo seli pimeja. (Every morning I drink coffee.)
mi wile sin e telo pi lape ala. (I need more coffee.)

THE LORD'S PRAYER

mama pi mi mute o, sina lon sewi kon.

nimi sina li sewi.

ma sina o kama.

jan o pali e wile sina lon sewi kon en lon ma.

o pana e moku pi tenpo suno ni tawa mi mute.

o weka e pali ike mi. sama la mi weka e pali ike pi jan
ante.

o lawa ala e mi tawa ike.

o lawa e mi tan ike.

tenpo ali la sina jo e ma e wawa e pona.

amen.

(Translated by Pije/Jopi)

PHILOLOGICAL FACTS

➤ Since it has very few root nouns, Toki Pona tends toward noun compounds in which a noun is modified by a following root—somewhat similar to German.
➤ At least 100 people speak Toki Pona fluently.

IF YOU'RE INTERESTED IN LEARNING THE LANGUAGE

The simple way to learn the simple language is to go to the web page: *http://en.tokipona.org/wiki/What_is_Toki_Pona%3F*.

FOR MORE INFORMATION

Review the resources listed in the bibliography and the web pages: "Dictionary toki pona—English" (*http://rowa.giso.de/languages/toki-pona/english/dictionary.php*) and "What is Toki Pona?" (*http://en.tokipona.org/wiki/What_is_Toki_Pona%3F*).

Trinary

SPOKEN BY

The language Trinary is used by Neo-Dolphins and sometimes humans.

DOCUMENTED BY

David Brin (1950–) chronicles the story of an Earth considered primitive by alien races who consider chimpanzees, dolphins, and dogs the most worthwhile species on the planet.

BEHIND THE WORDS

In the Uplift universe, a patron species will help prepare a nonuplifted species to achieve intergalactic travel. These patron species speak one of twelve Standard Galactic Languages and think little of the Anglic spoken on Earth. The story unfolds over six books: *Sundiver* (1980), *Startide Rising* (1983), *The Uplift War* (1987), *Brightness Reef* (1995), *Infinity's Shore* (1996), and *Heaven's Reach* (1998).

PHILOLOGICAL FACT

➤ In the short story "Temptation," Brin comments that Trinary is more suited to irony than is Underwater Anglic.

FOR MORE INFORMATION

Review the works listed above, the resources listed in the bibliography, and the website: Tomorrow Happens (*www.davidbrin.com*).

SPEAKING OF LANGUAGES

The knowledge of the ancient languages is mainly a luxury.

—John Bright

Troll

SPOKEN BY

Troll is spoken by the trolls on Discworld, a flat world that rests on the backs of four elephants that stand on the back of a giant turtle.

DOCUMENTED BY

Sir Terry Pratchett (1948–) chronicles the world of Discworld in the novels *The Colour of Magic* (1983), *The Light Fantastic* (1986), *Equal Rites* (1987), *Mort* (1987), *Sourcery* (1988), *Wyrd Sisters* (1988), *Pyramids* (1989), *Guards! Guards!* (1989), *Eric* (1990), *Moving Pictures* (1990), *Reaper Man* (1991), *Witches Abroad* (1991), *Small Gods* (1992), *Lords and Ladies* (1992), *Men at Arms* (1993), *Soul Music* (1994), *Interesting Times* (1994), *Maskerade* (1995), *Feet of Clay* (1996), *Hogfather* (1996), *Jingo* (1997), *The Last Continent* (1998), *Carpe Jugulum* (1998), *The Fifth Elephant* (1999), *The Truth* (2000), *Thief of Time* (2001), *The Last Hero* (2001), *The Amazing Maurice and His Educated Rodents* (2001), *Night Watch* (2002), *The Wee Free Men* (2003), *Monstrous Regiment* (2003), *A Hat Full of Sky* (2004), *Going Postal* (2004), *Thud!* (2005), *Wintersmith* (2006), *Making Money* (2007), *Unseen Academicals* (2009), *I Shall Wear Midnight* (2010), and *Snuff* (2011).

BEHIND THE WORDS

The trolls of Discworld are living "metamorphorical rock" and usually lie dormant during the daytime hours. They'd just as soon gesture as speak, and they prefer to punctuate their sentences with a rock to the head. Since they have diamond teeth, their diet is rock and stone (although quartz clogs the arteries).

A TASTE OF THE LANGUAGE

Aagragaah (noun)—forebodings
Aargrooha (noun)—the name of a sport not unlike soccer
Gahanka (noun)—a troll war beat made by banging clubs against the ground

Horug (noun)—an offensive term for dwarves
Taka Taka (noun)—a troll war club

PHILOLOGICAL FACTS

➤ In 2009, Terry Pratchett was knighted—after which he said, "You can't ask a fantasy writer not to want a knighthood. You know, for two pins I'd get myself a horse and a sword."

> Pratchett collaborated with noted author Neil Gaiman on *Good Omens*, a book about the Apocalypse, the onset of which is marred only by the fact that a demon and an angel have apparently mislaid the antichrist.

FOR MORE INFORMATION

Review the works listed above and the resources listed in the bibliography.

Tsath-yo

Tsath-yo is spoken by the Hyperboreans who once worshiped the god Tsathoggua.

DOCUMENTED BY

H. P. Lovecraft (1890–1937) wrote of the ancient Hyperboreans in the story "Through the Gates of the Silver Key."

BEHIND THE WORDS

Lovecraft's friend Clark Ashton Smith (1893–1961) wrote a series of stories set on the mythical continent of Hyperborea, which Smith identified with Greenland. Smith and Lovecraft borrowed freely from one another; Smith created the god Tsathoggua, which Lovecraft employed to good effect in the Cthulhu Mythos. As a tribute to Smith, Lovecraft referred in a story to the Atlantean high priest Klarkash-Ton, who recorded the myth cycle of the ancient Hyperboreans.

CHARACTERISTICS OF THE LANGUAGE

+ Many of the nouns end with -ath.

PHILOLOGICAL FACT

➤ As well as using the Hyperborea setting, Clark Ashton Smith published stories set in the fictional worlds of Poseidonis, Averoigne, and Zothique. Much of this was republished as part of the Adult Fantasy Series from Ballantine Books in the 1970s.

FOR MORE INFORMATION

Review the works listed above, the resources listed in the bibliography, and the web pages: "Cthulhu Files" (*http://baharna.com/cmythos/index.htm*), "The H. P. Lovecraft Archive" (*www.hplovecraft.com*), and "Tsath-Yo" (*www.yog-sothoth.com/wiki/index.php/Tsath-Yo*).

Ulam

SPOKEN BY
Ulam is spoken by the Ulam tribe.

DOCUMENTED BY
Linguist Anthony Burgess (1917–1993) was hired by the producers of *Quest for Fire* (1981) to create a language for a Neanderthal tribe.

BEHIND THE WORDS
When the Ulam tribe is attacked by the Wagabu, the Ulams lose the starter fire from which their working fires are made. Three of the Ulam are sent off on a quest to find a replacement.

PHILOLOGICAL FACTS

➤ Another language in the film—that spoken by the Ivaka, a more technologically advanced tribe than the Ulam—was based on random words from the language spoken by the Cree/Inuit people.

➤ The critic Martin Seymour-Smith wrote of Anthony Burgess that he "believes overplanning is fatal to creativity and regards his unconscious mind and the act of writing itself as indispensable guides. He does not produce a draft of a whole novel but prefers to get one page finished before he goes on to the next, which involves a good deal of revision and correction."

FOR MORE INFORMATION
Review the work listed above, the resources listed in the bibliography, and the web pages: "Anthony Burgess" (*http://en.wikipedia.org/wiki/Anthony_Burgess*) and "Anthony Burgess on the English Language" (*http://grammar.about.com/od/writersonwriting/a/burgesslang07.htm*).

Unglish

SPOKEN BY

Unglish is spoken by the people living in the Five Nations of Mong, which is located in the center of North America.

DOCUMENTED BY

Poul Anderson (1926–2001) made up three languages in *Orion Shall Rise* (1983): Angley, Ingliss, and Unglish. While each of the languages is rooted in English, each is nearly indecipherable to the speakers of the other two languages, owing to ways the languages developed over centuries of separation.

BEHIND THE WORDS

Several hundred years after a nuclear war, people—and nations—still have to find ways to deal with each other.

DERIVATION OF THE LANGUAGE

Unglish is derived from English, Russian, Chinese, and Mongolian.

FOR MORE INFORMATION

Review the work listed above, the resources listed in the bibliography, and the web page: "Thoughts on Poul Anderson" (*www.scifibookspot.com/markley/?p=48*).

Utopian

SPOKEN BY

Utopian is spoken by the people who live on Utopia.

DOCUMENTED BY

Thomas More (1478–1535) was a lawyer, philosopher, and statesman who coined the word *utopia* and wrote the utopian *Utopia* (1516).

BEHIND THE WORDS

The traveler Raphael Hythlodeaus (his name means *speaker of nonsense* in Greek) visits the imaginary island country of Utopia (which puns on both the Greek terms *ou-topos*, for *no place land*, and *eu-topos*, for *good place land*), where a peaceful society seems to have none of the strife then found in European countries.

DERIVATION OF THE LANGUAGE

The Utopian language is derived from Latin and Greek.

CHARACTERISTICS OF THE LANGUAGE

+ The word order in Utopian follows the subject-verb-object structure.
+ Nouns have at least three cases, and verbs, at least two tenses.
+ Pronunciation in Utopian follows the rules of Ecclesiastical Latin.

A TASTE OF THE LANGUAGE

The appendeum to *Utopia* contained a quatrain written by Peter Giles:

Vtopos ha Boccas peula chama polta chamaan.
Bargol he maglomi baccan oma gymno ophaon.
Agrama gymno ophon labarem bacha bodamilomin.
Voluala barchin heman la lauoluola dramme pagloni.

(The commander Utopus made me, who was once not an island, into an island. I alone of all nations, without philosophy, have portrayed for mortals the philosophical city. Freely I impart my benefits; not unwillingly I accept whatever is better.)

PHILOLOGICAL FACT

➤ Thomas More was one of the towering intellectual pillars of the English Renaissance as well as a prominent figure at the court of Henry VIII. He served as Henry's chancellor for a time, but the two men were driven apart by the king's demand for a divorce from his wife, Catherine of Aragon, so that he might marry Anne Boleyn. More refused to take an oath acknowledging the legitimacy of the divorce and, as a result of perjured testimony, was beheaded at the Tower of London. A sanitized version of his story is presented by Robert Bolt in the play *A Man for All Seasons*.

FOR MORE INFORMATION

Review the works listed above and the resources listed in the bibliography.

Verdurian

SPOKEN BY
Verdurian is spoken by the inhabitants of Verduria, on the planet Almea.

DOCUMENTED BY
Mark Rosenfelder created the language and history of Verduria.

DERIVATION OF THE LANGUAGE
Rosenfelder derived Verdurian originally from French and Russian, and was influenced by other constructed languages.

BEHIND THE WORDS
The planet Almea is home to many countries containing many peoples, all of whom speak their own languages and dialects. Verduria is a powerful state in the south of Almea. Its language derives from Cad'inor, which in turn comes from Proto-Eastern. The latter was spoken by invaders of the area now included in Verduria.

CHARACTERISTICS OF THE LANGUAGE

+ Verdurian contains twenty-one consonants and eight vowels.
+ The language uses a subject-verb-object structure.
+ Verdurian supports two genders, two numbers, and four cases.

A TASTE OF THE LANGUAGE

cloš (noun)—bell
crežen (verb)—to eat
cucec (verb)—to attack
dom (noun)—house
Ënomai (noun)—Sun
esta (noun)—summer
huvon (noun)—egg
iveri (noun)—winter
lef (noun)—wolf
mey (noun)—water

mlake (adjective)—black
nurža (noun)—food
prenan (verb)—to take
selë (noun)—river
šual (noun)—horse
šušče (noun)—death
taye (adjective)—brave
tecai (noun)—dagger
uazo (noun)—bird
verde (adjective)—green

PHILOLOGICAL FACT

➤ Mark Rosenfelder started constructing his own language after being introduced to the invented worlds of the game *Dungeons & Dragons* while he was in college.

IF YOU'RE INTERESTED IN LEARNING THE LANGUAGE

To get a good grounding in Verdurian, head over to Mark Rosenfelder's "Metaverse" website (*www.zompist.com*) or "Virtual Verduria" (*www.zompist.com/virtuver.htm*).

FOR MORE INFORMATION

Review the resources listed in the bibliography and the web page: "Virtual Verduria" (*www.zompist.com/virtuver.htm*).

Volapük

SPOKEN BY

Volapük is spoken by those who wish to learn the constructed language.

DOCUMENTED BY

The Roman Catholic priest Johann Martin Schleyer (1831–1921) created the international language Volapük, from 1879 to 1880.

BEHIND THE WORDS

Schleyer had had a vision in a dream in which God told him to create an international language. The result was Volapük, a language he said was "capable of expressing thought with the greatest clearness and accuracy." Interest in the language gradually spread across Europe, and Volapük conventions occurred in 1884, 1887, and 1889. At the time of the last convention, there were 283 clubs, twenty-five periodicals, and 316 textbooks about Volapük in twenty-five languages. It's estimated that at its height, more than 100,000 people spoke Volapük. Then came Esperanto, Ido, and Interlingua—all three easier for native English and Spanish speakers. By the year 2000, there were less than thirty people who still spoke Volapük, the international language.

DERIVATION OF THE LANGUAGE

Volapük is derived from English, German, and French. Although most of the words are based on English, Johann Martin Schleyer's preference for monosyllabic words and his dislike of the letter *r* mean that much of the language seems unfamiliar.

CHARACTERISTICS OF THE LANGUAGE

+ Volapük nouns have four cases: nominative, genitive, dative, and accusative.
+ Pronouns begin with *o-*.
+ Verbs can be conjugated in 1,584 ways in Volapük.

A TASTE OF THE LANGUAGE

böd (noun)—bird
deadam (noun)—death
dom (noun)—house
fat (noun)—father
fid (noun)—food
fidön (verb)—to eat
flumed (noun)—river
hitüp (noun)—summer
jipal (noun)—mother
klok (noun)—bell

kömön (verb)—to come
kuradik (adjective)—brave
lup (noun)—wolf
nifüp (noun)—winter
nög (noun)—egg
smil (noun)—laughter
sol (noun)—sun
sumön (verb)—to take
vat (noun)—water
zif (noun)—city

NUMBERING SYSTEM

bal—one
tel—two
kil—three
pol—four
lul—five

mäl—six
vel—seven
jöl—eight
zül—nine
bals—ten

THE LORD'S PRAYER

O Fat obas, kel binol in süls, paisaludomöz nem ola!
Kömomöd monargän ola!
Jenomöz vil olik, äs in sül, i su tal!
Bodi obsik vädeliki givolös obes adelo!
E pardolös obes debis obsik,
äs id obs aipardobs debeles obas.
E no obis nindukolös in tendadi;
sod aidalivolös obis de bad.
Jenosöd

PHILOLOGICAL FACTS

➤ When a Dane doesn't understand something, the person might say: "*Det er det rene volapyk for mig.*" ("It's pure Volapük to me.")

➤ In Volapük, every individual letter, including all vowels, must be sounded, which makes pronunciation of the language much easier.

IF YOU'RE INTERESTED IN LEARNING THE LANGUAGE

To learn Volapük, you might want to start with the ten-lesson online course (*http://personal.southern.edu/~caviness/Volapuk/VolVifik/volvif00.html*) before you jump into the "Handbook of Volapük" by Charles E. Sprague (*http://personal.southern.edu/~caviness/Volapuk/HBoV/*).

FOR MORE INFORMATION

Review the works listed above, the resources listed in the bibliography, and the web pages: "Johann Martin Schleyer" (*http://en.wikipedia.org/wiki/Johann_Martin_Schleyer*), "Volapük" (*www.homunculus.com/babel/avolapuk.html*), and "Volapük" (*http://personal.southern.edu/~caviness/Volapuk/HBoV/*).

Vulcan

SPOKEN BY

Vulcan is spoken by Vulcans in the Star Trek universe: in the television series [Gene Rodden-berry's *Star Trek: The Original Series* (1966–1969), *Star Trek: The Animated Series* (1973–1974), *Star Trek: The Next Generation* (1987–1994), *Star Trek: Deep Space Nine* (1993–1999), *Star Trek: Voyager* (1995–2001), and *Star Trek: Enterprise* (2001–2005)] and the film series [(*Star Trek: The Motion Picture* (1979), *Star Trek II: The Wrath of Khan* (1982), *Star Trek III: The Search for Spock* (1984), *Star Trek IV: The Voyage Home* (1986), *Star Trek V: The Final Frontier* (1989), *Star Trek VI: The Undiscovered Country* (1991), *Star Trek Generations* (1994), *Star Trek: First Contact* (1996), *Star Trek: Insurrection* (1999), *Star Trek Nemesis* (2002), and *Star Trek* (2009)].

DOCUMENTED BY

The Vulcan language and culture developed over time as various writers and directors included additional information in the stories they told.

BEHIND THE WORDS

The Vulcans were the first extraterrestrial species to make contact with human beings, as recounted in *Star Trek: First Contact*. As a species, the Vulcans prize logic above all, and *Star Trek: The Original Series* features a Vulcan, Mr. Spock, as the first officer on the *Enterprise*. Spock was not, however, the first Vulcan to serve on a Federation ship; that honor belonged to T'pol, who served aboard the first *Enterprise* under the command of Jonathan Archer.

CHARACTERISTICS OF THE LANGUAGE

+ The Vulcan language uses a verb-subject-object structure.

A TASTE OF THE LANGUAGE

Aluk (noun)—fish
Ek"zer (noun)—jewel
Fas-top (verb)—to cook
Ha-kel (noun)—home
Ifis-tor (verb)—to transport
Ko-mekh (noun)—mother
Lipau (noun)—knife

Nashiv-tor (verb)—to attack
Nem-tor (verb)—to take
Nesh-kur (adjective)—black
Salan (noun)—wind
Sa-mekh (noun)—father
Semek (adjective)—cold
Suk (adjective)—big

Temok (noun)—wall
Tev-tor (verb)—to fall
Yar-kur (adjective)—green
Yel (noun)—star

Yem-tukh (noun)—food
Yokul (verb)—to eat
Yon (noun)—fire

SOME USEFUL PHRASES

Tu'ash'voh svep. (Open the door!)
I'poprah fasei setebihk t'ovsotuhl-ozhika. (Now receive from us this symbol of total logic.)
Du vravshal srashiv t'Kolinahr. (You have not achieved Kolinahr.)
Dif-tor heh smusma. (Live long and prosper.)

NUMBERING SYSTEM

wahkuh—one
dahkuh—two
rehkuh—three
kehkuh—four
kaukuh—five

shehkuh—six
stehkuh—seven
ohkuh—eight
naukuh—nine
lehkuh—ten

PHILOLOGICAL FACTS

➤ In 1967, linguist Dorothy Jones Heydt constructed a Vulcan language for fans to use in writing Star Trek fan fiction. She also originated the *Star Trek Concordance*. The self-published fandom publication was later picked up by Ballantine Books.

➤ Vulcan, at the time of the events of *Star Trek* (in all its incarnations), was written in vertical columns running top to bottom and left to right. A more complex version of the script had been used in ancient times. A somewhat simplified version of Vulcan script, consisting of squiggles, spirals, and dots, was occasionally used in modern times.

IF YOU'RE INTERESTED IN LEARNING THE LANGUAGE

To learn Vulcan, click on over to the Vulcan Language Institute (*www.stogeek.com/ wiki/Category:Vulcan_Language_Institute*) and work your way through the lessons.

FOR MORE INFORMATION

Review the works listed above, the resources listed in the bibliography, and the web page: "Vulcan Language Institute Reclamation Project" (*www.stogeek.com/wiki/Category:Vulcan_Language_Institute*).

Wenedyk

SPOKEN BY
Wenedyk is spoken by the inhabitants of the fictional Republic of the Two Crowns.

DOCUMENTED BY
Translator Jan van Steenbergen constructed Wenedyk (2002) to see what might have happened if Polish had developed as a Romance language rather than a Slavic language. Linguist Grzegorz Jagodzinski assisted in a major overhaul of the language in 2005.

BEHIND THE WORDS
The premise is that the Roman Empire had claimed and managed the territories that would become Poland.

DERIVATION OF THE LANGUAGE
Wenedyk has a vocabulary and a morphology that reflect Romance influences; its phonology, orthography, and syntax reflect the Slavic influence that produced modern-day Polish.

CHARACTERISTICS OF THE LANGUAGE

+ Nouns, pronouns, and adjectives can have three genders (male, female, and neuter.)
+ Verbs are inflected for person, number, mood, and tense.
+ Wenedyk uses the thirty-two-letter Polish alphabet.

A TASTE OF THE LANGUAGE
fok (noun)—fire
jekwa (noun)—water
niegry (adjective)—black
omik (noun)—friend

ów (noun)—egg
pieszcz (noun)—fish
wucz (noun)—voice

PHILOLOGICAL FACT

➤ Hergé's Syldavian uses a similar premise to Wenedyk's. Syldavian develops out of the concept that German, and not Slavic, was the influencing language.

FOR MORE INFORMATION

Review the works listed above, the resources listed in the bibliography, and the websites: "Multilingual Mutterings" (*http://steen.free.fr/*) and "Wenedyk" (*http://en.wikipedia.org/wiki/Wenedyk*).

SPEAKING OF LANGUAGES

W ("double U") has, of all the letters in our alphabet, the only cumbrous name, the names of the others being monosyllabic. This advantage of the Roman alphabet over the Grecian is the more valued after audibly spelling out some simple Greek word, like epixoriambikos. Still, it is now thought by the learned that other agencies than the difference of the two alphabets may have been concerned in the decline of "the glory that was Greece" and the rise of "the grandeur that was Rome." There can be no doubt, however, that by simplifying the name of W (calling it "wow," for example) our civilization could be, if not promoted, at least better endured.

—Ambrose Bierce

Westron

SPOKEN BY

Westron is spoken by all (except the Elves) who inhabit the western lands of the Middle-earth.

DOCUMENTED BY

J. R. R. Tolkien (1892–1973) explored many languages and cultures as he told the stories of Middle-earth: *The Hobbit* (1937), *The Fellowship of the Ring* (1954), *The Two Towers* (1954), and *The Return of the King* (1955). (The last three are collectively called *The Lord of the Rings*.) After his death, his son Christopher Tolkien (1924–) edited *The Silmarillion* (1977) with the help of Guy Gavriel Kay (1954–). Christopher Tolkien then deeply analyzed his father's notebooks, letters, and drafts to produce an extended study of Middle-earth and its creation: *The Book of Lost Tales, Part One* (1983), *The Book of Lost Tales, Part Two* (1984), *The Lays of Beleriand* (1985), *The Shaping of Middle-earth* (1986), *The Lost Road and Other Writings* (1987), *The Return of the Shadow (The History of The Lord of the Rings, Part One)* (1988), *The Treason of Isengard (The History of The Lord of the Rings, Part Two)* (1989), *The War of the Ring (The History of The Lord of the Rings, Part Three)* (1990), *Sauron Defeated (The History of The Lord of the Rings, Part Four)* (1992), *Morgoth's Ring (The Later Silmarillion, Part One)* (1993), *The War of the Jewels (The Later Silmarillion, Part Two)* (1994), and *The Peoples of Middle-earth* (1996).

BEHIND THE WORDS

Westron—also called the Common Speech—is the language in which the Middle-earth stories are experienced. When we read the novels and stories, we presume we are reading stories originally written in Westron. It was widely spoken in Middle-earth, though there were some—for example, the Elves of Lothlorien—who purposely refrained from using it.

DERIVATION OF THE LANGUAGE

Westron derived from Adûnaic, the language of Númenor. It spread over the lands of Middle-earth with the exception of Mordor, which employed the Black Speech. This means that most of the characters encountered in *The Lord of the Rings* are effectively bilingual; Eomer, Eowyn, and Theoden, for instance, speak the language of the Rohirrim among themselves but readily communicate with the hobbits Merry and Pippin in Westron. (Curiously, Tolkien never invented a language for the hobbits, though there are words such as *mathom* that seem to be peculiar to their society.)

PHILOLOGICAL FACT

➤ Although the account of the events of *The Lord of the Rings* (primarily *The Red Book of Westmarch*) was originally written in Westron, Tolkien—so he tells us—has translated the book into English. Thus the Anglicized names given to some places and people (e.g., Brandywine River) are actually English translations of Westron names. (The Westron name for the Brandywine is, in fact, *Branda-nîn*, which means *border water*. The Sindarin translation is *Baranduin*, meaning *gold-brown river*.)

FOR MORE INFORMATION

Review the works listed above, the resources listed in the bibliography, and the web pages: "Ardalambion" (*www.folk.uib.no/hnohf/*), "Cirth" (*www.omniglot.com/writing/cirth.htm*), "How many languages did J.R.R. Tolkien make?" (*www.folk.uib.no/hnohf/howmany.htm*), "J. R. R. Tolkien: A Biographical Sketch" (*www.tolkiensociety.org/tolkien/biography.html*), "Sarati alphabet" (*www.omniglot.com /writing/sarati.htm*), "Tengwar" (*www.omniglot.com/writing/tengwar.htm*), and "Westron—the Common Speech" (*www.folk.uib.no/hnohf/westron.htm*).

Whitmanite

SPOKEN BY

Whitmanite is spoken by the Whitmanites, a sect that was evicted from Canada and emigrated to the planet Venus.

DOCUMENTED BY

Robert A. Heinlein (1907–1988) explored the idea of an alien invasion in *The Puppet Masters* (1951).

BEHIND THE WORDS

Alien slugs (the puppet masters) are invading the Earth, attaching themselves to humans high on their upper backs and controlling their minds. Sam, a member of a secret U.S. government agency, is assigned to save the president and the planet. Meanwhile, back on Venus, an invasion of the slugs is defeated by a plague of the Venusian Nine-Day Fever.

DERIVATION OF THE LANGUAGE

The Whitmanites, an anarchist-pacifist-religious sect, construct their own language.

PHILOLOGICAL FACTS

➤ The lone human survivor of the Nine-Day Fever on Venus was agent Allucquere, who had taken the alias "Mary" while on a mission, before marrying Sam. More than ten years after *The Puppet Masters* was published, a woman who lived near the Heinleins changed her name to "Allucquere."

➤ The original version of the novel was approximately 90,000 words; this was cut to 60,000 words at the request of the publisher. After Heinlein's death, an expanded edition of the book was published at around the same time that the publisher also released an expanded version of the Heinlein classic *Stranger in a Strange Land*.

FOR MORE INFORMATION

Review the works listed above, the resources listed in the bibliography, and the web page: "A Heinlein Concordance" (*www.heinleinsociety.org/concordance/index.htm*).

Zamgrh

SPOKEN BY

Zamgrh is spoken by zombies with the Death Rattle skill in the game *Urban Dead*.

DOCUMENTED BY

Urban Dead (*www.urbandead.com*) is a Massively Multiplayer Online Role-Playing Game (MMORPG) that was developed by Kevan Davis (*www.kevan.org*).

BEHIND THE WORDS

Create a character (survivor or zombie victim), and play for free. The game is set in an urban environment in one of three cities: Monroeville, Malton, or Borehamwood. Players, who can enter the game either as zombies or survivors, must try to kill survivors (if the player is a zombie) or escape the zombie hordes (if the player is a survivor).

DERIVATION OF THE LANGUAGE

Zamgrh is a low-impact language constrained by the types of sounds a zombie might make.

CHARACTERISTICS OF THE LANGUAGE

+ Zamgrh usually follows a subject-verb-object syntax.
+ The Zamgrh alphabet is limited to eight letters (*a, b, g, h, m, n, r,* and *z*) and various punctuation marks. (What, you were hoping to stage *Romeo and Juliet* in Zamgrh? They're zombies!)

A TASTE OF THE LANGUAGE

b!g (noun)—bird
baba (noun)—father
barb (noun)—knife
bragh (adjective)—black
brang (verb)—to take

ganarazharhbarn (noun)—factory
graan (adjective)—green
mama (noun)—mother
zan (noun)—sun
zhangh (verb)—to stab

A USEFUL PHRASE

Harm bang-bang man! (Kill all zombie hunters in the room!)

NUMBERING SYSTEM

Zombies use a base-five numbering system.

. — zero

! — one

? — two

= — three

, — four

!. — five

!! — six

!? — seven

!= — eight

!, — nine

PHILOLOGICAL FACT

➤ Sometimes it's just easier for a zombie to gesture or point to words on a sign.

FOR MORE INFORMATION

Review the works listed above, the resources listed in the bibliography, and the web pages: "Urban Dead" (*www.urbandead.com*) and "Zamgrh" (*http://wiki.urbandead.com/index.php/Zamgrh*).

Zaum

SPOKEN BY

Zaum was a term coined by Aleksei Kruchenykh (1886–1968) to describe experiments with language that he and other Russian Futurists were conducting to discover a primal Slavic tongue.

DOCUMENTED BY

Aleksei Kruchenykh wrote poetry in Zaum as well as writing the Zaum libretto for an opera, *Victory over the Sun* (1913). The prologue to the opera was written by Velimir Khlebnikov (1885–1922), who was central to the design of Zaum and who also wrote in his "language of the birds," "language of the gods," and "language of the stars."

BEHIND THE WORDS

Futurism, a twentieth-century artistic movement, was inspired by a manifesto written by the Italian Filippo Marinetti. Futurist movements arose in several European countries, but the movement found a strong appeal in postrevolutionary Russia. The movement placed great emphasis on the promise of technology, and rejected the past. Among those who embraced it in Russia was Boris Pasternak, author of the classic *Doctor Zhivago*.

Zaum provided an alternative language and concept during World War I and its aftermath. However, the death of Velimir Khlebnikov took the heart out of the movement, and Zaum quieted to a whisper, although in recent times it has seen something of a revival.

FOR MORE INFORMATION

Review the works listed above and the resources listed in the bibliography.

SPEAKING OF LANGUAGES

The great enemy of clear language is insincerity.

—George Orwell

PART II
CONSTRUCT YOUR OWN LANGUAGE

CHAPTER ONE

The Recipe for a Language

This book, like most others, is a product of space and time. Written in the United States of America (eastern Massachusetts) in 2011, the book is designed to be practical, informative, and efficient. Open *The Dictionary of Made-Up Languages* and you want to see the languages, organized in a way that's easy to access.

On the other hand, consider a cookbook. It is a collection of recipes divided into the types of foods: appetizers, main courses, and desserts. The recipes are divided into the types of information: ingredients, preparation instructions, and serving suggestions.

A few hundred years ago, recipes were narratives, with ingredients, instructions, and serving suggestions all mixed together in the story of creating the meal. If you lived in a community where only locally produced food was available and availability was based on the calendar, you would find a seasonal division to be a better organizing principle for a cookbook.

When constructing a language, you must produce something that both reflects your own space and time and serves the purpose for which you're creating it.

THE POWER OF SYMBOLS

Human beings have developed three basic approaches to communication: gestured, spoken, and written.

As a species and as individuals, we start with gestured communication. It's easy enough to point at an item and then point at yourself. Unfortunately, interpreting the gesture can be a challenging process with many false starts. You pointed at the item and then yourself. What does that mean? Are you asking for the item? Are you claiming ownership?

The next step is spoken communication. Now you can say why you're pointing at that item and what you want to happen next. Speaking is more effective than gesturing. But spoken communication has no permanence other than memory. It can go in one ear and out the other.

Finally, there is written communication. Now there's a record. There's permanence. What was written last week is still here now. Until the invention of recorded video to capture gestures and recorded audio to capture speech, written communication was the most effective way to distribute information to large groups of people.

One thing that gestured, spoken, and written languages have in common is a system of encoding: breaking concepts and ideas down into small units, the symbols that represent what's being communicated.

(In English, the letters of written communication represent the sounds of spoken communication. Not all languages work this way. In Chinese, for example, learning to read and write Chinese characters does not help you speak the language. This is something to keep in mind when you're trying to make up a language that's different from English.)

WHERE TO START?

As mentioned before, the order in which we develop communication methods is: gestured, spoken, and written. When you make up your own language, however, you usually reverse that order. Making lists of words that you can refer to is much easier than trying to remember exactly what you've said. Written communication can be practiced in private; spoken communication requires someone else to hear the words.

If you're creating a language for fictional purposes, you're probably disseminating the language through written materials. Even if your goal is to have the language eventually spoken aloud by actors, the words will need to be written long before that can happen.

The first thing you need to decide on is your alphabet, the set of symbols with which words can be built.

The simplest approach is to use the alphabet of the language you currently write. Some people prefer to develop their own alphabets. The downsides of this approach are composition (typesetting) and distribution. Even with the Internet, some constructed languages require readers to download language packs or install fonts; how many people actually make the extra effort?

If you decide to use your native alphabet, you can still mix things up to make the language appear more alien than it is. All lowercase looks very strange to me. How about capitalizing any consonant that follows a double vowel? Or making your language tonal and using upper- and lowercase to signify the correct sound?

You can change the letter distribution in your language. As *e*, *t*, and *a* are the most frequently used letters in English, refrain from using them when you build words. Load up your language with the letters *w* or *k* or *l*.

You can also add accent marks and umlauts and hooks (diacritics). They make words look foreign since only languages foreign to English speakers use them. But don't overdo it. Making up an alphabet that contains too many special characters, diacritics, and numbers may render the language laughable.

BINARY SYSTEMS

Computer machine language and Braille are both binary systems. At the root level, computers communicate in electrical bits that are on or off. In Braille, the six dots of each cell are raised or not.

We see the world in binary terms, in opposites. Things are on or off, black or white, up or down.

Just because our worldview is binary, however, doesn't mean that creatures from other worlds wouldn't think differently.

If you create your own alphabet from scratch, remember its purpose: to encode ideas. When blind Louis Braille (1809–1852) invented Braille in 1825 so that blind people would have a written alphabet, he chose to arrange the on/off dots in a two-by-three grid. Such a grid creates enough combinations to represent all the necessary letters.

If your alphabet is too complicated for common, daily use, it will evolve over time to become one that meets the needs of those trying to get their messages across as quickly as possible, although the fancier version might continue as a formal representation in official or religious documents where speed is not the issue. (Chinese characters, which take more time to create than typical Latin letters, represent whole words or ideas, not letters; that is how they pass the efficiency test.)

CHAPTER TWO

You Must Communicate

The success of a language is determined by how effectively it communicates. For communication to take place, three things are required:

+ The sender needs to be able to create a signal
+ The receiver needs to be able to receive a signal
+ There must be agreement on how to interpret the signal

Communication is not going to happen if I believe a single dot represents *a* and I'm sending a single dot to someone proficient in Morse Code; that person expects a single dot to represent *e*.

Unless you want the possibility of miscommunication to be present in your system, you must create an alphabet in which the symbols are easy to differentiate. That said, the process of differentiation can't come with too much cost.

For example, imagine you're creating a simple substitution cipher for the English alphabet. You will present each letter using a series of vertical lines. | is *A*, || is *B*, ||| is *C*, and so on. How do you translate the following three-letter word: ||||||||||||| ||||||||||||||| |||||||||||||? Considering how long it took to read that word, would anybody bother?

A society forced to work with the vertical-line alphabet would soon compress it. If ||||| is represented by ! then the word above becomes !!||| !!! !!|||, which is at least a start in the right direction.

NUMBERS AND PUNCTUATION

An alphabet is only one of the three symbol sets you need to think about. The other two are numbers and punctuation. Assuming your language is spoken before it is written, your numbers will be represented first by words, which will eventually be written alphabetically. As mathematics and number theory develop, numbers will probably need a separate set of symbols to simplify computations.

What symbols will be used for your numbers? How will you modify those symbols (if at all) to indicate negatives, fractions, and ordinals? What other qualities might you indicate for your numbers?

(Might you want to introduce a language where numbers do not have their own nonalphabetic symbol set? What impact would that have on the society that lives the language?)

What about punctuation? In English, we use periods not only to indicate the end of a sentence but also to indicate that a word has been abbreviated or reduced to an initial. The apostrophe is used to indicate ownership, a title (of a poem, story, or episode), missing letters formed by a contraction, and a quote within a quote (when single quotation marks are not used for this task). The apostrophe is also often used to symbolize characters in an alien language because although simple to make, a plethora of apostrophes adds an alien flavor to the text.

What punctuation marks will your language require? How will they appear and be used?

WORDS ARE POWER

A collection of agreed-upon symbols is necessary for written communication, just as a collection of agreed-upon sounds is necessary for spoken communication, and a collection of agreed-upon motions is necessary for gestured communication.

Those symbols, however, are not the message. They are used to *encode* the message so that the message can be communicated. The core units of the message are words.

In the beginning, we used words to describe things. "Cup," for example. We added words to represent desires. "I want the cup." We added words to represent commands. "I want you to bring me the cup." We added words to add motivation. "I want you to bring me the cup by the time I count to ten or else you're losing privileges."

Words have power. Compare the phrases *this toy* and *my toy* and *your toy*. There is a world of difference between *my toy* and *your toy*. Those simple possessive pronouns determine if you can play with the toy, how you can play with the toy, and whether you can take that toy and leave.

Words, as the core units of thought, are generally broken down into some basic types: nouns (person, place, or thing), verbs (actions or states of being), adjectives (describe a noun), and adverbs (describe a verb or another adverb). There can also be articles (*the* is a definite article indicating specificity, and *a* or *an* is an indefinite article indicating generality); pronouns standing in the place of nouns (*I* and *it* can be used in place of *Stephen D. Rogers* and *The Dictionary of Made-Up Languages*); conjunctions (*or* and *but* join words together); prepositions (*before* and *over* join words by indicating their relationship); and interjections—words that exclaim an emotion or sentiment (*wow* and *ugh* express a sentence's worth of emotion in a single word).

Which of the preceding types of words will you include in your dictionary? While nouns and verbs might seem like a given, how could a language develop that didn't include one or the other? Could the requirements of language still be met? In your language, can verbs be used as nouns? Can nouns be used as verbs? Imagine a language where the same root is used for nouns and verbs, the difference indicated by the root word being appended by an *-a* or an *-e*.

What kind of modifiers will each of the word types accept, if any? Nouns can be modified to indicate number, specificity, and gender. Verbs can be inflected to indicate number, aspect, and tense. Will your language include these types of word modifications, include others, or do away with modifications all together?

CORE WORD LIST

Linguist Morris Swadesh (1909–1967) compiled a list of 200-plus words that he said were core to all languages. Whether his glottochronological theories are valid or not, the list provides a good starting point when developing your own language.

What words will you include? How will the exclusion of others (such as *husband* and *wife*) reflect the society that speaks your language?

I	there	few	thick	man (human
you	who	other	heavy	being)
(singular)	what	one	small	child
he	where	two	short	wife
we	when	three	narrow	husband
you (plural)	how	four	thin	mother
they	not	five	woman	father
this	all	big	man (adult	animal
that	many	long	male)	fish
here	some	wide		bird

dog	hand	swim	salt	sharp
louse	wing	fly (verb)	stone	dull
snake	belly	walk	sand	smooth
worm	guts	come	dust	wet
tree	neck	lie	earth	dry
forest	back	sit	cloud	correct
stick	breast	stand	fog	near
fruit	heart	turn	sky	far
seed	liver	fall	wind	right
leaf	drink	give	snow	left
root	eat	hold	ice	at
bark	bite	squeeze	smoke	in
flower	suck	rub	fire	with
grass	spit	wash	ashes	and
rope	vomit	wipe	burn	if
skin	blow	pull	road	because
meat	breathe	push	mountain	name
blood	laugh	throw	red	
bone	see	tie	green	
fat (noun)	hear	sew	yellow	
egg	know	count	white	
horn	think	say	black	
tail	smell	sing	night	
feather	fear	play	day	
hair	sleep	float	year	
head	live	flow	warm	
ear	die	freeze	cold	
eye	kill	swell	full	
nose	fight	sun	new	
mouth	hunt	moon	old	
tooth	hit	star	good	
tongue	cut	water	bad	
fingernail	split	rain	rotten	
foot	stab	river	dirty	
leg	scratch	lake	straight	
knee	dig	sea	round	

DELINEATING CATEGORIES

In English, farmers grow wheat and consumers eat wheat, but farmers raise cattle and consumers eat beef. The words with which we describe our world say something about us. What will your language say about its speakers?

In English, the word *carrot* does not indicate whether you are talking about a carrot that's growing, a carrot that has been picked and thus has stopped growing, a carrot that has been cut into small pieces (changing its state of being in one way), a carrot that has been cooked (changing its state of being in another way), a carrot that is being eaten, and a carrot that is being scraped into the garbage. If carrots were the most important element of our diet, we might have different words for all these stages of a carrot.

Will the words in your language indicate category? You probably know that a tyrannosaurus rex and a stegosaurus are both dinosaurs. From that knowledge, you can guess that a borealosaurus is probably a dinosaur as well. (And you'd be right.) While English is not very big on categories, many constructed languages are developed with categories as a designing principle. Things that grow might all start with ag- or contain two syllables. The idea behind this is that new speakers don't have to memorize every word in order to have a basic understanding of what any word means.

We study the things that are important to us, and the more we study, the more components we can identify and label. Those who will speak the language you make up are probably no different.

HOW DIFFERENT IS DIFFERENT?

But maybe they're very different. We think in terms of words, of nouns and verbs. That's because we see things and we act. But what if a tree developed language, or a whale? Both those languages would probably be short on words and long on phrases that comment on weather or currents but that don't dwell on philosophical thoughts. Sure, your aliens might be humanoid, and might be obsessed with humanoid interests, but your aliens might also be *alien* aliens.

Imagine a race of creatures as unlike us as possible. What's their worldview? What are their concerns? What are their desires? How do your answers to those questions translate into language parameters?

Perhaps, rather than making up a completely new language, you want to modify one that currently exists. What will English sound like in a hundred years? Five hundred? A thousand? A time traveler leaves present-day Boston, Massachusetts, and goes fifty thousand years into the future. Will the people he encounters there still drop their *r*'s?

Glottochronology is the study of the relationship between language and time. Some proponents of the theory behind glottochronology believe that given a list of core words and how they've changed over time, you can produce a glottochronological constant that will allow you to know how the language will change in 1,000 or 10,000 years.

Whatever the currently accepted particulars of glottochronology are, you, William Shakespeare (1564–1616), and Geoffrey Chaucer (1343–1400) all have written in English. Read a few pages of their writing. How much has English changed in more than 700 years?

In 2,000 years, assuming something called *English* is still being spoken, you can be sure it will be close to indecipherable to someone from our times.

CHAPTER THREE

Taxing Syntax

Syntax is the arrangement of words within a sentence. In English, the typical sentence follows a subject-verb-object structure. That's *subject* (person, place, or thing), then *verb* (action or state of being), and then *object* (that which is acted upon). "Stephen drank a cup of coffee." *Stephen* is the subject, *drank* is the verb, and *a cup of coffee* is the object.

Another common structure in languages is subject-object-verb. "Stephen a cup of coffee drank." Some few languages use verb-subject-object, verb-object-subject, object-subject-verb, and object-verb-subject structures.

Just pick one. Whatever sentence structure you decide to use, ask yourself if that structure changes when the statement becomes a question. How about when the statement becomes a command? Does the structure change at any other times?

In your language, are sentences collected together in paragraphs? They could appear just one after the other, or every sentence could start at the left margin.

Do sentences start at the left margin or the right? Or are they read vertically, from top to bottom or bottom to top?

THE NEED FOR PUNCTUATION

Once you group words into sentences, you introduce the need for punctuation. What punctuation marks will you include in your language? What rules will define their use? How will speakers break and misuse those rules?

Do you need punctuation at all? If the verb is always the last word in a sentence, the appearance of the verb marks the stopping point. Or perhaps a sentence in lowercase is always followed by a sentence in uppercase; the pattern of alternating cases effectively indicates the beginning and endings of sentences.

Will you have a punctuation mark that indicates that the sentence is a question? Perhaps the placement of a particular word at the beginning of a sentence accomplishes that task, or a change in word order always indicates an interrogative.

The art of sentencing reflects our need to pause for breath and to close a thought so that we can process what we just read or heard. Perhaps your alien is capable of listening and speaking at the same time so that conversations are concurrent rather than sequential. How would you document that?

When writing, we organize our thoughts into paragraphs of linked sentences. (For the most part, we paragraph when we're speaking as well.) We approach the written and (to a lesser extent) the spoken word as occurring in a logical sequence.

"I went to the store. My mother dances. I bought a box of nails."

We assume that the first and third sentences are linked, and we try to guess how the second sentence fits in. The nails are needed to build something that will allow the mother to dance? The mother's dancing broke something that needs to be repaired? The mother danced in the store?

A human teacher or an editor would note that the second sentence should be moved to its own paragraph or cut if it's unrelated to the narrative of the store and the nails.

Perhaps your alien would find nothing unusual about those three lines. Perhaps an action sentence is always followed by a reflective sentence in the language your alien speaks.

Perhaps the sequential nature of sentences is even more ingrained in your alien's mind, creating the norm of sentences being linked. "I went to the store. The store carried the nails I need. I need the nails to build a wooden stage. The wooden stage will allow my mother to dance. Dance is the activity she most treasures."

PUTTING THE LANGUAGE IN CONTEXT

You're not just making up a language; you're making up the language of a society, one with a history and a culture. If you put some thought into the creatures that will be using the language, and some thought into the world in which they live, you'll find you have a better idea of how to answer many of the questions that arise when constructing a language.

The more details you have, the more they'll limit your choices. That's a good thing. When it seems as though there is only one logical way for the language to be developed, that's an indication that language might have developed naturally in the society you've described.

While languages might seem to take on a life of their own, actually they tag along on the heels of history. That's true of natural languages and of made-up ones as well.

Russian linguist Aleksandr Dulichenko (1941–), who compiled a list of more than 900 made-up languages, published his findings in *International Auxiliary Languages* in 1990. Twenty years have passed since then, and the Internet has turned a secret vice into a popular hobby. Today the number of constructed languages is probably well over 1,000.

The most successful made-up language is probably Esperanto. L. L. Zamenhof, its inventor, spread the message of Esperanto by using it when writing letters to people and including a few sample translations. He organized clubs and conferences and invented traditions around the green Esperanto flag and the green stars people wore to indicate that they were speakers of Esperanto. He created Esperantoland. He gave the made-up language a culture.

How we use language is affected by our culture. "Farmers always talk about the weather." "Men always talk about sports." "Preachers always talk about the Bible." Of course these are generalizations, but there's a kernel of truth in the idea that members of subcultures speak in ways that reflect their interests.

Many constructed languages claim to reduce waste and ambiguity. They assign one meaning per word and one word per meaning. But living cultures don't permit such precision in language.

VERTICAL DIVISIONS

In addition to horizontal divisions within a culture, let's also consider the vertical. There's what you say and how you say it to your friends. Then there's the more formal version of what you say and how you say it in business. There's even a rarified version of what you say and how you say it in the most important of ceremonies.

The beings that use your created language will make it their own. They will use the language to bond with some and to withdraw from others.

Think about how the characteristics of your culture will influence language changes—in what ways and how quickly. Languages can be expected to change more in action-oriented societies. Exploration, invention, and renovation can accelerate the creation of new words and phrases. A democratic society that has freedom of the press and that encourages individual expression will be driven by a language that evolves faster than that of a tyranny.

EVOLUTION AND REVOLUTION

To create a living language, you must simulate evolution by introducing appropriate slang, compression, regionalisms, and the effects of subcultures. How will these support or undercut the general impact of the culture at large?

Language evolves. It mutates. If you're interested in making up a language that could pass for a natural language, then you have to take the living nature of language into account.

Tolkien was a master conlanger not because he developed lists of words and rules of grammar but because he captured the evolution of his many constructed languages. What's the word for *cup*? That depends on which period of the language's history you're asking about.

What's the history of the culture that uses your created language? How has the society changed and evolved? What factions have separated? Which other languages have been absorbed?

How have changes in philosophy, sociology, and technology generated new words and new things to talk about? How have scientific advances influenced the metaphors of life?

What words and ideas have fallen out of favor?

How has propaganda shaped the linguistic frontier?

In what ways has the language been reinvented and recycled and reclaimed?

When do you intend to set it free?

PART III
LANGUAGE GAMES

For the most part, constructing a language is a serious business.

Imagine being one of the people who worked on universal auxiliary languages while the horrors of World War I and World War II unfolded around them. The people who constructed them believed they were working on an instrument that would put an end to war by putting an end to miscommunication. Amid all the slaughter and destruction of war, it's no wonder that a taste of some of those constructed languages leaves you feeling that your mouth is coated with a thin gray dust.

But it doesn't have to be that grim. Remember the first nonsense words that delighted you? Remember a passage from Dr. Seuss, Edward Lear, or Lewis Carroll that made you smile or even laugh out loud? Recall the secret language that you developed with your close friend or sibling; it allowed you to carry on conversations while grownups were in the room. They didn't even know what you were talking about!

Made-up languages can be fun. Words are fun. We joke and we pun and we double-entendre. We forward e-mails about mistakes in church bulletins. For years—more years than we care to admit—we giggled whenever we heard someone say "butt."

There's a wonderful sense of freedom that we can get from playing with language. For so many years, language wasn't quite the tool we needed to express ourselves. For so many years, language and the rules of language were things that were used against us. For so many years, there have been so many people who twisted our words, misunderstood what we said, or acted as though we hadn't said a thing.

Here are some language games.

Gibberish

Gibberish is a language game played in the United States, Canada, and Northern Ireland, although games with similar rules are played in Central and South America and in Eurasia from France to Russia.

The underlying concept of Gibberish is the inclusion of a given group of letters after the opening sound of each word in a sentence. The four most common dialects are created by inserting -itheg-, -idig-, -uddag-, or -uvug-.

"My name is Stephen D. Rogers" would be translated into Gibberish as follows:

+ With the -itheg- insert, "*Mithegy nithegame ithegs Sithegtephen Ditheg Rithegogers.*"
+ With the -idig- insert, "*Midigy nidigame idigs Sidigtephen Didig Ridigogers.*"
+ With the -uddag- insert, "*Muddagy nuddagame uddags Suddagtephen Duddag Ruddagogers.*"
+ With the -uvug- insert, "*Muvugy nuvugame uvugs Suvugtephen Duvug Ruvugogers.*"

But you can call me "Bob."

Jeringonza

Jeringonza is a Spanish language game played in Spain and Latin America.

The principle of Jeringonza is to insert a *p* after a vowel. The vowel is repeated after the inserted *p*. Why is there no *p* in the word Jeringonza? *No habla Español.*

If there are two or more vowels clustered together, some people insert the *p* only after the stressed vowel; others insert the *p* after every vowel; still others insert the *p*+vowel only after whole syllables.

"Please hand me the dictionary after you finish reading the index" would be translated into Jeringonza as follows:

+ Inserting the *p* after the stressed vowel, "*Plepeasepe hapand mepe thepe dipictipioniaparypy apafteper yopou fipinipish repeadiping thepe ipindepex.*"
+ Inserting the *p* after each vowel, "*Plepeapasepe hapand mepe thepe dipictipioponaparypy apafteper yopoupu fipinipish repeapadiping thepe ipindepex.*"
+ Inserting the *p*+vowel after every syllable, "*Pleasepe handpe mepe thepe dicpitionpiarypy aftpaerpe youpo finpiishpi readpeingpi thepe indpiexpe.*"

On second thought, I'll get my own copy.

Jst Cnsnnts

Jst Cnsnnts is a language game played in the United States.

In Jst Cnssnnts, vowels are dropped.

"Losing a bet, I gave him an IOU" would be translated into Jst Cnsnnts as follows:

"*Lsng bt gv hm n.*"

As you might guess, the game works best when played with people who together fashion a list of commonly used phrases to indicate words that become indecipherable when reduced.

Língua do Pê

Língua do Pê is a Portugese language game played in Brazil and Portugal.

The underlying concept of Língua do Pê is that *p* is inserted after a vowel and then the vowel is repeated after the included *p*. (Língua do Pê differs from Jeringonza because the former is a Portugese language game and the latter is a Spanish language game. Being called Língua do Pê, it also has a better name: The P Language.)

"I am spitting up a storm with all these *p* words" would be translated into Língua do Pê as follows:

"Ipi apam spipittiping upup apa stoporm wipith apall thepesepe p wopords."
I'll get you a towel.

Opish

Opish is a language game played in the United States.

To speak Opish, insert *op* after every consonant.

"I need pen and paper for this" would be translated as follows:

"I nopeedop popenop anopdop popapoperop foporop tophopisop."
Maybe I need a calculator.

Pig Latin

Pig Latin is a language game played in the United States.

To speak Pig Latin, move a beginning consonant to the end of a word and follow it with *-ay*. If the word begins with a vowel sound, add *-ay* (following a trailing consonant sound) or *-hay* (following a trailing vowel sound) at the end.

"My head is starting to hurt" would be translated into Pig Latin as follows:

"Ymay eadhay isay artingstay otay urthay."
Yes, my head is definitely hurting.

Rosarigasino

Rosarigasino is a language game played in Argentina.

The underlying concept of Rosarigasino is that *gas* is inserted after the stressed vowel and then the vowel is repeated.

"Rosario is the city where Rosarigasino is thought to have begun" would be translated as follows:

"*Rosarigaio igasis thegase cigasity whegasere Rosarigasino igasis thougasought togaso hagasave begasegun.*"

Are you sure it wasn't Pittsburgh?

Rövarspråket

Rövarspråket is a language game played in Sweden.

In Rövarspråket all consonants are doubled and an *o* is inserted between them.

"I think I would rather play jacks" would be translated into Rövarspråket as follows:

"*I thothinonkok I wowouloldod rorathotheror poplolay jojackocks.*"

Or maybe just tiddlywinks.

Sananmuunno

Sananmuunnos is a language game played in Finland.

The idea of Sananmuunnos is not unlike a spoonerism in English. The beginnings of two words are swapped to create a humorous or obscene phrase. (The morphology of Finnish allows better puns to be created than would occur in English.)

"A dictionary of made-up languages" would be sort of translated into Sananmuunnos as follows:

"*A dictionary of laid-up manguages.*"

Maybe you had to be there (in Finland).

Šatrovački

Šatrovački is a South Slavic language game played in the Serbian, Croatian, Bosnian, and Macedonian languages.

To play Šatrovački, reverse the syllables in two-syllable words. If the reversal produces a word that already exists, change the ending to differentiate the two.

"I finished my coffee" would be translated into Šatrovački as follows:

"I ishedfin my feecof."

Ubbi Dubbi

Ubbi Dubbi is a language game played in the United States.

When playing Ubbi Dubbi, *ub* is placed before the vowel sounds in each word. The game was perhaps invented but at least popularized by the PBS television show *ZOOM* (1972–1978, 1999–2005) in which actors spent part of each episode talking about or speaking Ubbi Dubbi—telling jokes, performing skits, and attempting to sing rounds.

"I really miss watching *ZOOM*" would be translated into Ubbi Dubbi as follows:

"*Ubi rubeally mubiss wubatchubing ZUBOOM.*"

Verlan

Verlan is a language game played in France.

The principle of Verlan is to reverse the syllables in a word. (The name Verlan is a Verlan of *l'envers* [the inverse]).

"I am getting pizza for dinner" translates into Verlan as follows:

"*I am tingget zappiz for nerdin.*"

Vesre

Vesre is a Spanish language game played in Buenos Aires and Uruguay.

Like Verlan, it involves reversing the syllables in a word.

"Should I get onion pizza or bacon?" translates into Vesre as follows:

"*Should I get ionon zappiz or conba?*"

Bibliography

Anderson, Stephen R. "How Many Languages Are There in the World?" Washington, DC: Linguistic Society of America, 2004.

Asimov, Isaac, ed., and Jonathan Swift. *The Annotated Gulliver's Travels*. New York: Clarkson N. Potter, 1980.

Bleiler, Richard, ed. *Science Fiction Writers: Critical Studies of the Major Authors from the Early Nineteenth Century to the Present Day*, 2nd ed. New York: Charles Scribner's Sons, 1999.

Bould, Mark, Andrew M. Butler, Adam Roberts, and Sherryl Vint, eds. *The Routledge Companion to Science Fiction*. London: Routledge, 2009.

Boyd, Brian. *On the Origin of Stories: Evolution, Cognition, and Fiction*. Cambridge, MA: Belknap Press of Harvard University Press, 2009.

Conley, Tim, and Stephen Cain. *Encyclopedia of Fictional and Fantastic Languages*. Westport, CT: Greenwood Press, 2006.

Harrison, Richard K., ed. *Invented Languages* (Summer 2008).

Lakoff, George, and Mark Johnson. *Metaphors We Live By*. Chicago: University of Chicago Press, 1980.

Le Guin, Ursula. *A Wizard of Earthsea*. New York: Bantam Books, 1968.

Lewis, M. Paul, ed. *Ethnologue: Languages of the World*, 16th ed. Dallas, TX: SIL International, 2009.

Martin, K Gerard. *Cerafina's Damiriak Language Handbook*. Kenosha, WI: Shouldercat Books, 2010.

Meyers, Walter E. *Aliens and Linguists*. Athens, GA: The University of Georgia Press, 1980.

Okrand, Marc. *The Klingon Dictionary*. New York: Pocket Books, 1985.

Okrant, Arika. *In the Land of Invented Languages*. New York: Spiegal and Grau, 2009.

Tolkien, Christopher, ed., and J. R. R. Tolkien. *The Lost Road and other Writings*. Boston: Houghton Mifflin, 1987.

Tolkien, J. R. R., *Parma Eldalamberon*, no. 11 (1995).

Westfahl, Gary, ed. *The Greenwood Encyclopedia of Science Fiction and Fantasy: Themes, Works, and Wonders*. Westport, CT: Greenwood Press, 2005.

APPENDIX A

Works, Language Creators, and the Languages Associated with Them

Acorna's People (1999) (see Linyaari)

Acorna's Quest (1998) (see Linyaari)

Acorna's Rebels (2003) (see Linyaari)

Acorna's Search (2001) (see Linyaari)

Acorna's Triumph (2004) (see Linyaari)

Acorna's World (2000) (see Linyaari)

Acorna the Unicorn Girl (1997) (see Linyaari)

Across the Zodiac: The Story of a Wrecked Record (1880) (see Martian)

Adams, Richard (see Lapine)

Adventures of Superman (1952–1958) (see Kryptonian)

The Adventures of Tintin: The Calculus Affair (see Bordurian)

The Adventures of Tintin: King Otto-kar's Sceptre (see Syldavian)

Agent of the Terran Empire (1965) (see Anglic [Galactic empire])

Alien Nation (1988) (see Tenctonese)

Alien Nation (1989–1990) (see Tenctonese)

Alien Nation: Body and Soul (1995) (see Tenctonese)

Alien Nation: Dark Horizon (1994) (see Tenctonese)

Alien Nation: The Enemy Within (1996) (see Tenctonese)

Alien Nation: Millennium (1996) (see Tenctonese)

Alien Nation: The Udara Legacy (1997) (see Tenctonese)

Always Going Home (1985) (see Kesh)

The Amazing Maurice and His Educated Rodents (2001) (see Troll)

Ambrov Keon (1986) (see Simelan)

Anderson, Poul (see Angley, Anglic [Galactic empire], Anglo-French [The Shield of Time], Ingliss, Unglish)

Atlantis: The Lost Empire (2001) (see Atlantean)

Avatar (2009) (see Na'vi)

Babel-17 (1996) (see Babel-17)

Babylon 5 (1993–2007) (see Interlac)

Ball, Margaret (see Linyaari)

Banks, Iain M. (see Marain)

Banner of the Stars (see Baronh)

Baptism of Fire (1996) (see Starsza Mowa)

The Beautician and the Beast (1997) (see Slovetzian)

Besson, Luc (see The Divine Language)

Betrayer (2011) (see Ragi)

Bionicle Adventures (see Matoran)

Bionicle Chronicles (see Matoran)

Bionicle Legends (see Matoran)

Blood of Elves (1994) (see Starsza Mowa)

Bök, Christian (see Eunoia)

bolo'bolo (1983) (see asa'pili)

The Book of Lost Tales, Part One (1983) (see Adûnaic, Avarin, Black Speech, Common Eldarin, Doriathrin, Goldogrin, Khuzdul, Nandorin, Primitive Elvish, Quenya, Sindarin, Telerin, Westron)

The Book of Lost Tales, Part Two (1984) (see Adûnaic, Avarin, Black Speech, Common Eldarin, Doriathrin, Goldogrin, Khuzdul, Nandorin, Primitive Elvish, Quenya, Sindarin, Telerin, Westron)

Bridwell, Edward Nelson (see Kryptonian)

Brightness Reef (1995) (see Anglic [Civilization of the Five Galaxies], Trinary)

Brin, David (see Anglic [Civilization of the Five Galaxies], Trinary)

Brisingr (2008) (see Ancient Language)

Brook, Peter (see Orghast)

Brown, Francie (see Slovetzian)

Brown, James Cooke (see Loglan)

Burgess, Anthony (see Nadsat, Ulam)

Burroughs, Edgar Rice (see Amtorian)

"The Call of Cthulhu" (see R'lyehian)

A Call to Arms (January 3, 1999) (see Interlac)

Cameron, James (see Na'vi)

Carpe Jugulum (1998) (see Troll)

Carreña 1: The Fall of Evanita (2010) (see Dahmek, Miramish, Mirsua, Nimiash)

Carreña 2: Lamina (2010) (see Dahmek, Miramish, Mirsua, Nimiash)

Carreña 3: Imperative Birth (2010) (see Dahmek, Miramish, Mirsua, Nimiash)

Carson of Venus, 1946 (see Amtorian)

Cat's Cradle (1963) (see Bokonon)

Caves, Sally (see Teonaht)

Cerafina's Damiriak Language Handbook (2010) (see Dahmek, Miramish, Mirsua, Nimiash)

Channel's Destiny (l982) (see Simelan)

Chanur's Homecoming (1986) (see Hani, Kiffish)

Chanur's Legacy (1992) (see Hani, Kiffish)

Chanur's Venture (1981) (see Hani, Kiffish)

Cherryh, C. J. (See Hani, Kiffish, Ragi)

Children of the Mind (1996) (see Stark)

Cilauro, Santo (see Molvanian)

A Clash of Kings (1998) (see Dothraki)

A Clockwork Orange (1962) (see Nadsat)

A Clockwork Orange (1971) (see Nadsat)

The Confusion (2004) (see Qwghlmian)

Consider Phlebas (1987) (see Marain)

Conspirator (2009) (see Ragi)

The Colour of Magic (1983) (see Troll)

"The Courtyard" (2003) (see Aklo)

The Crest of the Stars (see Baronh)

Crossroads of Twilight (2003) (see The Old Tongue)

A Crown of Swords (1996) (see The Old Tongue)

Cryptonomicon (1999) (see Qwghlmian)

A Dance with Dragons (scheduled for 2011) (see Dothraki)

The Day of Their Return (1973) (see Anglic [Galactic empire])

Deceiver (2010) (see Ragi)

Deep Wizardry (1985) (see The Speech)

Defender (2001) (see Ragi)

Delany, Samuel R. (see Babel-17)

Deliverer (2007) (see Ragi)

Destroyer (2005) (see Ragi)

de Wahl, Edgar (see Occidental)

The Dispossessed: An Ambiguous Utopia (1974) (see Iotic, Pravic)

Doctolero, Suzette (see Enchanta)

The Dragon Reborn (1991) (see The Old Tongue)

Duane, Diane (see Rihannsu, The Speech)

"The Dunwich Horror" (1928) (see Aklo)

The Earth Book of Stormgate (1978) (See Anglic [Galactic empire])

Earth: Final Conflict (1997–2002) (see Eunoia)

An Earthly Crown (see Chapalli)

Earthsong (1993) (see Láadan)

Eldest (2005) (see Ancient Language)

Elen, Sonja (see Toki Pona)

el-Gheithy, Said (see Ku)

Elgin, Suzette Haden (see Láadan)

Elliot, Kate (see Chapalli)

The Empty Chair (2006) (see Rihannsu)

Encantadia (2005) (see Enchanta)

Ender in Exile (2008) (see Stark)

"Ender's Game" (1977) (see Stark)

Ender's Game (1985) (see Stark)

Ender's Shadow (1999) (see Stark)

Equal Rites (1987) (see Troll)

Eragon (2003) (see Ancient Language)

Eric (1990) (see Troll)

Escape on Venus (1946) (see Amtorian)

Etheria (2005–2006) (see Enchanta)

Excession (1996) (see Marain)

Explorer (2002) (see Ragi)

The Eye of the World (1990) (see The Old Tongue)

Far-Seer (1992) (see Quintaglio)

The Farthest Shore (1973) (see Hardic, Kargish, Language of the Making, Osskili)

A Feast for Crows (2005) (see Dothraki)

Feet of Clay (1996) (see Troll)

The Fellowship of the Ring—The Lord of the Rings (1954) (see Adûnaic, Avarin, Black Speech, Common Eldarin, Doriathrin, Goldogrin, Khuzdul, Nandorin, Primitive Elvish, Quenya, Sindarin, Telerin, Westron)

The Fifth Element (1997) (see The Divine Language)

The Fifth Elephant (1999) (see Troll)

The Fires of Heaven (1993) (see The Old Tongue)

First Channel (1980) (see Simelan)

First Meetings (2002) (see Stark)

First Warning (2005) (see Linyaari)

Flandry of Terra (1965) (see Anglic [Galactic empire])

Foreigner (1994) (see Quintaglio, Ragi)

Fossil Hunter (1993) (see Quintaglio)

Fromer, Paul (see Na'vi)

Fromkin, Victoria (see Pakuni)

The Game of Empire (1985) (see Anglic [Galactic empire])

A Game of Thrones (see Dothraki)

Garrett, Randall (see Anglo-French [Lord Darcy stories])

The Gathering (February 22, 1993) (see Interlac)

The Gathering Storm (2009) (see The Old Tongue)

Gleisner, Tom (see Molvanian)

Going Postal (2004) (see Troll)

The Great Hunt (1990) (see The Old Tongue)

Greg, Percy (see Martian)

Guardians of Ga'Hoole Book 1: The Capture (2003) (see Krakish)

Guardians of Ga'Hoole Book 2: The Journey (2003) (see Krakish)

Guardians of Ga'Hoole Book 3: The Rescue (2004) (see Krakish)

Guardians of Ga'Hoole Book 4: The Siege (2004) (see Krakish)

Guardians of Ga'Hoole Book 5: The Shattering (2004) (see Krakish)

Guardians of Ga'Hoole Book 6: The Burning (2004) (see Krakish)

Guardians of Ga'Hoole Book 7: The Hatchling (2005) (see Krakish)

Guardians of Ga'Hoole Book 8: The Outcast (2005) (see Krakish)

Guardians of Ga'Hoole Book 9: The First Collier (2006) (see Krakish)

Guardians of Ga'Hoole Book 10: The Coming of Hoole (2006) (see Krakish)

Guardians of Ga'Hoole Book 11: To Be a King (2006) (see Krakish)

Guardians of Ga'Hoole Book 12: The Golden Tree (2007) (see Krakish)

Guardians of Ga'Hoole Book 13: The River of Wind (2007) (see Krakish)

Guardians of Ga'Hoole Book 14: Exile (2008) (see Krakish)

Guardians of Ga'Hoole Book 15: The War of the Ember (2008) (see Krakish)

Guards! Guards! (1989) (see Troll)

Gulliver's Travels (1726) (see Houyhnhnm)

Harry Potter and the Chamber of Secrets (1998) (see Parseltongue)

Harry Potter and the Deathly Hallows (2007) (see Parseltongue)

Harry Potter and the Goblet of Fire (2000) (see Parseltongue)

Harry Potter and the Half-Blood Prince (2005) (see Parseltongue)

Harry Potter and the Order of the Phoenix (2003) (see Parseltongue)

Harry Potter and the Philosopher's Stone (1997) (see Parseltongue)

Harry Potter and the Prisoner of Azkaban (1999) (see Parseltongue)

A Hat Full of Sky (2004) (see Troll)

'The Haunter of the Dark" (1935) (see Aklo)

Havel, Ivan M. (see Ptydepe)

Havel, Václav (see Ptydepe)

Heaven's Reach (1998) (see Anglic [Civilization of the Five Galaxies], Trinary)

Heinlein, Robert A. (see Whitmanite)

Hergé (see Bordurian, Syldavian)

The Hexer (2001) (see Starsza Mowa)

Heydt, Dorothy Jones (see Vulcan)

High Wizardry (1990) (see The Speech)

Hildegard of Bingen (see Lingua Ignota)

Hiroyuki, Morioka (see Baronh)

His Conquering Sword (see Chapalli)

The Hobbit (1937) (see Adûnaic, Avarin, Black Speech, Common Eldarin, Doriathrin, Goldogrin, Khuzdul, Nandorin, Primitive Elvish, Quenya, Sindarin, Telerin, Westron)

Hogfather (1996) (see Troll)

Honor Blade—#96 (2000) (see Rihannsu)

House of Zeor (1974) (see Simelan)

Hughes, Ted (see Orghast)

The Illuminatus! Trilogy (1975) (see Aklo)

Infinity's Shore (1996) (see Anglic [Civilization of the Five Galaxies], Trinary)

Inheritance (2011) (see Ancient Language)

Inheritor (1996) (see Ragi)

Interesting Times (1994) (see Troll)

The Interpreter (2005) (see Ku)

In the Beginning (January 4, 1998) (see Interlac)

Invader (1995) (see Ragi)

Inversions (1998) (see Marain)

I Shall Wear Midnight (2010) (see Troll)

James Cameron's Avatar: The Game (2009) (see Na'vi)

Jaran (see Chapalli)

Jingo (1997) (see Troll)

Johnson, Kenneth and Juliet (see Tenctonese)

Jordan, Robert (see The Old Tongue)

Jovovich, Milla (see The Divine Language)

The Judas Rose (1987) (see Láadan)

Khlebnikov, Velimir (see Zaum)

The Kif Strike Back (1985) (see Hani, Kiffish)

Knife of Dreams (2005) (see The Old Tongue)

A Knight of Ghosts and Shadows (1974) (See Anglic [Galactic empire])

Krofft, Sid and Marty (see Pakuni)

Kruchenykh, Aleksei (see Zaum)

Kurland, Michael (see Anglo-French [Lord Darcy stories])

Kwapis, Ken (see Slovetzian)

Lady of the Lake (1999) (see Starsza Mowa)

Land of the Lost (1974–1977) (see Pakuni)

Land of the Lost (1991–1992) (see Pakuni)

Land of the Lost (2009) (see Pakuni)

The Languages of Pao (1958) (see Pastiche)

The Last Continent (1998) (see Troll)

The Last Hero (2001) (see Troll)

The Last Wish (1993) (see Starsza Mowa)

The Law of Becoming (see Chapalli)

The Lays of Beleriand (1985) (see Adûnaic, Avarin, Black Speech, Common Eldarin, Doriathrin, Goldogrin, Khuzdul, Nandorin, Primitive Elvish, Quenya, Sindarin, Telerin, Westron)

The Legend of the Rangers (To Live and Die in Starlight) (January 19, 2002) (see Interlac)

LEGO Group (see Matoran)

Le Guin, Ursula K. (see Hardic, Iotic, Kargish, Kesh, Language of the Making, Osskili, Pravic)

Let the Spacemen Beware (The Night Face) (1963) (see Anglic [Galactic empire])

Lewis, C. S. (see Old Solar)

Lichtenberg, Jacqueline (see Simelan)

The Light Fantastic (1986) (see Troll)

Ling, Van (see Tenctonese)

Lingua Ignota per simplicem hominem Hildegardem prolata (see Lingua Ignota)

Logan, John (see Eloi)

Lois & Clark: The New Adventures of Superman (1993–1997) (see Kryptonian)

The Long Night (1983) (See Anglic [Galactic empire])

Look to Windward (2000) (see Marain)

Lord Darcy Investigates (1981) (see Anglo-French [Lord Darcy stories])

Lord of Chaos (1994) (see The Old Tongue)

Lords and Ladies (1992) (see Troll)

Lorrah, Jean (see Simelan)

Lost on Venus, 1935 (see Amtorian)

The Lost Road and Other Writings (1987) (see Adûnaic, Avarin, Black Speech, Common Eldarin, Doriathrin, Goldogrin, Khuzdul, Nandorin, Primitive Elvish, Quenya, Sindarin, Telerin, Westron)

Lovecraft, H. P. (see Aklo, Black Speech, R'lyehian, Tsath-yo)

Machen, Arthur (see Aklo)

Madison, R. Ben (see Talossan)

Mahogany Trinrose (1981) (see Simelan)

Making Money (2007) (see Troll)

Martin, George R. R. (see Dothraki)

Martin, K Gerard (see Dahmek, Miramish, Mirsua, Nimiash)

Maskerade (1995) (see Troll)

Matter (2008) (see Marain)

McCaffrey, Anne (see Linyaari)

The Memorandum (1966) (see Ptydepe)

A Memory of Light (scheduled for 2012) (see The Old Tongue)

Men at Arms (1993) (see Troll)

Mirkheim (1977) (See Anglic [Galactic empire])

Morgoth's Ring (The Later Silmarillion, Part One) (1993) (see Adûnaic, Avarin, Black Speech, Common Eldarin, Doriathrin, Goldogrin, Khuzdul, Nandorin, Primitive Elvish, Quenya, Sindarin, Telerin, Westron)

Molvania: A Land Untouched by Modern Dentistry (2004) (see Molvanian)

Monstrous Regiment (2003) (see Troll)

Moore, Alan (see Aklo)

More, Thomas (see Utopian)

Mort (1987) (see Troll)

Morwood, Peter (see Rihannsu)

Moving Pictures (1990) (see Troll)

Murder and Magic (1979) (see Anglo-French [Lord Darcy stories])

My Enemy, My Ally—#18 (1984) (see Rihannsu)

Myst (see D'ni)

Native Tongue (1984) (see Láadan)

Night Watch (2002) (see Troll)

Nineteen Eighty-Four (1948) (see Newspeak)

Nineteen Eighty-Four (1956) (see Newspeak)

Nineteen Eighty-Four (1984) (see Newspeak)

Okrand, Marc (see Atlantean, Klingon)

Orghast (1971) (see Orghast)

Orion Shall Rise (1983) (see Angley, Ingliss, Unglish)

Orwell, George (see Newspeak)

The Other Wind (2001) (see Hardic, Kargish, Language of the Making, Osskili)

Out of the Silent Planet (1938) (see Old Solar)

Paolini, Christopher (see Ancient Language)

The Path of Daggers (1998) (see The Old Tongue)

The People of the Wind (1973) (see Anglic [Galactic empire])

The Peoples of Middle-earth (1996) (see Adûnaic, Avarin, Black Speech, Common Eldarin, Doriathrin, Goldogrin, Khuzdul, Nandorin, Primitive Elvish, Quenya, Sindarin, Telerin, Westron)

Perelandra (1943) (see Old Solar)

Personal Recognizance (2011) (see Simelan)

Peterson, David J. (see Dothraki)

Pirates of Venus (1934) (see Amtorian)

The Player of Games (1988) (see Marain)

p.m. (see asa'pili)

Pratchett, Sir Terry (see Troll)

Precursor (1999) (see Ragi)

Pretender (2006) (see Ragi)

The Pride of Chanur (1981) (see Hani, Kiffish)

The Puppet Masters (1951) (see Whitmanite)

Pyramids (1989) (see Troll)

Quest for Fire (1981) (see Ulam)

Quicksilver (2003) (see Qwghlmian)

Reaper Man (1991) (see Troll)

Remi, Georges Prosper (see Syldavian)

RenSime (1984) (see Simelan)

The Return of the King—The Lord of the Rings, (1955) (see Adûnaic, Avarin, Black Speech, Common Eldarin, Doriathrin, Goldogrin, Khuzdul, Nandorin, Primitive Elvish, Quenya, Sindarin, Telerin, Westron)

The Return of the Shadow (The History of The Lord of the Rings, Part One) (1988) (see Adûnaic, Avarin, Black Speech, Common Eldarin, Doriathrin, Goldogrin, Khuzdul, Nandorin, Primitive Elvish, Quenya, Sindarin, Telerin, Westron)

Rihannsu: The Bloodwing Voyages (2006) (see Rihannsu)

Riven (see D'ni)

The River of Souls (November 8, 1998) (see Interlac)

Roddenberry, Gene (see Eunoia, Klingon, Vulcan)

The Romulan Way—#35 (1987) (see Rihannsu)

Rosenfelder, Mark (see Verdurian)

Rowling, J. K. (see Parseltongue)

Sanderson, Brandon (see The Old Tongue)

Sapkowski, Andrzej (see Starsza Mowa)

Satan's World (1969) (see Anglic [Galactic empire])

The Saturn Game (1989) (see Anglic [Galactic empire])

Sauron Defeated (The History of The Lord of the Rings, Part Four) (1992) (see Adûnaic, Avarin, Black Speech, Common Eldarin, Doriathrin, Goldogrin, Khuzdul, Nandorin, Primitive Elvish, Quenya, Sindarin, Telerin, Westron)

Sawyer, Robert J. (see Quintaglio)

Scarborough, Ann (see Linyaari)

Schleyer, Johann Martin (see Volapük)

Scott, Orson Card (see Stark)

Second Wave (2006) (see Linyaari)

Shadow of the Giant (2005) (see Stark)

Shadow of the Hegemon (2001) (see Stark)

Shadow Puppets (2002) (see Stark)

The Shadow Rising (1992) (see The Old Tongue)

The Shaping of Middle-earth (1986) (see Adûnaic, Avarin, Black Speech, Common Eldarin, Doriathrin, Goldogrin, Khuzdul, Nandorin, Primitive Elvish, Quenya, Sindarin, Telerin, Westron)

The Shield of Time (1991) (see Anglo-French [The Shield of Time])

The Silmarillion (1977) (see Adûnaic, Avarin, Black Speech, Common Eldarin, Doriathrin, Goldogrin, Khuzdul, Nandorin, Primitive Elvish, Quenya, Sindarin, Telerin, Westron)

The Sime-Gen Universe (see Simelan)

Sitch, Rob (see Molvanian)

Small Gods (1992) (see Troll)

Smallville (2001–2011) (see Kryptonian)

Smith, Andrew (see Brithenig)

Snuff (2011) (see Troll)

Something ends, Something begins (2000) (see Starsza Mowa)

Soul Music (1994) (see Troll)

Sourcery (1988) (see Troll)

So You Want to Be a Wizard (1983) (see The Speech)

Speaker for the Dead (1986) (see Stark)

Star Trek II: The Wrath of Khan (1982) (see Klingon, Vulcan)

Star Trek III: The Search for Spock (1984) (see Klingon, Vulcan)

Star Trek IV: The Voyage Home (1986) (see Klingon, Vulcan)

Star Trek V: The Final Frontier (1989) (see Klingon, Vulcan)

Star Trek VI: The Undiscovered Country (1991) (see Klingon, Vulcan)

Star Trek (2009) (see Klingon, Vulcan)

Star Trek: The Animated Series (1973–1974) (see Klingon, Vulcan)

Star Trek: Deep Space Nine (1993–1999) (see Klingon, Vulcan)

Star Trek: Enterprise (2001–2005) (see Klingon, Vulcan)

Star Trek: First Contact (1996) (see Klingon, Vulcan)

Star Trek Generations (1994) (see Klingon, Vulcan)

Star Trek: Insurrection (1999) (see Klingon, Vulcan)

Star Trek: The Motion Picture (1979) (see Klingon, Vulcan)

Star Trek Nemesis (2002) (see Klingon, Vulcan)

Star Trek: The Next Generation (1987–1994) (see Klingon, Vulcan)

Star Trek: The Original Series (1966–1969) (see Klingon, Vulcan)

Star Trek: Voyager (1995–2001) (see Klingon, Vulcan)

Stargate (1994) (see Ancient)

Stargate: Atlantis (2004–2009) (see Ancient)

Stargate Infinity (2002–2003) (see Ancient)

Stargate SG-1 (1997–2007) (see Ancient)

Stargate Universe (2009–2011) (see Ancient)

Startide Rising (1983) (see Anglic [Civilization of the Five Galaxies], Trinary)

The State of the Art (1991) (see Marain)

Stephenson, Neal (see Qwghlmian)

A Stone in Heaven (1979) (See Anglic [Galactic empire])

A Storm of Swords (2000) (see Dothraki)

The Story Untold and Other Stories (2011) (see Simelan)

Sudre, François (see Solresol)

Sundiver (1980) (see Anglic [Civilization of the Five Galaxies], Trinary)

Supergirl (1984) (see Kryptonian)

Superman II (1980) (see Kryptonian)

Superman III (1983) (see Kryptonian)

Superman IV: The Quest for Peace (1987) (see Kryptonian)

Superman (1978) (see Kryptonian)

Superman/Batman: Apocalypse (2010) (see Kryptonian)

Superman Returns (2006) (see Kryptonian)

Surface Detail (2010) (see Marain)

The Swallow's Tower (1997) (see Starsza Mowa)

Swift, Jonathan (see Houyhnhnm)

Sword of Destiny (1992) (see Starsza Mowa)

Swordhunt—#95 (2000) (see Rihannsu)

The System of the World (2004) (see Qwghlmian)

Tales from Earthsea (2001) (see Hardic, Kargish, Language of the Making, Osskili)

Tehanu: The Last Book of Earthsea (1990) (see Hardic, Kargish, Language of the Making, Osskili)

The Terminal (2004) (see Krakozhian)

That Hideous Strength (1945) (see Old Solar)

Thief of Time (2001) (see Troll)

Thirdspace (July 19, 1998) (see Interlac)

Third Watch (2007) (see Linyaari)

"Through the Gates of the Silver Key" (see Tsath-yo)

Thud! (2005) (see Troll)

The Time Machine (2002) (see Eloi)

Times of Contempt (1995) (see Starsza Mowa)

To Kiss or to Kill (2011) (see Simelan)

Tolkien, Christopher (see Adûnaic, Avarin, Black Speech, Common Eldarin, Doriathrin, Goldogrin, Khuzdul, Nandorin, Primitive Elvish, Quenya, Sindarin, Telerin, Westron)

Tolkien, J. R. R. (see Adûnaic, Avarin, Black Speech, Common Eldarin, Doriathrin, Goldogrin, Khuzdul, Nandorin, Primitive Elvish, Quenya, Sindarin, Telerin, Westron)

The Tombs of Atuan (1971) (see Hardic, Kargish, Language of the Making, Osskili)

Too Many Magicians (1966) (see Anglo-French [Lord Darcy stories])

Towers of Midnight (2010) (see The Old Tongue)

Trader to the Stars (1964) (see Anglic [Galactic empire])

The Trouble Twisters (1966) (see Anglic [Galactic empire])

The Truth (2000) (see Troll)

Tweehuysen, Rolandt (see Spocanian)

Twenty Thousand Leagues Under the Sea (1870) (see Nautilus Language)

The Two Towers—The Lord of the Rings (1954) (see Adûnaic, Avarin, Black Speech, Common Eldarin, Doriathrin, Goldogrin, Khuzdul, Nandorin, Primitive Elvish, Quenya, Sindarin, Telerin, Westron)

The Treason of Isengard (The History of The Lord of the Rings, Part Two) (1989) (see Adûnaic, Avarin, Black Speech, Common Eldarin, Doriathrin, Goldogrin, Khuzdul, Nandorin,

Primitive Elvish, Quenya, Sindarin, Telerin, Westron)

Unseen Academicals (2009) (see Troll)

Unto Zeor, Forever (1978) (see Simelan)

The Uplift War (1987) (see Anglic [Civilization of the Five Galaxies], Trinary)

Urban Dead (see Zamgrh)

Use of Weapons (1990) (see Marain)

Utopia (1516) (see Utopian)

Vance, Jack (see Pastiche)

van Steenbergen, Jan (see Wenedyk)

Verne, Jules (see Nautilus Language)

Victory over the Sun (1913) (see Zaum)

Vonnegut, Kurt (see Bokonon)

Walk the Plank (2003) (see Nautilus Language)

A War of Gifts: An Ender Story (2007) (see Stark)

The War of the Jewels (The Later Silmarillion, Part Two) (1994) (see Adûnaic, Avarin, Black Speech, Common Eldarin, Doriathrin, Goldogrin, Khuzdul, Nandorin, Primitive Elvish, Quenya, Sindarin, Telerin, Westron)

The War of the Ring (The History of The Lord of the Rings, Part Three) (1990) (see Adûnaic, Avarin, Black Speech, Common Eldarin, Doriathrin, Goldogrin, Khuzdul, Nandorin, Primitive Elvish, Quenya, Sindarin, Telerin, Westron)

War of the Wing-Men (The Man Who Counts) (1958) (see Anglic [Galactic empire])

Watership Down (1972) (see Lapine)

The Wee Free Men (2003) (see Troll)

Wells, H. G. (see Eloi)

"The White People" (1899) (see Aklo)

Wilson, Robert Anton (see Aklo)

Winter's Heart (2000) (see The Old Tongue)

Wintersmith (2006) (see Troll)

"The Witcher" (1986) (see Starsza Mowa)

The Witcher (1990) (see Starsza Mowa)

Witches Abroad (1991) (see Troll)

A Wizard Abroad (1993) (see The Speech)

A Wizard Alone (2002) (see The Speech)

A Wizard of Earthsea (1968) (see Hardic, Kargish, Language of the Making, Osskili)

A Wizard of Mars (2010) (see The Speech)

The Wizard of Venus (1964) (see Amtorian)

Wizards at War (2005) (see The Speech)

The Wizard's Dilemma (2001) (see The Speech)

Wizard's Holiday (2003) (see The Speech)

Wood, Aaron (see Sandic)

Wyrd Sisters (1988) (see Troll)

Xenocide (1991) (see Stark)

Zelerod's Doom (1986) (see Simelan)

Glossary

Accusative—the case of a noun that acts as the object. In English, *me* is the accusative form of the first-person pronoun.

Adjective—a word or affix that modifies a noun. In English, adjectives usually precede the noun being described. "I owned a little red wagon." *Little* and *red* are adjectives.

Adverb—a word or affix that modifies a verb or another adverb. In English, adverbs can appear in several places in relation to the verb being described. Note how the adverb *quickly* moves: "Quickly I drank the coffee," "I quickly drank the coffee," and "I drank the coffee quickly."

Affix—characters that appear before, after, within, or around a stem word to modify its meaning. In English, placing an affix before the stem (a *prefix*) and placing the affix after the stem (a *suffix*) are very common. Not so common are placing the affix within the stem (an *infix*) or around the stem (a *circumfix*).

Affricative—when the airflow is modified to form a stop plus a fricative when forming a consonant. In English, "j" is an example of this.

Agglutination—the process of adding multiple prefixes and suffixes to a stem to produce single words with complicated meanings. An example in English (not a very agglutinating language) is *homelessness* to mean *the state of not having a home.*

Agreement—a cross reference between two parts of a sentence. In English, if the noun *he* is changed to *I*, then the verb *runs* has to change to *run* to keep the noun and verb in agreement.

Alveolar—when airflow is blocked behind the teeth to form a consonant. In English, "t" is an alveolar consonant.

Animacy—the way that a language indicates whether something is animate or inanimate. In English, the pronouns *he* and *she* usually represent animacy, while *it* represents inanimacy.

Approximants—when the airflow is barely impeded when forming a consonant. In English, "r" and "l" are examples of this.

Article—a type of adjective that indicates definiteness in English. *A* and *an* are called *indefinite articles*, and *the* is called a *definite article*.

Artlang—a language constructed for artistic, esthetic, or fictional purposes.

Aspect—the way that a language indicates the flow of time. In English, "I used to write" and "I have written" reflect different aspects (but the same past tense).

Aspiration—whether stops are released lightly or with a puff when forming a consonant.

Auxlang—a language constructed to serve as an auxiliary to natural languages already in use, either with the intention of replacing other languages or providing a neutral meeting point.

Canon—the officially recognized core of a constructed language. When fans of the language add words to fill in the blanks, these additions are considered noncanonical.

Case—indicates the grammatical function of a noun or pronoun. In English, "I helped him" has two examples of case different from "He helped me." For examples of 72 different cases used by various languages, take a look at the "List of grammatical cases" (*http://en.wikipedia.org/wiki/List_of_grammatical_cases*).

Circumfix—characters that are added before and after a stem word to modify its meaning. A rare example from English is found in the word *embolden* where the stem is *bold* and the circumfix of *em- -en* changes the meaning to *give someone courage.*

Clause—a phrase containing a subject and predicate.

Clusivity—indicates whether the subject or object is inclusive or exclusive. In English, "We went outside" indicates the speaker is included, "You went outside" indicates the speaker was excluded but the addressee was included, and "They went outside" indicates the speaker and the addressee were both excluded.

Conjunction—a word that joins two or more words. In English, *and* and *or* are two of the joining words.

Definiteness—indicates whether something is being referred to in specific or general terms. In English, *the cup* is specific and *a cup* is general.

Degree of comparison—how a language indicates scale. In English, there's *hot, hotter*, and *hottest*, but also *tender, more tender*, and *most tender*.

Dental—when airflow is blocked by teeth to form a consonant.

Diachronic linguistics—the study of how a language changes over time.

Diacritics—the extra markings that adorn some letters. (When designing an alphabet, consider how easy the letters will be to replicate on keyboards.)

Diphthong—two vowel sounds in a single syllable.

Evidentiality—how a language indicates what evidence (if any) exists for a statement. In English, "I heard someone fell" indicates second-hand reportage, while "I heard someone fall" indicates firsthand knowledge.

Focus—how a language indicates the most important concept in a sentence. In English, the following two sentences emphasize a different part of the sentence: "I drank from the cup that was red." "I was the one who drank from the red cup."

Fricatives—when the airflow is impeded enough to create audible friction. In English, "f" and "sh" are examples of this.

Glottal—when airflow is blocked at the back of the throat to form a consonant. In English, "h" is a glottal consonant.

Grammatical gender—the situation where the gender of a person or an item (that is defined as having a gender) affects other parts of the sentence. In English (a generally gender-free language), a ship is considered feminine, and so one starts *her* engines.

Grammatical number—the method of indicating number by modifying a word. In English, *more than one* is usually indicated by adding *-s* (or *-es*) to the end of a word.

Infix—characters that are added inside a word to modify its meaning. In English, the only examples are found in slang expressions, such as inserting an obscenity in the middle of *abso-lutely* to indicate the heightened degree of absolute.

Inflection—the use of an affix to modify some grammatical property of a stem. In English, *cup* is inflected by the addition of *-s* to form *cups* to indicate more than one, and *swallow* is inflected by the addition of *-ed* to form *swallowed* to indicate past tense.

Interjection—a word that exclaims heightened emotion or attention. In English, *wow* and *psst* are interjections.

IPA—the International Phonetic Association (*www.langsci.ucl.ac.uk/ipa/index.html*). "The aim of the IPA is to promote the scientific study of phonetics and the various practical applications of that science. In furtherance of this aim, the IPA provides the academic community world-wide with a notational standard for the phonetic representation of all languages—the International Phonetic Alphabet (also IPA)."

Isolating language—a language where most words consist of a single sound. In English, early reading books containing only one-syllable words come close to representing an isolating language.

Labial—when airflow is blocked by lips or lips and teeth to form a consonant. In English, "w" and "f" are labial consonants.

LCS—the Language Creation Society (*www. conlang.org/lcs.php*). "Its goal is to promote conlangs and conlanging through offering platforms for conlangers to publish high-quality work of interest to the community, raising awareness about conlanging amongst the general public, organizing work for professional conlangers and people in the entertainment industry interested in adding more depth to their alternative worlds, and providing a central place for reliable contacts and information to those seeking to learn more."

Loglang—a constructed language created to serve logical functions.

Mirative—an element that indicates expectedness. In English, an exclamation point is used to differentiate a simple statement from a surprise. "The coffee was hot." "The coffee was hot!"

Modality—the type of information and how that information is communicated: auditory, diagrammed, gustatory, kinesthetic, mapped, olfactory, tactile, visual, and written. (There is also another *modality* that is more closely related to *mood*.)

Monophthong—a single vowel sound in a syllable.

Mood—indicates the attitude of the speaker to the subject. In English, there are three moods: indicative, subjunctive, and imperative. (The Nenets language of northern Russia has sixteen.) Compare "drink your coffee" to "if you had drunk your coffee."

Morphology—the study of words, stems, and affixes.

Nasalization—when the airflow travels through the nose as well as the mouth when forming a consonant. In English, the oral airflow of "m" and "b" are blocked, but "m" still has airflow through the nose.

Nominative—the case of a noun that acts as the subject. In English, *I* is the nominative form of the first-person pronoun.

Noun—a word that represents a person, place, or thing.

Palatal—when airflow is blocked at the top of the palate to form a consonant.

Palatalization—whether the tongue is raised toward the palate when forming the consonant.

Palato-alveolar—when airflow is blocked further back from the teeth to form a consonant. In English, "r" is a palato-alveolar consonant.

Person—indicates the relative participation of a subject. In English, pronouns are used to indicate whether the speaker (*I*), the addressee (*you*), or both (*we*) is being discussed.

Phonetics—the study of how a language's sounds are created and perceived.

Phonology—the study of a language's sound system.

Polarity—how a language indicates an affirmative or negative attribute. In English, both *impossible* and *not possible* indicate negativity.

Predicate—the part of the sentence that modifies the subject. In English, the noun is the subject and the rest of the sentence is considered the predicate.

Prefix—characters that are added before a word to modify its meaning. In English, adding *un-* before an adjective negates the meaning of the adjective.

Preposition—the word in a prepositional phrase that defines the relationship between the subject and the object. In English, some common prepositions are *of*, *to*, *in*, *for*, and *on*. (Other languages use postpositions or circumpositions.)

Resonating space—the internal shape of the mouth limits what sounds are possible to make. Moving the tongue alters that shape, allowing distinct sounds to be produced. In human English, the placement of the tongue is described as *front* or *back*, and *high*, *middle*, or *low*.

Sapir-Whorf Hypothesis—the hypothesis states that not only does the available language shape a society, it also shapes the thinking available to the members of the society that speaks the language.

Semantics—the study of meaning.

Stem—the root part of a word that accepts affixes that modify the word's meaning.

Stops—when the airflow is completely blocked when forming a consonant. In English, "p" and "k" are examples of this.

Stress—emphasis given to a syllable within a word or a word within a sentence.

Subject—the part of the sentence that is modified by the predicate. In English, the subject is usually the noun.

Suffix—characters that are added after a word to modify its meaning. In English, adding *-able* after a verb means the achievement is possible.

Syntax—the study or rules of sentence structure.

Tense—how a language indicates the relationship between the event and the reporting of the event. In English, *I wrote* indicates that writing occurred before the statement was made, and *I will write* indicates that the statement was made first.

Tone—shifting pitch to change or differentiate the meaning of a word. In Mandarin Chinese, four words that look the same are spoken with different tones: high, rising, low falling, and high falling.

Topic—how a language indicates what a sentence is about. In English, *the carrier brought the mail* is about the carrier, and the *mail was brought by the carrier* is about the mail.

Transitivity—refers to whether a verb can take an object or not. In English, *I run* (transitive) can stand as a complete sentence, but *I throw* (intransitive) is not a complete sentence until an object is added.

Unvoiced sounds—those sounds created when the process of speaking does not cause air to vibrate the vocal cords. In English, the consonants "c," "f," "g," "h," "j," "k," "q," "s," "t," "w," and "x" are unvoiced when they are letters in a spoken word.

Uvular—when airflow is blocked far back in the mouth to form a consonant.

Velar—when airflow is blocked at the back of the mouth to form a consonant. In English, "k" is a velar consonant.

Verb—an action word or a word that defines a state of being.

Voice—how a language indicates the relationship between the verb and the noun. In English, *was* or *were* is placed before the verb to indicate a passive voice. In "Robin jumped" (active voice), Robin performs the action of jumping. In "Robin was jumped" (passive voice), Robin receives the action of being jumped.

Voiced sounds—those sounds created when the process of speaking causes air to vibrate the vocal cords. In English, all vowels are voiced, as are the consonants "b," "d," "l," "m," "n", "r," "v," "y," and "z."

Index

DAILY BENDER

Want Some More?

Hit up our humor blog, The Daily Bender, to get your fill of all things funny—be it subversive, odd, offbeat, or just plain mean. The Bender editors are there to get you through the day and on your way to happy hour. Whether we're linking to the latest video that made us laugh or calling out (or bullshit on) whatever's happening, we've got what you need for a good laugh.

If you like our book, you'll love our blog. (And if you hated it, "man up" and tell us why.) Visit The Daily Bender for a shot of humor that'll serve you until the bartender can.

Sign up for our newsletter at

www.adamsmedia.com/blog/humor

and download our Top Ten Maxims No Man Should Live Without.